Robin Hood Was Right

Robin Hood Was Right

A Guide to Giving Your Money for Social Change

Chuck Collins and Pam Rogers
with Joan P. Garner

Preface by Alfre Woodard

W. W. Norton & Company
New York London

For information about permission to reproduce selections from this book,
write to Permissions, W. W. Norton & Company, Inc., 500 Fifth Avenue,
New York, NY 10110

The text of this book is composed in Bembo with the display set in Meta
Composition by Allentown Digital Services
Manufacturing by The Maple-Vail Book Manufacturing Group
Book design by Chris Welch

Library of Congress Cataloging-in-Publication Data
Collins, Chuck, 1959–
Robin Hood was right : a guide to giving your money for social change / by
Chuck Collins and Pam Rogers, with Joan P. Garner; preface
by Alfre Woodard.
p.   cm.
Rev. ed. of: Robin Hood was right / Vanguard Public Foundation, © 1977.
Includes bibliographical references and index.
ISBN 0-393-04827-6
1. Philanthropy—United States.   2. Endowments—United States.   3. Social
change.   4. Social action.   I. Rogers, Pam, 1950–   II. Garner, Joan P.,
1951–   III. Vanguard Public Foundation. Robin Hood was right.   IV. Title.
HV25.V36   2000
361.7'4'0973—dc21   99-053150

W. W. Norton & Company, Inc., 500 Fifth Avenue, New York, N.Y. 10110
www.wwnorton.com

W. W. Norton & Company Ltd., 10 Coptic Street, London WC1A 1PU

1 2 3 4 5 6 7 8 9 0

To you, the reader, in the hope that this book will inspire you to greater generosity and a deeper commitment to a freer, kinder, more just world

Contents

Part I   The Politics of Giving

Part II: Your Money, Yourself

Part III   Getting from Here to There— Nuts and Bolts

Part IV: Decisions, Decisions

Acknowledgments

Our appreciation for the enthusiasm and assistance that we received as *Robin Hood* took form is boundless. We thank our editor at W. W. Norton, Edwin Barber, whose personal commitment to giving is admirable and whose insistence on the crisp and concise is correct, although not always easy to achieve. Thankfully Mr. Barber was infinitely patient. Tom Bissell, our assistant editor, was patience personified. Our literary agency, Linda Chester and Associates, particularly Judith Ehrlich, believed the message of *Robin Hood Was Right* needed to move into the larger world. They took us under their capable wings and educated, cajoled, pumped up, and at times bossed us around. All to the good.

Since the Merry Men of Sherwood Forest were unavailable, we were blessed by a cast of writers whose work appears as follows: Ellen Bikales laid a firm foundation for the technical chapters in Part II; Lynne Gerber wrote Chapter 4, made Chapter 5 sing, and wrote many of the social change group vignettes; Jean Riesman interviewed most of the people whose quotes spark our book; Kathy Pillsbury enhanced Chapter 10 and Part IV with her insight and experience; and Nikki Lessin-Joseph arrived at crunch time with her writing, editing, and organizational skills. Patricia Maher wrote, reviewed, and fielded the often asked question "Why is it taking them so long?" Our "grassroots" editors were Virginia Rogers (who wrote "shame" when a writer, who shall remain unnamed, misused "affect") and Patricia Maher.

Our "infrastructure" team gave the book much of its shape and content. Elliot Ratzman, Kurt Shaw, Daniel P. Delany, and the Data Center provided research. Our technical assistance roster included: Vivian Bianchi, Lynne Brandon, Marcia Gallo, Susan Goodman, Julie Goodridge, Ellen Gurzinsky, Ron Hanft, Judy Hatcher, Jeffrey Hewatt, Fred Humphrey, Zach Klein, Jenny Ladd, Sally Levering, Joy Linscheid, Shelley Mains, Kate Mills, Christopher Mogil and the Impact Project (largely responsible for the bibliography), Burt Nadler, Scot Nakagawa, Susan Ostrander, Pamela Prodan, George Pillsbury, Elaine Reily, Sharon Rich, Nan Rubin, Rick Schwartz, Marilyn Stern, Jan Strout, Cathy Suskin, Mary Tiseo, Jean Weiss, Angela Wessels, and the staffs of the Funding Exchange member funds.

People whose brains we picked included: Sue Anderson, Brad Armstrong, Janet Axelrod, Gerardo Ayala, David Becker, Roxie Berlin, Sue Blaustein, Chela Blitt, Susan Bower, Leslie Brockelbank, Robert Brown, Kimo Campbell, Eliza Critchlow, Joe and Jean Crocker, Diana Dillaway, Wendy Emrich, Carmen Febo-San Miguel, Tracy Gary, Leslie Goldstein, Jack Gray, Tracy Hewat, John Hickenlooper, Janet Hicks, Allen Hunter, Randi Johnson, Kim Klein, John Lapham, Pamela Lichty, Sue and Art Lloyd, Kim Lund, Shirley Magidson, June Makela, Carolyn McCoy, Margaret McCoy, Jim McDonnell, Rob McKay, Nancy Meyers, Madeline Moore, Ed Nakawatese, Esther Nieves, Teresa Odendahl, Sarah Pillsbury, Francisco Ramos, Catherine Reid, Peter Reilly, Shad Reinstein, Lucy Rogers, Rosemary Santos, David Schecter, Naomi Schwartz, Kristine Smith, Marjorie Smith, Lally Stowell, Miven Booth Trageser, Cora Weiss, Judy Weiss, Bob Weissbourd, and Helen Wolcott.

Our readers were: Christie Balka, Hillary Goodridge, Ellen Gurzinsky, Anne H. Hess, Andrei Joseph, Karl Bruce Knapper, Melissa Kohner, Mark Melchior, Torie Osborn, Ian Simmons, and Lisa Port White.

Chuck thanks: Pam Rogers for her humor, friendship, determination, and patience. Tricia Brennan and Nora Collins, his family. Michael Brennan, whose time as a writer was all too short. George Pillsbury, June Makela, and Janet Axelrod, who built this movement of alternative funds and made it possible for him to do this work. David Hunter, who inspires him to carry on.

Pam thanks: her family, Andrei Joseph, for his politics, his heart, and his habit of bringing home flowers; Nina and Nikki; her parents who understood when she couldn't visit, or even call; and her sister, Joan (Po-Po). Hillary Goodridge, Pam Flood, Nora Janeway, Bonnie Tumulty, Eurydice Hirsey, Shari Zelkind, and Debi Adams: There are not enough words to thank each of you. Roberta De Estachio, Claude Rosenberg, and Greg Bates, all of whom gave us votes of confidence at critical junctures; Annie Hoffman, whose spirit of generosity inspires her; Pat Maher for creative intellectual sparring; and the Haymarket People's Fund staff. Finally, thanks to the people she has met over seventeen years of coordinating Haymarket Conferences. Much of this book has come from all of them.

Preface

Robin Hood was right. Tipping the balance of resources to include more of humanity is an adventurous, thrilling, and worthwhile pursuit. Charity is good, but supporting and creating social change are about power. Power can infuse lives with purpose and dignity. That opens up the possibility of joy. The life of the giver, as well as that of the receiver, is transformed. So this book trumpets a vital message. No matter who we are, no matter how much money we have, whatever our color, gender, age, religion, or language, we can bring change to the world around us. We can open our minds, roll up our sleeves, and reach out our hands.

Giving isn't a posture reserved for the rich or powerful. It is the responsibility and privilege of every man, woman, and child to participate in the task of building more just and humane societies. We all have the ability to use our talents, our resources, our voices, and our sweat to create positive change in our own communities and in the larger world around us.

There are traditions of giving and activism in every culture, in all quadrants of the globe. In metropolises and in remote villages, in tony suburbs and in blighted ghettos, busy hands and tireless feet are on the move, teaching a skill, putting money in the church plate, holding up a protest sign, caring for the orphaned, honoring the elderly. I got my activist schooling as a knobby-kneed girl in North Tulsa, Oklahoma, from my parents, whose mantra was: You can fully judge how good your life is only by considering the quality of the people's lives around you.

I believe that generosity is a natural instinct that beats, however faintly, in every human heart. Those of us who act on our hunger for justice, who get creative with our righteous anger, who connect and comfort with our empathy, are very fortunate indeed. Generosity links us, beyond time and place, to people of conscience and action everywhere who have made our world freer, kinder, and more just. Philanthropy and activism are a gift to one's self. By giving, we lessen our own cynicism and alienation.

There is an incredible economic divide in our country. The majority of wealth is in the hands of only 1 percent of the population. In our prosperous, democratic nation, children are hungry, people live on the streets, toxins choke our air and water, gays and lesbians do not have equal rights under the law, Native American sacred sites are routinely destroyed, and more African American men go to prison than to college. The imbalance of access and justice is so pronounced it's a wonder the whole country doesn't roll into the polluted sea. Yes, comparatively we have made progress, but the task is a life's work, a work in process. It also demands that we stay with it. The great Martin Luther King, Jr., wrote: "Injustice anywhere is a threat to justice everywhere. We are caught in an inescapable network of mutuality, tied in a single garment of destiny. Whatever affects one directly, affects all indirectly." Many of us recognize that charity begins at home, but home is the entire planet. There is glorious work to be done.

As we enter the twenty-first century, the world is indeed becoming a much smaller place. It's more and more evident we can no longer live in isolation. Varying cultures, beliefs, lifestyles, and agendas converge and collide on a daily basis. People in every nation are deeply impacted by decisions made in countries far away or in boardrooms they can't enter. In a time when we can phone or fax or E-mail across continents, many people still don't cross the lines into neighborhoods inhabited by communities of other classes or colors. Activism opens up these byways. Along with philanthropy for social change, it helps tip the scales. It amplifies the voices traditionally ignored and disregarded. It puts the power to solve problems in the hands of the people who bear the brunt of them. It holds governments and corporations responsible, letting them know the eyes of the world are watching. It advocates for decisions that have positive impacts rather than negative consequences. Giving for social change connects us beyond the borders that separate us. It allows people of different classes, of different cultures to work together on equal footing.

After learning that U.S. companies had more than fifteen billion dollars invested in the South African economy, thereby upholding the apartheid regime, I could not sit still. I joined with other American artists and activists to found Artists for a New South Africa, to help advocate for sanctions and the cultural boycott. At the time most of us in the international antiapartheid movement never thought Nelson Mandela would live to be free or see his people liberated. Nonetheless we marched and lobbied and sang and spoke out. We raised money, and we raised a ruckus, simply because it was the right thing to do. It echoed the struggles of our own parents and grandparents, as they marched on Selma, fled Nazi Germany, survived life on reservations, built labor unions, buried loved ones, and faced hardship in a myriad of forms. Something within our hearts and our consciences would not allow us to remain silent when our brothers and sisters in South Africa—young and old, black, brown, and white—were enduring relentless suffering, sacrificing all for their freedom: their sweat, their blood, their tears, their lives, and the lives of their children.

Then, in 1994, something truly unbelievable happened. Against all odds, the will of the people triumphed. Democracy replaced tyranny. Peace prevailed over violence. Reconciliation gained the upper hand over retribution. A once-pariah nation became a global model for seeking truth and justice. On April 27, 1994, like many around the world, I sat glued to my television, watching the miracle of South Africa's first free elections. Masses of people stood for ten and twelve hours in long, snaking lines as they waited to cast their ballots. Twenty-one million black people were voting for the first time in their lives.

After eighty years of protest, apartheid had gasped its last, and its final moments were wondrously peaceful. A few weeks later I was in Pretoria when the world's most famous political prisoner was inaugurated as president. I've always had faith in the power of people to change the world. That day I witnessed a glorious verification.

But in South Africa, as in America, the work doesn't end with the gaining of legal rights. The effects of tyranny and bigotry and exploitation and abuse don't disappear overnight. The painful legacy of apartheid is that most South Africans live in crushing poverty. I have met so many people there who live in desperate conditions, yet still possess profound hope and courage, people who believe in the possibility of beating the odds and are bravely facing the challenges of rebuilding their own lives and their nation. South Africa has proved once again that people can organize, fight inequity, and forever alter the balance of power.

When dramatic world events give way to the steadier process of rebuilding, many turn away, thinking the task is complete. In fact, the fight simply clears the way for the work to take place, the work of alleviating the ills of disparity. Tearing down employs emotion, reaction, and righteous zeal. Building up demands a progressive stance. It asks for focus and heart. Doing good takes more than good intentions. It requires listening to and building partnerships with the people affected by the problems. It demands patience and resolve. It requires funding. Even small amounts of money, given in strategic places, can have a lasting impact.

Creating social change is exciting. It's proof that we are alive and thinking. What could be better than to work for a future where fairness is the bottom line? Creating social change can give everyone the right to have decent housing, a good education, gainful employment, and respect. It will allow people an equal say in the decisions that directly impact on their lives. Social change will ensure gender equality and will guarantee each girl and woman the space to reach for their potential and raise healthy families, safe from abuse and discrimination. Social change will eliminate police brutality in communities of color and inhumane immigration policies. Social change will bring living wages to all who work. It's about building a society that nurtures and supports all the individuals who constitute it. It is the process of bringing forth a world in which no one is disregarded or discarded.

I hope that you, the reader, will be inspired by this book and fired up by its stories of organizing. I hope you will join me in contributing to groups that work for social change. Together, let's support the progressive community funds and the partnerships they have developed to make change. I trust that you will give with faith and love, with dignity and righteousness. I know you will be enriched in the process.

Robin Hood was right. And he had a damn good time.

Peace,
Alfre Woodard

Introduction

This book is about how to give money to create a better world. This is not the sort of giving that is a reflexive response to guilt, like plucking out a splinter because it hurts, or about giving to gain recognition. It's about learning to give in creative ways, by targeting the root causes of problems. It's about giving in ways that build bridges, that transform us as givers as well as improve the quality of the communities around us. It is about giving in a way that deepens our connection to one another.

Our world has big problems that need attention: environmental devastation, access to quality education and health care, homelessness and poverty, hate and violence. We don't claim to have the answers, but we know that we cannot leave the solutions up to the politicians. We also know that there are thousands of grassroots organizations throughout the country developing creative solutions to these and other societal issues.

Pro-gres-sive:—*adj.* 1. moving forward or onward 2. continuing by successive steps. . . . 5. favoring, working for, or characterized by progress or improvement, as through political or social reform.— *n.* a person who is progressive, esp. one who favors political progress or reform.

A Book for Givers of All Sizes and Shapes

The first *Robin Hood Was Right* was published by the Vanguard Public Foundation more than twenty years ago. It was a book you could hand to a friend or family member and say, "Read this! It describes a movement I want to join. I thought you might be interested too." That book, which sold twenty thousand copies by word of mouth, played a major role in the growth of a movement of social change givers and progressive foundations.

This new *Robin Hood* will give you tools to give for effective change. It is for people who have from one thousand dollars a year to give (possible if your annual income is thirty thousand dollars) to the sky's the limit. Although some of the technical information is targeted to people with substantial wealth, the rest of the book applies to anyone. We sincerely believe that everyone can be a philanthropist.

What Is Activism?

Activism is not issue-specific.

It's a moral posture that, steady state,
    propels you forward, from one hard
hour to the next.

Believing that you can do something
    to make things better, you do
something, rather than nothing.

You assume responsibility for the
    privilege of your abilities.

You do whatever you can.

You reach beyond yourself in your
    imagination, and in your wish for
understanding, and for change.

You admit the limitations of individual
    perspectives.

You trust somebody else.

You do not turn away.

June Jordan

Who We Are

In the years since the original *Robin Hood Was Right* was published, funders and activists have joined together as a network of social change foundations. Since 1979, these foundations and the Funding Exchange, their umbrella fund, have contributed more than sixty-four million dollars to locally based organizations working to advance economic and social justice and to protect the environment. At the same time they have provided community, assistance, and support to thousands of people who want their money to make a difference. The Funding Exchange is fortunate to have a wide array of sister foundations throughout the country.

In *Robin Hood Was Right,* we have attempted to impart the collective experience that social change givers and progressive foundation grantmakers and staff people have gained in the last twenty-five years. The "we" in Robin Hood clearly means many people; each chapter passed through several hands. In the end the mouthpieces are Chuck Collins, Pam Rogers, and Joan P. Garner. All of us are connected to the Funding Exchange network. Chuck is the codirector of United for a Fair Economy, a grant recipient of the Funding Exchange and its member fund Haymarket People's Fund. Pam has been a staff person at Haymarket for more than seventeen years, primarily working with donors. Joan was executive director of the Fund for Southern Communities in Atlanta, as well as co-director of the National Network of Grantmakers. She is now executive director of Southern Partners Fund, a foundation created and governed by experienced grassroots leaders that funds Southern communities in an eleven-state region. All are regular givers.

A Guide through Sherwood Forest

Here's what you can expect. Part I, "The Politics of Giving," examines the difference between traditional philanthropy and social change giving and the impact social change giving has had on shaping history and our lives today. The final chapter in the section gives you a taste of current social change organizing. We had so many great organizing stories that we decided to place one between each chapter.

Part II, "Your Money, Yourself," examines some of the personal issues that affect our giving, issues of hope and vision, of attitudes toward money and giving. Chapter 5 is a somewhat irreverent look at the roadblocks that can stop or slow you down on your path to effective giving.

Part III, "Getting from Here to There—Nuts and Bolts" is a practical road map to taking control of your money, investing, and tax-wise giving. For those whose financial situation precludes these concerns, dive into the last chapter of the section, "Organizing . . . and Beyond."

Part IV, "Decisions, Decisions," examines different methods you

"We're from Mexico, and my parents used to buy used clothes and take them when we drove down to central Mexico to see family. We would give them to kids along the way, to the kids who would clean our car windows. . . . Once my mother took a sweatshirt off my back and gave it to a kid. She definitely was a model, and she taught us a profound lesson. It's that we always have something to give."—*Gerardo Ayala, Fund for Santa Barbara*

can use to give and presents you with a giving plan to tailor to your vision. Our final chapter explains the qualities of a really great giver.

The Appendices have lists of more than 150 great social change groups, progressive social change foundations, and resources, resources.

We hope *Robin Hood Was Right* will lead you to greater joy and satisfaction in your giving.

Let us know what you think. fexexc@aol.com

Part I

The Politics
of Giving

Chapter 1

Understanding Charity

We are a nation of givers. Contradicting the mistaken notion that human nature is selfish, we are a generous species. We care about our families, our friends, and our communities, and we consistently reach out to others in need. Millions volunteer their time in hospitals, provide rides for the elderly, or coach soccer and Little League teams. Frequently our caring takes the form of donating money. Last year Americans gave $109 *billion* to charity.[1]

But is all this money making a difference? Are we spending our charitable dollars effectively? We give to help the poor, but poverty prevails. We contribute to save the environment, but corporate destruction of our land and waters continues. We donate to shelters, but millions remain homeless. We provide for health care research, but cancer and AIDS still claim our loved ones.

Despite these monetary gestures of humanity and compassion, we often feel increasingly isolated from the people around us. With each passing year, more of us live in cities where neighbors remain strangers and the sense of community we long for remains elusive. We en-

> "When I was in high school, I made forty dollars a week. My parents expected me to make contributions to the church—ten percent, four dollars a week."—*Esther Nieves, donor, Crossroads Fund*

counter but feel distant from those whose race, class, or sexual orientation differs from our own. We cannot help noticing that income, wealth, and possessions are distributed unevenly. Those on one side of that great social class canyon find it hard to see the needs and goodwill of those on the other side.

It is time to reassess our assumptions about charity. Even if charitable donations doubled, private philanthropy would have a hard time replacing the social service programs that the government has cut. We must take a second look at the aims and approaches of traditional charity, rethinking the prevailing wisdom about who is deserving. It is time to reevaluate what our money can and cannot do. We believe that giving can be one of the most joyous and rewarding of all human experiences. Done consciously and with one eye always on the goal of attaining social and economic justice, it can be one of the most satisfying ways of all to spend money.

Traditional Charity

What is charity? In the United States traditional charity has its roots in specific moral attitudes from the upper classes in Europe. This version of charity has rendered invisible traditions of giving that exist in every culture. For most of the nineteenth and twentieth centuries charity was defined by the attitude of noblesse oblige. This attitude, which originated among European nobility, holds as its central tenet that along with the accumulation of money, the wealthy take on an obligation to improve the lot of people "beneath" them. Needless to say, the concept is more moralistic than altruistic. Early patrician do-gooders viewed poor people as moral failures, who needed only to be exposed to the high moral standards of successful people like themselves to be "redeemed." Notions of social and economic justice played no part in this "noble" undertaking; indeed the highborn opposed giving any kind of financial aid to the poor.

Later cries for justice were answered with the declaration that science could rectify the plight of the poor. Robert Treat Paine, a Boston philanthropist, advocated a more methodical and systematic approach in which "experts," graduates of elite colleges and universities, would provide services to the less enlightened. Poverty was still viewed as a result of individual shortcomings, but now the experts, with their purportedly superior knowledge, could both "diagnose" the problem and impose a "remedy" for the basically passive individual. Paine's and others' efforts eventually led to the professionalization of philanthropy and social work.

Today we have arrived at a historic moment when the stock market is reaching unprecedented heights and government is ending its sixty-year social contract with the needy. Governmental aid to the poor is being dismantled by representatives of both major political parties. Politicians and commentators encourage us to perceive the poor as unworthy of charity, arguing that they lack the will to get ahead. Most poverty and social problems, we are told, result from the bankruptcy of morality at the individual level, otherwise known as a loss of family values. This stereotyping dehumanizes the poor. They are falsely identified as living it up on our hard-earned tax dollars. The demand is for "workfare, not welfare" and for strict limits of benefits, even for those in dire need. A generation ago Lyndon Johnson's administration spoke of a War on Poverty. Today the war is on the poor.

In the immigrant Vietnamese community of Worcester, Massachusetts, a group of women pool money to create a loan fund so that local Vietnamese youth can attend college. They then pool the interest from the low-interest loan payments to support other community projects, keeping financial resources in the community.

"Charitable" Giving?

Charity is not all that charitable when it derives from an assumption that our money or our status somehow makes us more worthy than members of the communities we seek to benefit. Yet this may be precisely what we do when as givers we retain exclusive authority to decide where the money will go. Rarely have donors entertained the notion that they might share decision-making power with informed, active members of the populations or communities they wish to support. We simply assume that it is for a donor to decide what's best, even when he or she has little or no contact or familiarity with the recipient community.

The private charitable giving that does exist today is not what it appears to be at first glance. Some would argue that when closely analyzed, many tax-deductible donations are made not merely from deep generosity but also from self-interest. When donors give money to the prep schools they hope their children will attend or to land conservancies that will protect the views from their decks, they feel generous. But they also get tax deductions and are giving to institutions and causes that directly benefit *them*.

Charity is not exactly "charitable" when we expect something back. Like industry, charity is big business. Large charities have learned to court donors just as large businesses court customers. They pursue press coverage and seek support through expensive mass mailings. They also distribute tokens of gratitude and put on high-profile displays of recognition, sometimes with such vigor that these public tributes eclipse the importance of the underlying cause.

We donate in ever-increasing amounts, but the wealthiest give smaller portions of their assets than do the poorest. One in four top earners gives nothing at all. Moreover, contrary to public perception, only about 13 percent of the philanthropic pie goes to direct public benefit and human services programs.[2] The lion's share goes to churches, the arts, elite private colleges and universities, and hospitals.[3] We are giving more but sharing less. Moreover, despite our prosperous economy, the gap between rich and poor in both income and net worth is widening. Real income for the poorest 20 percent of the population is declining. (The United States actually leads the world in economic inequality.[4])

At the same time that some donors are motivated by self-interest,

others do give from a deep sense of generosity. We give food and clothing to a homeless shelter; we purchase a "brick" to help pay for the construction of a hospice for people with AIDS; we donate to the local theater company. We give to build and sustain our communities. Such long and proud cultural traditions as tithing in Christianity, tzedakah in Judaism, and zakat in Islam embody this spirit and remind us of our deep connection with and responsibility to our broader human family.

> " I give because someone gave to me when I needed it most."—*Tommie Hollis-Younger, board member, Cooperative Economics for Women*

Diverting Our Attention

There is nothing wrong with these forms of traditional charity viewed narrowly and without a historical perspective. No one could argue with feeding people in soup kitchens or treating children for lead poisoning. All should be able to appreciate the joy that art and music bring us. Traditional recipients of charity such as museums and universities are worthy institutions, and most human service organizations do provide valuable services to assist people in need.

Much of our giving is limited to "safe" causes as we support services that provide temporary relief but do not challenge the status quo. Believing that there is nothing more we can do, we see only limited, individual "solutions." Health care is not a guaranteed right, so we buy policies just for ourselves. It doesn't occur to us to take on the HMOs or government policy makers. Children in faraway places are hungry, so we "adopt" one to clothe and feed "for only pennies a day." We don't ask about the trade policies that produce widespread scarcity and shortages. Our efforts temporarily alleviate problems, but in the end they allow the symptoms we see today to grow tomorrow. As Dr. Martin Luther King said, "Philanthropy is commendable, but it must not cause the philanthropist to overlook the circumstances of economic injustice that make philanthropy necessary."

Redefining Charity

"I give when I can, and sometimes when I can't."—*Luz Santana, The Right Question Project*

Thus we are looking to redefine charity and to promote new traditions of giving and sharing that affirm and empower the ignored and disregarded. We must move beyond our notion of self-interest to include the interests of people in our wider community. Under this new definition, charity is an effort to close the divide between rich and poor. It works for social and economic justice and for greater equity in the distribution of wealth and other resources. This new charity moves us from giving solely to issues within our own experience to opening up the whole universe of populations, issues, and activities that lack access to the resources we may take for granted.

For all the good it does, we see modern philanthropy reinforcing what *is,* instead of working toward what *could be.* We see it focusing on immediate *symptoms* or *results* of social and economic problems, rather than on root *causes.* This is why charitable efforts often fail to achieve lasting solutions. In our view, it's time for a new focus on change, not charity, and we would like to see far more giving dollars flowing in this direction.

We yearn for the whole process of giving to operate more democratically, with those communities in need participating in decision making about how charitable dollars are spent. Otherwise, we fear, American philanthropy, however well intentioned, will fail to address the fundamental needs of our society. You may not always agree with our perspective, but we hope that it will at least provoke you to think long and hard about how, when, and with whom you share your money. In this process we hope to convince you that as a giver you can contribute to a new, just society that will benefit us all.

The Newtown Florist Club

The Newtown Florist Club in Gainesville, Georgia, was started more than fifty years ago by African American churchwomen who brought flowers to sick people in their congregation. Newtown, the Black community in Gainesville, is built on the old city dump. Eighteen out of twenty emission-producing industries are in Newtown. The ladies who took flowers to the sick noticed that nearly all of them had environmentally related diseases. There was an unusually high incidence of miscarriage, infant mortality, cancer, lead poisoning, respiratory problems, and lupus.

The women began to give "toxic tours" of Newtown for visitors, mark houses with purple ribbons where people had died of environmental illnesses, and take visitors to talk with families affected by unclean air and water in Gainesville. It's been an eye-opener for many folks to see environmental racism firsthand.

The Newtown Florist Club sued Ralston Purina for Environmental Protection Agency (EPA) violations and obtained an injunction that reduced the pollution. Other industries, afraid the environmental "terrorists" disguised as church ladies (they are mostly elderly, and all still wear hats and gloves) would sue them as well, agreed to reduce emissions and, in one case, to relocate.

The Florist Club then sued the local school district for violating civil rights laws and also filed a voting rights suit. In 1996 the American Civil Liberties Union of Georgia recognized the Newtown Florist Club as the most effective citizens' advocacy group in Georgia.

The club members still take flowers to their sick neighbors and still conduct "toxic tours." In some cases the original members' daughters are carrying on the work.

Their first grant was from the Fund for Southern Communities, a social change foundation based in Atlanta.

Chapter 2

Change, Not Charity

Y ou have been a witness to social change. Twenty years ago most domestic violence was hidden away and treated as a private concern. Today it is a recognized crime. While women are still battered, the need for battered women's shelters and other services is a given. Twenty years ago Love Canal and hazardous waste, Three Mile Island and nuclear power became household words. By the end of the 1980s hazardous waste policy was moving to break from the traditional format of pollution *control* toward the superior logic of pollution *prevention,*[1] and by the early 1990s there were no more plans to build nuclear power plants. Twenty years ago the civil rights of gay men, bisexuals, lesbians, and transgendered (GBLT) people were barely a blip in public discourse. Today some states and municipalities have begun to enact legislation to protect GBLT people against discrimination in employment based on sexual orientation and to guarantee their partners the same employment benefits as those of married couples. While smoking is not yet history, corporate lies and conspiracies have been exposed. Now there are many public places where you can breathe smoke-free air, and tobacco companies are being held responsible for massive public health costs.

At the same time conservative forces have pursued a strategy that has culminated in another type of social change: the end of the safety net for poor people, an increase in tax relief for the wealthy and for corporations, a campaign to end affirmative action, an attack on public education, and an escalating war against reproductive rights.

In both progressive and conservative cases, change occurred neither on a random, individual level nor simply because of one charismatic leader. Rather, it occurred when groups of people joined together in organizations to transform the rules of society. The dedication and commitment of these activists were nourished by money donated to their cause. Donors have made and can still make a huge difference.

Social Change Kicks the Status Quo

Social change can be a slight shift, an alteration or a reversal in the status quo, that brings about institutional, or systemic, change. Common understandings about what is right and true can change. Social change is embodied in new laws, procedures, and policies that alter the nature of institutions and, in time, the hearts and minds of people. Social change affects how we treat each other (African Americans no longer must give up their seats on buses to whites); what is considered "normal" (girls *can* play competitive sports in school); and established ways of doing things ("experts" are no longer trusted to make environmental decisions without community input).

Progressive social change is characterized by its insistence on addressing the root cause(s) of problems rather than the alleviation of symptoms. Because the goal is systemic change, conflict with those who hold power is often inevitable. The power that social change organizations bring to the table is their ability to organize, to educate, and to mobilize.

Examples of Change vs. Charity

Charity: Focus on individual needs.
Change: Focus on institutions and policy.

Charity: Give to the fine arts museum.
Change: Give to an organization working to ensure National Endowment for the Arts (NEA) funding for the arts.

Charity: Donate a dollar a day to help one child in Guatemala.
Change: Donate to development projects focusing on building up the local economy in Guatemala.

Charity: Support shelters for battered women.
Change: Support conflict resolution and antiviolence programs for junior high and high school students to prevent battering.

Charity: Fund Toys for Tots during holidays.
Change: Fund organizing for a livable wage so parents can afford to buy toys for their kids.

How Social Change Happens

Progressive social change is profoundly democratic. At its best, people of different racial and ethnic backgrounds, different sexual orientations, different abilities, and a wide range of ages participate in developing creative solutions to social problems. Organizing amplifies the voices of those whose interests are usually not heard.

Money alone does not bring about change; neither do individuals. But when individuals band together and form organizations to focus their collective power, social change can happen. When a large number of organizations work together toward a common goal, that's a movement. Movements make change.

When you give for social change, you give to organizing. To organize, according to a paraphrase of *Webster's,* is:

- → To arrange or form into the coherent unity of a functioning whole.
- → To persuade to join in some common cause or enlist in some organization.
- → To arrange by systematic planning and united effort.
- → To arrange elements into a whole of interdependent parts.

That's organizing! All these pieces—to urge others to join, to develop a unity of purpose (goals), to make plans and strategies, and to build and strengthen ties among members of the organization—all these activities build organizations.

The goals of social change organizing (and giving for change) are to:

- → Aim at root causes, not symptoms.
- → Build collective responses, not individual solutions, to problems.
- → Change attitudes, behavior, laws, policies, and institutions the better to reflect values of inclusion, fairness, and diversity.
- → Insist on accountability and responsiveness in such institutions as government, large corporations, and universities.

Charity: Give to a telethon for services for people with disabilities.
Change: Give to a group of disabled people and their allies pushing their elected officials to make public buildings accessible.

Charity: Donate to cancer research
Change: Donate to a group organizing to clean up the toxins in our environment and to pressure polluters.

Charity: Send money to a shelter for homeless families.
Change: Send money to a housing coalition working for affordable housing.

Charity: Give to a senior citizen center.
Change: Give to a senior action council working for home health aid coverage to enable older people to remain independent as long as possible.

Charity: Fund a scholarship for one high school student to attend college.
Change: Fund a student association organizing to ensure that higher education is affordable for everyone.

→ Expand democracy by involving those closest to social problems in determining their solution.

Organizing projects comes in all shapes and sizes. Some are small neighborhood-level efforts; others are national or even international in scope. Some focus on single issues; others link related issues, building coalitions that work to advance common interests. Some lobby; some litigate; some educate.

Successful social movements are built from the ground up. That's why we concentrate most of our attention on grassroots organizing. National organizations can provide expertise and resources to local efforts, coordinate regional and national activities, and, at times, supply leadership for movements. But without participation from the grassroots, the "base," national organizations have little impact.

People organize around all the familiar issues of our day, including race, health care, safety in the workplace, the environment, international and peace issues, housing, sexism, human rights, public education, and economic justice. Perhaps an issue close to your heart! Who are the constituents? Elders, youth, workers, people of color, GBLT people, people with disabilities, and all who long for a better world.

What do social change organizations do? They must analyze and agree on the root cause(s) of the situation or problem, determine goals, decide on a course of action, educate and organize their constituents, and raise money. People join social change organizations out of both self-interest and compassion for others. The act of coming together to hammer out strategies and goals builds unity.

Analyzing the root causes of why a situation exists is a primary difference between charity and social change. Charities don't ask why. Social change organizations do. Here are the kinds of questions these progressive organizations ask:

Why are there thirty million poor children in the United States?
Why do we have a health care system in which doctors are often obligated to act more like gatekeepers than healers? Why do more than forty million Americans have no health insurance at all?

Charity: Donate to a food pantry to provide supplemental food for lower-income working families.
Change: Raise the minimum wage so people can afford to purchase the food they need.

Charity is not a bad thing. But social change can ultimately eradicate the need for most charity.

One vision: People grow old with dignity, without fear of want. Quality education and access to decent health care are rights. Our economy builds prosperity and security for all. People are treated with dignity at work, and they earn livable wages. Everyone feels safe in his or her home, at work, and on the street. Our democracy has been invigorated and enlarged by eliminating the influence of money in politics and through the active involvement of the people closest to the consequences of political decisions. The principles of fairness and equality of opportunity for all are the foundation of our government and our nation's institutions. As a nation we take a long view of how to build environmental sustainability and, with other countries, are committed to do what is necessary to reverse environmental destruction. Our foreign policy is built on respect for the sovereignty of other countries, the promotion of human rights, and the willingness to accept international treaties and oversight, such as the United Nations and the World Court. As a people we have an abiding commitment to peace and disarmament.

Why have the richest 1 percent of households doubled their share of the wealth since 1975, owning more wealth than 95 percent of the population?

Why are nearly two million people in prison or jail in the United States? Why are there five times as many Black men in prison as in four-year colleges and universities?

Why do many people no longer feel secure in their jobs? Why is the largest private employer in the United States, Manpower, Inc., an agency for temporary workers?

Why do even those of us who have "won the rat race" often feel beleaguered and without enough time to enjoy our friends and families?

"Why" is a provocative and not always popular question, but the answers to it can become the foundation for strategy and action. What will a group do to convince others that its vision is the right one and is viable? How will it find the information and the allies that it needs? What steps will it take to realize its goals? The answers to these questions are never carved in stone; organizations must continually reassess their strategies and tactics.

Successful organizing may require courage. Imagine what it was like twenty years ago for "ordinary" people to gather around kitchen tables and in church basements and decide they were going to confront large corporations and government officials to stop nuclear power. Imagine the courage it takes for gay men and lesbians to "come out," to be visible, to their families and coworkers.

Along with courage and vision, what social change groups need is money. Financial resources are critical to organizing yet difficult to raise. Instant gratification doesn't exist for the social change organization or for its donors. When you give to social change organizing, you invest in the future.

Movements Make History . . . and Money Helps

"Philanthropy should . . . twist the tail of the future."—*Paul Ylvisaker*

Did you have an enjoyable weekend? Thank the labor movement, the folks who brought you the eight-hour day and the weekend. Have you voted recently? Thank the women's suffrage and African American civil rights movements for opening up our democracy to all citizens. Happy that your salad is free of DDT? Thank the United Farm Workers, whose union contract specified DDT's original ban.

On the surface, social change movements appear to be spontaneous bursts of energy, a sweep of people, outraged, rising to demand a change. But in truth they flow from careful organizing, massive public education, sustained agitation, and at times inspired collaboration across the divides of race, gender, and class. These movements are driven by human energy, intelligence, courage—and money.

Donors have played a significant role in the history of progressive social change. For instance, you probably remember the roles of Patrick Henry and Paul Revere in the American Revolution. But many of us forget that the colonists had no power to tax and raise money for the Continental army. Raising money from individuals was vital. Wealthy patriots financed and bought supplies from international dealers to back the independence movement. Ben Franklin secured loans and gifts, *well over a billion in today's dollars*, from private individuals in France.

In the movement to end slavery, a clandestine group of men calling themselves the Secret Six funded different wings of the abolitionist movement. The six included two Unitarian ministers, Theodore Parker and Thomas Higginson; Julia Ward Howe's husband, Samuel Howe; a former U.S. representative, Gerrit Smith; Franklin Sanborn; and George Stearns, one of the richest men in America. Publicly the Secret Six helped elect abolitionist activist Charles Sumner to Congress, supported the work of Frederick Douglass, and financed the abolitionist newspaper the *Liberator*, published by William Lloyd Garrison. They also funded the attempted insurrection at Harper's Ferry led by John Brown.

Social movements are built on donations both large and small, but their financial bases come from their members. The labor movement built itself through membership dues. Cesar Chavez, founder of the

United Farm Workers, collected $1 a month from farm workers who had little to spare. The contributions and sacrifices of African Americans, much of it funneled through networks of Black churches throughout the country, were the backbone of support for the civil rights movement. For example, the Congress of Racial Equality (CORE), founded in the forties by Bayard Rustin, had twelve thousand donors by the late fifties who gave an average of $4.83 each. In 1960, when Harry Belafonte and Eleanor Roosevelt stepped in to help raise funds, CORE's income skyrocketed.

Both the farm workers and civil rights movements received significant financial support from individuals' penny jars, allied organizations, wealthy individuals, and small progressive foundations. This behind-the-scenes funding helped finance movements: printing pamphlets and independent newspapers, renting meeting halls, making banners, raising bail money, and paying rent and utility bills for offices and the woefully inadequate salaries of organizers. As movements gain in strength and visibility, others not directly affected by the problem, or those who may seem to benefit from the status quo, may decide to join out of moral outrage or a reasoned commitment to the cause. Sometimes they help with money, and sometimes they give their time too.

Progressive social change ideas are often initially greeted by the larger society as dangerously radical or outrageously impractical. This was true when abolitionists argued that slavery was immoral. It was true when reformers tried to end child labor and suffragists claimed women should have the right to vote. In the 1930s, facing a nationwide depression, workers demanded jobs, unemployment insurance, a minimum wage, and government relief for the millions who were starving and homeless. Once more these "radical" demands were met with disbelief and outrage. Conservatives railed that these reforms would lead the country down the slippery slope to socialism. But rallying in a widespread movement, workers and their allies successfully pressured a scion of the wealthy, President Franklin D. Roosevelt, to develop the New Deal. By the end of the decade what had once been considered revolutionary had been enacted as government regulation. The rules had changed. These organizing efforts would not have succeeded without the vision and dedication of millions of people and significant amounts of financial support.

Social change can be maddeningly slow. The forces of the status quo are mighty. It took the women's suffrage movement seventy-odd years to secure the right of women to vote. Numerous campaigns, spearheaded by what is now the League of Women Voters, led to the adoption of the suffrage amendment by Congress in 1920. Women used a variety of tactics to win, ranging from massive hunger strikes to voting anyway and then being arrested. Thousands of women and men lent support, financial and otherwise, and dozens of wealthy women left bequests to the movement in their wills.

A Wider Generosity

To give to social change is to expand the notion of who is a member of your "family." Laurent Parks Daloz writes in her essay "Can Generosity Be Taught?": "Perhaps what distinguishes people committed to the common good is not so much a greater generosity as a wider one. Their giving, it would seem, extends not only to those within, but also to those beyond their own tribe. If we wish to expand our generosity, perhaps we have only to broaden our notion of who 'we' are."[2]

The quality of our lives is linked to the quality of the lives of people everywhere. This was abundantly clear from the Chernobyl accident, when people in Scandinavia and eastern Europe became sick. And there is now almost no place in North America, according to a recent federal study, to escape airborne toxic chemicals. The consequence? Every time you draw a breath in the great outdoors, you increase your risk of cancer. Truly we are all in this together.

The Movement to End Child Labor in the United States

In the early 1900s, after she had passed her seventieth birthday, Mother Jones, the most successful labor organizer in U.S. history, took up a new battle. Horrified by the hunched backs, dismembered limbs, and hopeless eyes of working children in textile mills, she organized the Children's March, a month-long protest against child labor.

With no money in her pockets, Mother Jones led hundreds of children through Pennsylvania, New Jersey, and New York. At each town she and the children told of machines designed for children's small hands, of eight-year-olds working sixteen hours a day, of arms ripped off by machinery.

The march also showed Mother Jones's genius for fund raising; through the donations of shopkeepers' wives, rural women, and the wives of Trenton, New Jersey, police officers, she fed and clothed the children as never before. As they ate better, they spoke more damningly of their suffering in the factories.

Less than a year after the children had returned to their families, with new clothes and full bellies, Pennsylvania passed the most progressive child labor law in the nation. Other states soon followed.

Our Mission, Should We Choose to Accept It . . .

"Even if all the money given to the social change world were given instead to meet immediate needs, that only would be a drop in the ocean of real need. So you have to give to those organizations actually trying to change the rules of the game—the way wealth is distributed in this country and the way services are provided. If you change the rules of the game sufficiently, if you decrease economic inequality and inequality of power, then more people would be able to create adequate, even pleasurable lives for themselves and less money would have to go into immediate needs."—*Allen Hunter, donor, Wisconsin Community Fund*

Of all the giving in America, only between 2 and 4 percent goes to progressive social change work. On the other hand, tens of millions of dollars of corporate and individual contributions have been underwriting the conservative movement. Money has clearly made a difference to the political right wing. Twelve key foundations and individuals have provided focused funding for an infrastructure of conservative and extremist think tanks, advocacy groups, and grassroots organizing efforts.

Our challenge is to move more money into social change organizing and progressive social change foundations. We are about movement building and grassroots organizing that will always be the basis for deep and lasting change. For people concerned about the health of the environment, a fair economy, a healthy democracy, and equal rights for all, there is a lot of work to be done . . . *and more history to be made.*

The Coalition for Human Dignity

A national white supremacist strategy known as the "Northwest Imperative"
called on white supremacists to turn the Northwest into a white homeland.
They believed that there were so few people of color in our region that there
would be no resistance.
They were wrong.

"The Coalition for Human Dignity organized in response to the
brutal murder of an Ethiopian student, Mulugeta Seraw, at the hands
of neo-Nazi skinheads," says Scot Nakagawa, the group's first staff
person. "Generally, when a murder of this kind occurs, law enforcement cracks down, putting a chill on hate groups and causing a reduction in hate activity. But in Portland, Oregon, as a result of police
reports claiming there were no racist skinhead hate groups here and
the indecisiveness of a city concerned about tourism revenues, hate
crimes rose. Our city was dubbed the hate crimes capital of the United
States.

"The coalition mounted a campaign to expose white supremacists
and organize neighborhood opposition to the hate groups. We compiled personal testimony, photographs, neo-Nazi literature, record-
ings of telephone hate lines, and other evidence to prove that there
was active neo-Nazi recruitment in Portland and throughout the
state. Our research became the basis of a campaign to draw attention
to a problem that eventually garnered international media attention."

One of the coalition's first efforts was to assist in organizing a chapter of Anti-Racist Action, a youth group opposed to white supremacy
and neo-Nazis. Anti-Racist Action and the Coalition for Human Dignity led a campaign in the city's alternative rock and roll venues to oppose the skinhead groups that were successfully recruiting supporters
at rock and roll shows. By organizing in the alternative music scene,
youth activists were able to recruit a base of opposition to hate groups
among young people who were tired of being intimidated and ha-

rassed by neo-Nazi thugs. Anti-Racist Action also organized their own concerts to recruit additional support and led a young people's march through downtown Portland to send a message through the media concerning the youths' opposition to hate. These activities forced hate groups to abandon their strategy of recruiting disaffected young people at rock and roll shows.

The coalition also worked with neighborhood associations to build local opposition. It was able to demonstrate that neo-Nazi organizing was the source of much of the violence taking place in neighborhoods. Coalition activists shared information with neighborhood leaders and helped inspire neighborhood canvasses and demonstrations to draw attention to the problem.

A highlight of the coalition's early work was the March for Dignity and Diversity, the largest antiracist march and rally in the Pacific Northwest at the time. More than two thousand people turned out to "celebrate unity in diversity" and to oppose hate crimes. The march coincided with the start of the Southern Poverty Law Center's civil rights lawsuit against national neo-Nazi leader Tom Metzger for his involvement in the murder of Mulugeta Seraw. The event was covered in print and electronic media, from *Good Morning America* to *Parade* magazine and through news outlets in Japan, the Netherlands, France, Italy, Germany, Britain, and Mexico.

The cumulative impact of this work was profound. The Portland Police Department succumbed to public pressure and changed its policies in regard to white supremacist groups, establishing a special hate crimes unit. When the Oklahoma City bombing occurred, the national news media turned to the coalition to assist in understanding the militia phenomenon.

The success of the coalition, and the research materials it produced on white supremacy in Oregon, helped launch a number of other groups, including the Rural Organizing Project, the People of Faith against Bigotry, and the Homophobic Violence Documentation Project, as well as the antibigotry coalitions still active in some Portland neighborhoods.

"Until McKenzie River Gathering came along and provided us with our very first grant, no foundation would support the then-controversial work of the coalition. Everyone from mainstream foundations to the local police was claiming that hate groups weren't active in Portland and weren't a serious threat," says Scot Nakagawa. "Now the organization is a regional think tank providing data and information to organizations and government agencies throughout the Northwest region and internationally."

Chapter 3

What's Going On Out There

Community Organizing Strategies

Arts and cultural work can transform people's understanding of past or present conditions through the use of theater, music, and community participation in designing and producing arts events.

Thousands of groups and organizations are working for change, not charity, and new ones form every day. Their strategies and constituencies vary, but their successes give us singular cause to cheer. It's inspiring to see the range of options progressive givers have for putting their money to work. Here we share some real-life examples so you can see what a difference your money can make. (The organizations we highlight in the book and in the appendices should not be looked at as the A list. They are wonderful and there are thousands of other great groups making a difference all over the country.)

Let's start our tour in Washington, D.C.

"*What CAYA does is so important . . . it allows each and every participant to look inside themselves and find out who they are and what they stand for. CAYA gives us the tools to become better at whatever it is we want to do. However, more important, they make us realize that nobody can change something for us. We have to do that ourselves.*"—*Ruxandra Georgiana Gecui, Wilson High School student*

The Community Alliance for Youth Action (CAYA) builds the next generation of social change activists. In some of the most economically disadvantaged schools in Washington, D.C., classroom teaching is now connected to the real world. Through Community Action Tours about social justice concerns, such as Environmental Justice and Alternatives to Violence, students learn more about neighborhood issues and are challenged to take action. Community Action Tours embody the belief that people are more engaged in learning when they are actually doing something.

The Environmental Justice tour begins by exploring a problem. Students may go to an illegal dump site, do water testing in a local river, or visit a neighborhood that has elevated cancer rates because it is next to an incinerator. Their vision of what is possible is developed by experiencing the beauty of the environment through outdoor activities (e.g., canoeing), meeting with activists, and creating their own images of what a clean environment would be like. The "connection" step comes through workshops at which students explore the ways environmental pollution affects their lives. The high rate of asthma in their neighborhoods, for example, is a visceral connection for many. Ideas about action emerge from meetings with activists, government representatives, corporations, and others involved in the problem. Participants then choose an action step that they implement with CAYA's support.

The students choose different actions. Two schools have started Coalitions against Racism, and one organized conflict resolution workshops in the schools. Student groups have testified at city council meetings, developed recycling projects, and started urban gardening programs. One class organized a cleanup project during which forty-five students removed two hundred tires from a creek next to their school. In the wake of continued illegal dumping in the creek, the students created an Environmental Justice Group, the EJs. Their goals are the installation of No Dumping signs and a regular trash pickup schedule in their neighborhood.

CAYA has received funding from the Funding Exchange.

In the last decade, issues of environmental justice—the illegal dumping of hazardous wastes and the hugely disproportionate numbers of

Constituency organizing is community organizing based on who you are rather than on where you live or what you do. Many identity-based organizations work in coalition with other groups because most societal issues have an impact on us all.

Coalition building is making an alliance of organizations that work together for joint action. Together they will have more visibility, they can share resources, and they can build a stronger base of support for their campaigns.

Film, video, and radio productions are used by organizations and independent producers to make issues vivid and understandable to people. When designed as an organizing tool, these types of communication can be an effective way to explain a complex story.

polluting factories and power plants in poor neighborhoods and communities of color—have vastly expanded and invigorated the traditional environmental movement. Here's another grassroots response to environmental devastation:

"We used to go down here to the river to catch frogs. . . . We used to hear them croak, but I have not seen a frog here for the longest time. My grandchildren have never seen a live frog."—ISABEL TRUJILLO RENDO, resident of Arroyo Hondo, Amigos Bravos Oral History Project

In the last fifty years the Rio Grande watershed has changed from a vital, healthy source of water to a serious health hazard. In 1993 it was named the Most Endangered River in North America. Industrial and government waste, sewage discharge, poor management, mining, and nonsustainable grazing practices have led to the river's decline. But the memory of a healthy river that supported communities lives on, and Amigos Bravos/Friends of the Wild Rivers is committed to restoring it.

Amigos Bravos was organized in response to a plan by Molycorp, a mining company that is the source of much of the river's pollution, to develop a tailing facility on Guadeloupe Mountain, a pristine, undeveloped piece of land. Molycorp already had a dismal history with its tailing facilities. (After ore is processed, the leftovers, or tailings, are pumped away from the mine site, mixed with water, and pumped into "lakes" and "ponds" that are essentially repositories for this highly toxic sludge.) Amigos Bravos was the lead plaintiff in an appeal filed by the Sierra Club Legal Defense Fund challenging Molycorp. It won, and the proposal was rescinded, although Molycorp and its abuse of the river remain a central issue.

Amigos Bravos provides a range of technical support to indigenous communities throughout the Rio Grande watershed in New Mexico through its outreach and education program. It supports a volunteer program that organizes its members to participate in cleanup efforts and the replanting of native vegetation. The organization looks to communities for cultural resources that can provide models and directions toward making the rivers sustainable. Its oral history project interviews elders about their memories of the river and its uses. The information it gathers is used both to support its work and to inform its plans. For example, Molycorp claims that the condition of the river has always been the same as it is now. Historical information about the community's use of the river for drinking water within people's memory gives Amigos Bravos tools with which to challenge the company. The rapid changes in the environment increase the value of historical information that could easily be lost with the passing of a generation.

Amigos Bravos has been bridging the gap between largely white urban environmentalists and Latino and Native American rural communities that are often pitted against one another in environmental struggles. It maintains "that environmental justice and social justice go hand-in-hand," believing that "the way to protect and reclaim the river ecosystem and the quality of our water is through the empowerment of the populations that are sustained by that water."

Amigos Bravos shows that groups can work together for common goals, even if their perspectives are very different. This kind of coalition building is difficult, but when it works, it can really make a difference, as our next example shows.

Amigos Bravos also received Funding Exchange support.

In the spring of 1991, thirty-four organizations in Pittsburgh, ranging from unions to gay and lesbian organizations to local chapters of the National Association for the Advancement of Colored People (NAACP) and the American Civil Liberties Union (ACLU) to religious and community-based groups, organized the Alliance for Progressive Action (APA). Their intention was to provide a network of mutual support and to respond in a unified voice to issues of common concern.

When issues came up, organizations called on other groups within the alliance, and the numbers of people supporting each action increased significantly. A strike at a major food store received broader support than the local union could have mobilized on its own. At the time of the Rodney King decision APA was able to mobilize five thousand people in forty-eight hours for a peaceful rally.

The alliance has helped develop a number of proactive campaigns.

and services in protest of a company's actions. In 1995 the threat of a boycott was enough to move the Gap to force factory owners in Central America to improve working conditions in plants from which the company purchases clothes.

»→ *Community economic development* recognizes the need for "ordinary" people to hold the vision for what community is and how community needs will be met. It can result in affordable housing, jobs, and a more actively involved community.

»→ *Divestment campaigns* are organized efforts to get individuals and institutions (such as pension funds) to sell off their stock in companies whose business practices undermine human rights, ruin the environment, or create harmful products.

Electoral work can force the political structure to live up to its ideals by responding to those who have been

traditionally left out. Voter
registration and participation drives, campaign fi-
nance reform, third-party
organizing, and campaigns
to promote proportional
representation are strategies that social change
groups are using to increase
democratic participation.

G*rassroots lobbying* is
essential for making
and keeping the govern-
ment accountable. Organi-
zations lobby to create laws
that protect our civil rights,
our communities and envi-
ronments, our workplaces,
and our children. There is
also lobbying to pressure
government to use its re-
sources to provide for
human needs.

G*rassroots organizing*
means working with
people directly to involve
them in an issue, a cam-
paign, or a movement.
Whether grassroots organizing is done by
small local or
large na-
tional orga-
nizations, the

When a study found that Pennsylvania had one of the highest level of hate activities in the country, APA spawned the Coalition to Counter Hate Groups. It spun off yet another coalition, Citizens for Police Accountability (CPA), which succeeded in a campaign to establish an independent citizen police review board. The Alliance for Progressive Action shows what careful movement building can accomplish. It has received support from the Three Rivers Community Fund.

The response to the agenda of the radical right is at this time primar-ily coming from the grassroots. The Coalition to Counter Hate Groups, which the alliance formed, the Coalition for Human Dignity (profiled after Chapter 2), and others are working on issues that many of us—and most traditional foundations—would rather pretend do not exist. History shows us otherwise. Below is another response to the right-wing agenda, whose end is to change forever the content and nature of public education.

"*What the best and wisest parent wants for his own child, that must the community want for all its children. Any other ideal for our schools is narrow and unlovely. . . ."—John Dewey, leader in progressive ed-ucation,* The School and Society

In the mid eighties a group of Milwaukee-based teachers and ac-tivists came together to study the connections between schools and broader community problems. In a city dominated by a preeminent provoucher educational policy institute, these educators searched for ideas and practical tools for school reform based on values of equity and justice. When they didn't find any in the prominent educational publications, they started their own. *Rethinking Schools* began in a Mil-waukee kitchen with a mission of creating a newspaper to which a range of voices involved in education, from practicing teachers to parents to researchers, could come to address the educational, practi-cal, and policy concerns currently facing America's schools. Originally envisioned as a Milwaukee-based project, *Rethinking Schools* has de-veloped into a national voice for proequality educators.

The quarterly *Rethinking Schools* has taken on a wide spectrum of educational issues. It has published extensively on vouchers and school "choice," standardized testing and its impact on educational achievement, and the complicated problem of school funding. As an organizing vehicle for people committed to democracy, it also continually confronts, discusses, and exposes right-wing educational agendas and the many ways they are manifested, from abstinence only sex education programs to the introduction of creation science as an alternate scientific perspective into biology curricula. *Rethinking Schools* also publishes materials that take on many of these issues in great depth, providing analysis, resources, and action steps to address the politics of education.

The mission of *Rethinking Schools* is based in a vision of schools as the place where our experiment in democracy is constantly worked and reworked. Its materials reflect a belief that "classrooms can be places of hope, where students and teachers gain glimpses of the kind of society we could live in and where students learn the academic and critical skills needed to make that vision a reality." The Wisconsin Community Fund has supported this project.

It's amazing how many stories about the origin of social change groups begin with "We met around a kitchen table." Our next story, one that highlights the role of progressive legislation, is about a group of women who challenged the notion of gender-based jobs. They organized after several years of potluck dinner discussions.

"One of the biggest challenges we face is getting the world as a whole to acknowledge that there's no such thing as women's work and men's work," says Lauren Sugarman, Chicago Women in Trades director. "Empowerment is the key. If we had not organized on our own behalf, no one would have taken on these issues."

Chicago Women in Trades (CWIT) helps women enter and remain in high-wage, high-skilled jobs still predominantly held by men and also develops proactive legislation ensuring the fair treatment of women in the workplace. Through direct service programs (e.g., career fairs, preapprenticeship courses, and career awareness workshops for schoolgirls) it helps women pursue careers in the trades. Its adult training programs enable women to develop the kinds of networks,

key element is to involve people at the local level—in action and decision making.

Long-range planning and strategic development are important since the results of social change work may be slow in coming. A long-range plan keeps an organization's work manageable while holding the goal clearly in sight.

Mass mobilization is a strategy to show visible widespread support for an issue. Mobilizations of hundreds of thousands of people were critical in stopping the Vietnam War.

Infrastructure encompasses organizations that support grassroots organizations. Sometimes it takes place behind the scenes through critical strategic development, training, or media work. Sometimes it's in the forefront, exposing issues and proposing solutions. Infrastructure can include:

⇥ *Technical assistance,* to train groups how to organize, fund-raise, do media work, develop leaders, and build organizations. Even Rosa Parks received training at the Highlander Center of Tennessee before she refused to give up her seat on the bus.

⇥ *Internet site development,* to provide us with access to information, and to get the word out about actions and strategies.

⇥ *Funding networks,* to help us expand the financial resources for the movement for progressive change.

⇥ *Research,* to provide organizations with the facts.

⇥ *Think tanks,* to help social change groups to develop strategic thinking and policies.

⇥ *Progressive media,* to create a forum for debate. Investigative journalism, including magazines, journals, news services, television, and radio, raises issues before they reach the mainstream press.

like mentorship opportunities, that men in trades have always had. It also builds the next generation of tradeswomen by offering hands-on project-oriented workshops for girls and concrete links between young women training for trade positions and women working in the field.

CWIT also moves beyond direct service by advocating for implementation of equitable work conditions and policies by unions, employers, and government agencies. Breaking New Ground: Work Site 2000, a research project aimed at developing positive legislation, identified the range of barriers to women's long-term retention in the trades and painted a picture of what a gender-equitable workplace would be like. This vision and analysis are a foundation for both local and national legislation. It has also inspired women to take the lead in building networks of support at work sites by reaching out to new women workers and ensuring that women's issues are addressed on the job. From the leadership role that members play in supporting tradeswomen in Chicago to the impact of their research and action on policy, Chicago Women in Trades demonstrates the many ways that groups of people can make progress on the issues that affect their lives. CWIT has received support from the Crossroads Fund.

The Chicago tradeswomen are an example of how it is often necessary for people to organize around their identities. This is even more powerful when identity-based organizations bring their constituencies' needs and experiences into the larger world of organizing. The next two examples, both from New York City, show how this can happen.

The Audre Lorde Project (ALP) is a multipurpose center for lesbian, gay, bisexual, two-spirit, and transgender (LGBTST) people of color. Located in Brooklyn, ALP organizes, advocates, and promotes coalition building around issues of social and economic justice for LGBTST people of color and other communities struggling for justice. Initiatives and program areas include:

⇥ *Countering homophobia/heterosexism.* ALP conducts workshops in communities of color (including immigrants and refugees) to counter stereotypes and prejudice against the LGBTST community.

> → *Valuing Families/Building Community Documentation Project.* This volunteer-led working group documents organizing efforts and family and community structures within the LGBTST community, using video, photography, and oral history.
> → *Working Group on Immigrant Rights and Education.* This group educates, mobilizes, and supports LGBTST immigrants, migrants, and refugees of color and others around broader immigrant and LGBTST issues.

The ALP serves as a "home base" for LGBTST people of color to organize, to work in coalition and across differences.

The second New York identity-based organization is known as JFREJ.

More than a decade ago, Nelson Mandela visited New York City for the first time. Because of his past association with Yasir Arafat, Mandela was officially shunned by the Orthodox Jewish population of New York, a relatively small but vocal group. Infuriated that a man who was such a symbol of hope and freedom was snubbed and outraged at the general tendency of the Orthodox Jews to presume to speak for the entire Jewish community in New York, a group of communal leaders, rabbis, educators, writers, and activists organized the Jews for Racial and Economic Justice (JFREJ).

JFREJ, a grantee of the North Star Fund, mobilizes the progressive Jewish population in New York not only around issues affecting their own community but also around crosscultural struggles, through connecting their work to communities of color. Examples include:

> → *Supporting the ongoing struggle to end segregation in the housing units in Williamsburg, Brooklyn.* African American and Latino people make up 85 percent of the population there, yet through "arrangements" between the New York City Housing Authority and the conservative Hasidic Jewish community, more than 70 percent of the housing units are given to Orthodox Jewish families. JFREJ has takes a great risk as an organization in this struggle, saying that the abolition of these illegal "arrangements" was not anti-Semitic but rather a civil rights issue.
> → *Active organizing to end police brutality.* JFREJ was one of the first groups to advocate the creation of a Civilian Complaint Board and

***

Labor organizing has been critical in creating social change, not only for unionized workers but for all workers. Labor organizing can bring about decent wages, safer working conditions, fair labor practices, and basic dignity and human rights in the workplace.

Leadership development is best explained by the saw that "Organizers organize organizations." The job of an organizer is to recruit and train people affected by a problem so they can mobilize others, determine strategy, and speak for the organization. Effective leadership development results in many people sharing

power and acquiring skills, rather than just a few running the show.

has worked with communities of color within New York to demand police accountability. JFREJ produces a 'zine (a self-published magazine) aimed at Jewish teenagers on police brutality, and more than seventy-five Jewish community leaders, rabbis, and activists participated under JFREJ's banner in a civil disobedience action to demand justice for the 1999 murder of Amadou Diallo by white police officers.

Says Cindy Greenburg of JFREJ: "Our religious and secular history as Jews teaches us to be accountable to others, to care for others, and that the struggles of 'marginalized' people today *are* our struggles."

Since you don't often hear about this kind of cutting-edge local organizing through the mainstream media, how do you find about it? How do you find organizations that touch your heart, your values, and your vision? You may hear of amazing groups through the Internet, magazine articles, journals, and newspapers. Contact groups you are interested in, and ask them to send you information. Friends and people who work in the field can be a good source of information too.

We suggest you contact local or national social change foundations (see Appendix B). Their annual reports generally have summaries of organizations they have funded. Call them. *You can do this even if you have no plans to become further involved with them.* Their main goal, like yours, is to move money out to movements for change.

Colorado Cross-Disability Coalition

"Charity has been damaging to people with disability. It has kept them in a powerless position. For example, instead of giving people access to the resources necessary to hire an assistant to help them get out of bed, charity forces them to depend on the goodwill of a volunteer. If the goal is to integrate people with disabilities into the mainstream world, economic empowerment, not charity, is the key."

—Julie Reiskin, director, Colorado Cross-Disability Coalition

The Americans with Disabilities Act (ADA) was a huge victory for people working on issues of disability and equal access. Finally there was a legal tool to bring about the kinds of changes necessary to level the playing field for people with disabilities. Activists in Denver, Colorado, wanted to make sure that the victory wasn't hollow for lack of enforcement. They formed the Colorado Cross-Disability Coalition (CCDC) to make ADA a meaningful law. One of its first acts was to sue the state legislature for its lack of compliance with ADA. CCDC won, and a strong grassroots voice for disability rights started making itself heard.

CCDC organizes and advocates for people with disabilities in Colorado. It is a significant force in the state legislature. In the last legislative session it monitored 169 bills, reporting on their status to CCDC members on a daily basis. CCDC members worked for, and achieved, the creation of a pilot program allowing people to keep Medicaid when they get jobs, removing a significant barrier to employment. In the realm of consumer legislation, they have supported bills that allow people to hire their own home health care workers and have helped create a wheelchair lemon law. They've also squared off against the Social Security Administration (SSA) in their effort to eliminate the PASS (Plan to Achieve Self Sufficiency) work incentive program. This program, passed by Congress, allowed people to save a portion of their disability payments to pay for things that would enable them to work, such as a van for a person in a wheelchair or college tuition. However, SSA made changes that cost people their health coverage, forced them to sell specialized equipment, and charged people—years later—for earlier participation in the program. Through effective legislative pressure CCDC was able to get at least 50 percent of the most detrimental policies overturned in Colorado.

The backbone of CCDC is its highly organized constituency, particularly in rural areas throughout the state. The coalition informs communities about its work and encourages local leadership. When leadership emerges and people are ready to work, CCDC helps them develop the programs needed in their community. The work of these chapters ranges from educational forums to independent living centers to legislative actions.

All chapters work to hold their state representatives accountable to the disability agenda. At last year's first annual Grassroots Summit, CCDC's community leaders developed a broad-based disability platform for candidates to respond to. This has been used in candidate forums and electoral education programs to inform citizens about legislative issues related to disability and to pressure candidates and elected officials to support a positive disability agenda.

In 1996 the CCDC board decided that if companies were going to comply voluntarily with ADA, they already would have done it. So it developed a legal program by recruiting lawyers with an interest in disability and suing noncompliant companies. Currently it is developing a tester program that will train people with disabilities to test access in different locations and within various industries. The initial group of testers has focused on taxi companies, highlighting issues of accessibility to transportation.

This balance of advocacy and organizing is critical to CCDC's success. Director Julie Reiskin says, "Advocacy won't work if you don't have the constituency base. And why have the base if you're not going to do anything with it? Grassroots organizing gives people the tools and confidence to be politically involved. Once they become active, their whole lives come together. People with disabilities are so conditioned to think that *they're* the problems and that *they* need to change. When they start advocating for other people with disabilities, they begin to unravel those messages and learn that they aren't the problem; systems are."

For more information on the Colorado Cross–Disability Coalition, please contact the Chinook Fund (see Appendix A).

Part II

Your Money, Yourself

Chapter 4

Vision + Belief = Action for Change

Giving money to social change is fundamentally an act of vision. It is a demonstration of belief in the possibility of a more just and equitable world. Developing a commitment to social change requires a positive vision of the future and a belief that change is possible. Yet vision and belief are not always easy to come by.

To become a good giver, it is critical to become a visionary. So, in addition to sharing information and inspiration on giving, we want to help you develop some of the intangibles that are essential to create and sustain dynamic giving plans. In this chapter we look at the role that vision and belief play in working for change. Along the way we also examine at our cultural addiction to cynicism and how it can drain our hopes for change. We'll offer practical suggestions about how you can bolster and maintain your vision and your belief in change.

> "I see conditions everywhere I want to change. One block away people are out on the street with no place to live. Well, I don't have that much money; I can't make that much of a difference. But then there's what the Talmud said: 'It is not incumbent on you to finish the work, neither is it permitted to desist from the work altogether.' "
> —Donor, Bread + Roses Community Fund

Cynicism: Why Belief Is Hard to Hold On To

We live in a world where change often seems unlikely. The magnitude of social problems, the complexity of each issue, and the apparent strength of the status quo can seem overwhelming, especially because organizing for social change is rarely heard about in the mainstream media. For instance, an annual vigil takes place at the School of the Americas (SOA), a U.S. Army facility that trains tens of thousands of police and military personnel from dictatorships in Latin America. The vigil commemorates the murder of six Jesuit priests at the hands of a Salvadoran army unit made up primarily of SOA graduates. Each year the protest grows. In 1998 more than seven thousand religious people, young folks, and concerned citizens participated in three days of nonviolent protest at the site. More than twenty-three hundred people risked arrest by walking onto Fort Benning land. But barely a word or image of this demonstration of outrage and sorrow was heard or seen by anyone in the nation.

It is easy to understand why many are cynical about change. These days cynicism is viewed as the logical choice for those who know better than to hope. There is a kind of hipness in "believing" that change is impossible, a social ridicule aimed at those gullible or naïve enough to take seriously the possibility of a better world. But individual cynicism is rarely a simple response to the perceived inevitability of the status quo. It is often an easy out for people who are daunted by the immensity of the challenge. Or it can be a protective stance for those who fear being taken in by false hope or who have been deeply disappointed by having had their hopes dashed. Maintaining a vision of change and a belief in its possibility requires that we respond to some of these real forces in ways that don't immobilize us.

Our culture fans the flames of cynicism and hopelessness. The futility of change is unremittingly drilled into our heads by media that emphasize what is terrible in our communities and offer only individualized solutions, rarely exploring the possibilities that exist in collective responses or the progressive experiments that work. Pundits and commentators are caught up in their own version of the "more cynical than thou" ethos that sheds a doubting light on any sign of positive action. The bankruptcy of many of our elected officials gives us plenty of reason to abandon hope. Also, consumer culture—the advertising industry in particular—has been stunningly successful at reducing significant movements for change into opportunities to sell products. The use of images, ideas, and slogans of these movements to market the latest innovation in detergent, appliances, or personal hygiene products trivializes the vision and the successes of these movements. (If you just relied on advertisements for information, you could conclude that the most significant achievement of the entire women's movement is a newfound freedom to choose what brand of tampons to buy.)

People find the strength to work for change in many places. Some take inspiration from their understanding of the dynamics of history and earlier movements for change. Others are moved by a deeply held set of values and sense of morality. The spirit of resistance motivates many to refuse to participate in systems that are destructive, leading to the many "Not in Our Name" campaigns that bring awareness to critical concerns. Spirituality and faith traditions are another source of inspiration, where vision and belief are used to bring spiritual truths into material form.

> "As I understand the Christian Gospel and its Jewish roots, justice is absolutely central to what God is about, and building human community is also central, and those two go together. The whole concept of shalom, of health or wholeness, is a social, communal, and personal expression of what it means to be human and to be faithful."—*Art Lloyd, donor, Wisconsin Community Fund*

Developing Vision

To inspire and sustain hope, you need to work with both the material and the abstract, analysis and imagination. Analysis helps us understand what's wrong, how it got that way, and, most important, how change can occur. Imagination enables us to envision new possibilities.

Analyzing the Situation

Look at your own experience. What do you need for a good life? Once you've established your standard of what you need in order to thrive, you can analyze why those needs aren't being met for everyone. An analytical path toward developing a vision takes a systematic approach to evaluating the current state of society. The foundation of

The next time you feel overwhelmed by the challenge of change, remember this:

In 1905 the American Woolen Company built the largest cloth-producing factory in the world in Lawrence, Massachusetts. Thousands of immigrants were lured there by posters promising good jobs and future wealth. This dream of a better life became a nightmare. Women and children worked fifty-four-hour weeks at ten cents an hour.

On January 12, 1912, *thirty-five thousand* mill hands walked off their jobs in protest of a cut in their meager wages. Despite inadequate food, beatings, shootings, and jail sentences, the men, women, and children of Lawrence, *speaking twenty-seven different languages,* stood firm. On March 12—sixty-three days later—the American Woolen Company gave in, and the workers won a raise and improved conditions. At one of the many rallies during the strike, women carried a banner proclaiming WE WANT BREAD, BUT ROSES TOO.

this perspective is found in some basic questions: What is the reality of the situation? Why is it that way? What can be done, or is currently being done, about it? What does history teach us about similar situations? Your answers to these questions are the building blocks of a comprehensive vision of change.

Opening Your Mind

Spiritual practice, such as meditation or prayer, can be an effective way to open your mind (and your heart) to the real possibility of change. These practices often cultivate a concrete, bodily understanding of our fundamental interconnection with all life and the role we can play in the healing or suffering of "the whole." Spirituality helps us see how much of life, both personal and social, is the result of human choices, not of divine decree. Many spiritual traditions offer the vision, or give the imperative, that different choices can and must be made. Traditions of faith—Judaism, Christianity, Buddhism, Islam—can connect us with an important source of our values about equality, justice, and environmental respect. Some believe that hope and despair are fundamentally concerns of the spirit. If you have a spiritual outlook, you know that faith in things unseen requires risk. When one faces the kind of despair that may arise while one takes risks for change, tools of faith, which acknowledge "the dark night of the soul," can be indispensable in keeping hope alive.

Visions for change need to be developed on a community as well as an individual level. The visions that sustain movements emerge from the hopes and aspirations of large groups of people that are willing to work hard to make them real. In developing a vision for change, it's important to synthesize our individual dreams into a collective image of the future. The "Twenty-five Year Visioning Exercise" from

Bridging the Class Divide, by Linda Stout (see Appendix G: Books about Social Change) can be used with any group to help it work together and take seriously its ability to claim the future by first articulating a vision.

Cultivating Belief

Belief that change is possible is the fuel of social movements. Opponents of progressive change know this, and a common strategy for undermining a movement is to generate a sense of futility in its members. Sustaining belief is critical to develop a long-term commitment to social change giving. The history of positive change is often obscured. Take the time to learn about it, and claim it as your heritage. Read about social change movements and how much has truly been achieved when people work together for justice.

A good way to connect to the spirit of change is to read the biographies, autobiographies, and memoirs of people touched by social change movements. These personal histories allow you to experience the power of moments of social transformation. Reading people's stories can make tangible the large-scale agendas, strategies, and his-

> "Kids have an innate sense of justice ('Daddy, that not *fair!*'). By the values we hold and the actions we take as parents, we can help connect that belief in justice beyond the home to the larger society."— *George Pillsbury, donor, Funding Exchange*

tories of mass movements, and learning of their struggles can inspire your own.

Alternative media can help you understand social change, both past and present. Although not always easy to come by, alternative film, video, and radio can provide compelling illustrations of a wide range of issues. There is also a diverse list of wonderful magazines and newspapers in Appendix G that can be an ongoing source of education and inspiration.

Take Hope Personally

Our sources of hope, and of despair, are often deeply connected to our personal experiences. One way to cultivate a hope for societal change is to reflect on how hope lives in your life. Understanding your sources of hope can help you identify resources you can call on when it falters. Hope can be strengthened by your looking at your own history. When did you feel hope as a child? Did you have experiences in which your hopes were dashed? Did the people you were raised by encourage or discourage your hopes? How has that affected your feelings about acting on your beliefs today? What makes you feel hopeful now? The more we develop our inner resources, the stronger we can be in the face of external challenge to our beliefs.

Pitch In

A visceral way of seeing that change is possible is to join social change organizations. This can give you a sense of how difficult and frustrating the work can be, but it will also connect you to amazing people for whom change is not only possible but is occurring. Experiencing that commitment, and seeing results, can be invaluable.

"There is such an incredible adrenaline rush to be in a group of mindful people that believe they can create change. I can make more than a financial contribution by being an activist and feeling part of making that change. It is a complete win!"—*Tracy Gary, coauthor,* Inspired Philanthropy

Acknowledge Despair, but Hope Anyway

When despair hits hard, remember that ultimately unjust systems buckle under the weight of their contradictions. Philosopher Cornel West speaks to this kind of hope, distinguishing it from optimism. He writes:

> [H]ope is not the same as optimism. Optimism adopts the role of the spectator who surveys the evidence in order to infer that things are going to get better. Yet we know that the evidence does not look good. Hope enacts the stance of the participant who actively struggles against the evidence in order to change the deadly tides of wealth inequality, group xenophobia, and personal despair. Only a new wave of vision, courage, and hope can keep us sane and preserve the decency and dignity requisite to revitalize our organizational energy for the work to be done. To live is to wrestle with despair yet never to allow despair to have the last word.

"In the Dharma there are no oughts. They disappear in the realization of dependent co-arising. [T]here is the simple, profound awareness that everything is interdependent and mutually conditioning—each thought, word and act, and all beings too, in the vast web of life. Once there is insight into that radical interdependence, certain ways of living and behaving emerge as intrinsic to it."—*Joanna Macy*, In Indra's Net

The Women's Cancer Resource Center

"So many advancements in understanding and treating breast cancer, from
increased research dollars to new treatments, have happened because
women have organized and demanded them."
—Barbara Weiner, executive director, Women's Cancer Resource Center

The rate of cancer, and breast cancer in particular, has grown exponentially. Today one out of three Americans gets cancer. At the turn of the century it was one in one hundred. In 1970 one in twenty American women was diagnosed with breast cancer. Now it's one in eight.

In 1993 the Women's Cancer Resource Center (WCRC) was organized in the Twin Cities by women with cancer. Besides offering information about cancer and its treatment, the founders were concerned about the reasons behind the sharp increase in cancer rates.

Today WCRC is an information, support, and advocacy organization for women with any kind of cancer. "The medical experience has really stripped away women's feeling of their own personal power," observes Weiner. "Getting accurate information is essential for women to feel in control of their own health care decisions." The center offers various programs: a phone information and referral line, research support, a massage program, and a lending library. It organizes support groups that are difficult to find in mainstream cancer support organizations. These range from groups for lesbians with cancer to women exploring alternative and complementary treatments to women coping with recurrence or long-term survival. Women's empowerment is central to their mission.

WCRC's work is not limited to support. Advocacy and activism are a key piece of what it does. In particular, it focuses on the links between cancer and the environment and what individuals can do to affect policy and clean up the environment.

Cancer activism takes different forms. For some people it means working to increase the amount of research money. Others make sure that there is solid legislation ensuring that medical rights and insurance needs are protected. WCRC is currently helping forward a national campaign titled "Health Care without Harm." This project helps hospitals reduce their use of environmental pollutants. The incineration of medical waste is a particular concern because burning plastics releases dioxin, a known carcinogen. WCRC sponsors conferences for hospital administrators to discuss change and offers hospitals follow-up support.

The center develops political understanding of cancer by looking at the part that industry, insurance, pharmaceutical, and health care corporations may play in promoting and profiting from cancer. It challenges "the cancer industry" by asking hard questions: Who's receiving the money for research? Who has what to gain from the outcome of the research? How are clinical trials being done? Who is paying for those trials? Answers to these questions inform both WCRC's programs and organizing agenda. "There's tremendous profit to be made from cancer on many levels," according to Weiner. "We have seen corporations involved in cancer on every level, from producing carcinogens to screening to treatment."

"One of the most rewarding parts of this work," says Weiner, "has been to see people become politicized through the cancer process. Cancer can be an incredible door for people to make transformations in their lives. Many people we work with have never thought about the environment, spraying their lawns, using household chemicals, or investments corporations have in profiting from cancer. Asking the questions about who's profiting from cancer and seeing the connections makes people angry. And it gives them an opportunity to give back and make a difference."

For more information on the Women's Cancer Resource Center, please contact the Headwaters Fund (see Appendix A).

Chapter 5

Roadblocks to Action . . . and Moving Ahead

G iving money for social change is relatively easy. As long as you have money to give, making financial plans and learning about social change organizing are straightforward tasks with tremendous personal paybacks of satisfaction. But sometimes the process of giving can raise questions and concerns that keeps us from acting.

Herein lies Robin Hood's Top Ten Roadblocks, which may stop some people in their giving tracks, along with hints on how to move ahead. If you don't need this chapter, skip it! (Or quickly scan the roadblocks, and stop to read the ones that resonate for you.) Or when you are ready to implement your giving plan, you might want to peruse this chapter since creating a giving plan and actually implementing it can be two different things.

Roadblocks to Giving

Roadblock 1: How Much Is Enough

For many givers, the biggest conundrum is the part-practical, part-technical, part-philosophical, and entirely subjective question "How much is enough?" How much is enough for you, your family, and your loved ones? How much can you afford to share in the larger world? This question can require deep reflection. Although we have no secret formula to figure it out, attention to the three considerations below may help you find your answer:

Personal Values and Lifestyle Choices

➻ What kind of lifestyle do you want to maintain?

➻ How do you find comfort and security? Is it related to the amount of money you have and what you own?

➻ What are your personal beliefs on the limits of accumulation, both financially and materially?

Social Analysis

➻ How can you bring your personal values and lifestyle choices into a dialogue with needs you see in the larger world?

➻ How could resources be allocated to help bring about a fairer economic reality?

➻ How can you and your contributions participate in that (or any other) change you are committed to?

Financial Planning and Number Crunching

➻ Given your values and choices around lifestyle, your understanding of the social issues, and the reality of your current financial situation, how much can you afford to give this year? Over the next ten years? A competent financial planner, accountant, or attorney can answer that question for you once you have a rough idea of how you want to live and what you have to live on.

> "There are all different levels at which to give. How many resources are you going to use? Everyone has to make his or her own decision. Even *Newsweek* is noticing the growing gap between the rich and the poor. We have to look at the concept of having more than our share again and again."—*Sue Blaustein, donor, Wisconsin Community Fund*

IT'S THE

AMERICAN WAY!

If you are wealthy, consider a challenge to the Classic Financial Law, Never to Be Questioned by Mortals or Divine Beings: "Don't touch the principal." We know people—stay with this image a moment—who have dipped into principal when giving and have actually survived. And thrived! No matter how much money you have, remember that traditional financial advice is predicated on the preservation and expansion of capital, rather than on the use of capital to invest in a better world.

Roadblock 2: Kids, Catastrophes, and Other Unknowns

Concerns about unanticipated financial needs may surface as you consider giving or increasing your present giving. These worries may mask larger questions of security. The insidious economic insecurity that permeates our society can make it difficult to think rationally about your real financial needs and situation.

To move this roadblock, consult a financial professional. When developing your long-term goals and plans, sketch a range of scenarios from most optimistic to worst case, and see what impact each has on your bottom line. Understanding the spectrum of possibility and the numbers that correspond to each point can help you gauge what level of catastrophe planning is appropriate and what borders on paranoia.

The larger question of building internal, or emotional, security may be more difficult to address. What are your sources of nonmaterial security? Are they your family, friends, and community? Your faith? Your job or hobby? Your volunteer work? You may find that cultivating nonmaterial security will lessen your fears about unknowable financial crises, freeing you to share your money joyfully.

> "If you feel deprived in some way, no matter what you have, it will not feel like enough."
> —Rosemary Santos, director, United Black and Brown Fund of Rhode Island

Roadblock 3: Guilt and Money

> "*Why should I have so much more than other people? Why should my children have so much more? I don't completely buy the argument that I worked hard for it, although I did. Other people work hard, and they don't have much at all.*"—Marjorie Smith, donor, North Star Fund

Marjorie is talking facts, not guilt. But you can see how facts like these could easily lead to guilt.

Robin Hood, as you know, can be an irreverent fellow. When asked his opinion on guilt and money, he replied: "Some people think of guilt as the great motivator; others characterize it as a big waste of emotional energy, tending toward the paralytic. However it manifests itself in your life, here's a suggestion of how to move through it:

"*There are approximately seven hundred eighty-six million hungry people in this world.* You can feel guilty that you aren't one of them, or you can get involved to change this reality with your time and your money. Guess which feels better and is more effective?

> "It's important to see money as a tool and not as the tie that binds. Money is money. Strip it of its symbolic power, and separate it from caring, loyalty, feelings of obligation, and all other ways families are emotionally connected."
> —Nora Janeway, donor, Haymarket People's Fund

"Transform guilt into responsibility—not the 'should' kind that masquerades as guilt. No, I mean the kind of responsibility that sees extra money as a resource you can use to stimulate and support social change, the kind of responsibility that can bring you fulfillment.

"If, on a personal level, you have guilt about how you earn your money or how you inherited your money or the fact you have more money than your parents, or any other emotional or financial issue, take it to a highly recommended therapist. Life is too short to live with guilt, and there is a lot we have to do!"

Roadblock 4: When Money Is Symbolic

Money can be entangled in family, emotional, or cultural dictates or myths. When money becomes loaded down with symbolic meaning, its value as a resource can be lost. Here are several experiences and messages about money from the family front:

- Money is the way my family showed or withheld love.
- Money is a ticket to a better life. If you don't have it, you can't be happy. If you do have it, you have no reason to be anything but happy.
- You can't ever have too much money.
- Money must stay within the family.
- What women know about money is how to spend it.
- Money: Here today, gone tomorrow! Hoard it; hold tight.
- Your net worth is also a measure of your self-worth.

For young people, family messages and invisible strings around money can be difficult, particularly for those who have inherited. Miven Booth Trageser, a Liberty Hill Foundation donor, recounts her story: "At one point, I knew ten or fifteen people like me, between twenty and thirty, all withdrawing and not dealing with their money. For each of us, the money represented unfinished business with our families. One friend was always told to beware because people would like her only for her money. Another felt like the money was a living legacy of her beloved grandfather: She wouldn't touch it."

None of us has escaped contradictory or confusing messages about money. You might want to write down everything you remember being told about money and giving from your childhood. Decide what is valid, and dump the rest. Resolve to follow *your* beliefs and values as you make choices about your money.

Roadblock 5: Isolation

Some people are blocked from action because they think the questions they want to raise about money and giving would put them too far out on a limb. The secrecy surrounding money can add to this isolation. Some people may find themselves taking political or financial stances that differ significantly from those of partners, family members, or friends, thus cutting themselves off from major sources of support. If you're not taking action because you feel as if you're the only person on earth who wants to use your money in a nontraditional way, find others in your situation. Progressive social change foundations, conferences on giving and social change, and adult education courses on socially responsible investing are good places to meet people who will support your values.

Roadblock 6: Not Knowing Enough

This roadblock can be legitimate. Sometimes you really need more information about your financial situation, about the issues you want to support, or about the methods of giving. The rest of this book will give you the tools you need to make good giving decisions.

This concern becomes a roadblock if perfectionism and control keep you from making any choices for fear of not doing it a-b-s-o-l-u-t-e-l-y right. Resist this! There is only so much you need to know to be a really great giver. By the time you've finished *Robin Hood,* you will know how to analyze requests and review budgets, what questions to ask, and which criteria are important to you. This is good enough. Like anyone else, you will make mistakes from time to time, but you will also learn to make better decisions from your mistakes. Don't get sidetracked in a never-ending quest for more information.

Roadblock 7: Knowing Too Much

Becoming overwhelmed can stop you cold. There is a staggering range of organizations you could fund. Learning the language of social change work and the strategies and tactics organizations use makes

"Don't let perfectionism turn into passivity. Take a stab at things and start small. People say, 'I don't have enough to be giving it away.' Everybody has enough to be giving, and even wealthy people can start small."—*Emily Morgan, donor, McKenzie River Gathering Foundation*

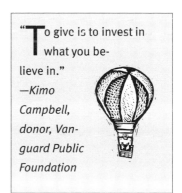

"To give is to invest in what you believe in."
—*Kimo Campbell, donor, Vanguard Public Foundation*

some people feel as if stepping into this world requires a lifetime involvement in grassroots activism. Add decisions about the kinds of giving options that are available, and you could easily end up on overload.

If this is your prime roadblock, pick a specific issue and geographic area you feel passionate about—like organizing for racial justice in your city—and stick with that for the time being. You'll become knowledgeable about that area and may decide to expand your giving boundaries later. Another option is to give through a progressive social change foundation. This way your money can affect a range of concerns without your becoming an expert on each. Seeing the impact of your giving can inspire you to learn more about the issues closest to your heart.

Roadblock 8: To Be or Not to Be . . . Anonymous

The question of whether or not you want to be known as a donor may be a significant concern for those with wealth. It is a very personal choice and, unlike other giving decisions, cannot be changed easily. If you decide to be visible and then change your mind, it's not a graceful switch.

Being Anonymous: The Advantages

Longtime givers identify several advantages in anonymity. The most obvious one is that people won't ask you for large donations or prod you to do things that visible donors are asked to do. Also, if you remain anonymous, you can have the security of knowing that people around you don't relate to you because of your money. For some, giving is an intensely private experience. These individuals simply want no recognition. For them, the satisfaction comes from the giving itself, not from the attention garnered as a result of the gift. Anonymity guarantees privacy.

Being Anonymous: The Disadvantages

There are some disadvantages to remaining anonymous. First, it can be a hassle. You have to take precautions and remember who (if anyone) knows and who doesn't. Second, in a small town or close community people may figure out anyway that you make large donations. Some will respect your decision to be anonymous. Others may feel uneasy around you because of this not-so-secret secret. Third, you don't get the opportunity to influence others—friends and perhaps family—through your giving if no one knows about it. Finally, if you are wealthy, the decision to remain anonymous may come at the cost of your self-esteem. Being wealthy, either by good fortune and hard work or by the luck of the draw, is a part of who you are.

Being Visible

Stand the list of disadvantages of anonymity on its head, and you have the advantages of visibility. Here are things to keep in mind when being "out" as a giver:

→ Be specific about your funding goals so you have an easy answer to phone calls and visits from fund raisers ("I'm sorry. I don't give to X. I fund only Y"). If you develop some expertise in your funding areas, you will make better decisions than if you open yourself up to anything that comes down the road.

→ Just because someone asks doesn't mean you have to say yes. If you dislike fund-raising parties, don't go. Some people appreciate the opportunity to hear an update on a campaign to get money out of politics, for example. Some prefer one-on-one meetings. Others want to read grant proposals in the quiet of the living room, with their feet up and a cat on their lap. Know your style.

→ Maintain a circle of friends who have absolutely no relationship to the projects seeking funding from you.

Roadblock 9: Uncertainty about the Impact of Your Gifts

Many givers, especially when they are just starting to fund social change, feel uncertain about how to make decisions and how to ensure that their funding gives them the most impact for their bucks. Should they defer to the judgment of activist decision makers, or do it themselves? Make lots of small grants or a few big ones? In what area will their funding be most effective? When you fund social change, how do you know you are having an impact?

Like some of the other roadblocks, these concerns have a valid place, and the rest of the book will equip you to deal with them, but at some point they just become fodder for inaction. Let's be real. There *is* uncertainty when quantifying outcomes where social change giving is concerned. Social change groups, unlike your alma mater, op-

> " Give strategically, and take pride in the impact of your giving. No one of us can remedy all injustice, no matter how much money we give. I can, however, be among the millions of givers who together fund most social change."—*Tracy Hewat, director, the Comfort Zone*

Robin Hood and Maid Marian Associates surveyed dozens of people about why they were stuck in their giving. An executive summary of the findings:

1. "My finger freezes when trying to make telephone calls related to my money."

2. "The way the stock market is going, if I wait a week, I can give away more money."

3. "I'm afraid of being laughed at for my information request."

4. "First, I need to organize all these papers on my desk alphabetically."

5. "I could learn something tomorrow that might inform my decision. I'd be foolhardy to act today."

erate in the messy arenas of institutional power, public opinion, and economic insecurity. They may not have nice buildings, consistent staffing, or stable financial support. Results aren't instantaneous by any means. Nonetheless hundreds of thousands of people work for better schools, affordable housing, and a cleaner environment. We think their work is worth betting on, even when some victories may be small or hard to measure.

Roadblock 10: Slacking

AKA just putting it off. Some of your most creative thinking may have been to come up with reasons for not making giving choices and acting on them *now*. Often there seems to be no rush ("The world will go on with or without my giving"). Moreover, when every issue in the world is pitched as absolutely vital, a real sense of what's urgent can be lost in the rhetoric.

If you're slacking, you may want to build some accountability into your life and set up some external prods to motivate yourself.

Set Goals

Robin Hood Was Right will help you develop clear giving goals. Fill out the giving plan. Keep your goals in front of you: Tape them to the wall; E-mail them to your friends; do what you need to in order to stay inspired and motivated by them.

Name That Block

Many times your obstacles dissipate simply by your identifying them, hauling them out for examination in the light of day, and understanding the concern that lies underneath. Once you do, you'll be able to move ahead with joy and confidence.

Get Help

The single biggest mistake givers can make is to think that they have to move ahead completely on their own. In fact, if you "move ahead" in isolation, you may be limited in your perspective. There are creative resources available for assistance, such as events, conferences, and workshops related to money and giving. Check out Appendix A for the closest local progressive foundation that can connect you to these resources.

Consequences for Inaction

One reason for paralysis is that there is often no external accountability. Years can go by, and no one will ask you what choices you've made about your money. It's up to you to move.

Sometimes an extreme consequence might be needed to get unstuck. Perhaps negative reinforcement will do the trick, like deciding that you'll give up chocolate (or something you love) until a task is accomplished!

"When I started giving, it felt like an opening up."—*Lucy Rogers, donor, Headwaters Fund*

Act!

If you're feeling stuck, act anyway. Act on a small manageable piece of what you want to do. Or do something outrageous to break out of your rut. Invite friends over, and together figure out how to make gifts to organizations totaling five hundred, five thousand, fifty thousand, or five hundred thousand dollars. Then make them! Shake up your patterns of stagnation, and get yourself and your money moving.

Moving On

You don't have to figure out everything before you get moving. *Au contraire!* If you want to make a significant gift, all you *must* do is figure out the anonymity question and be sure you can still pay the rent or mortgage and buy food for the foreseeable future. Once those things are determined, anything is possible.

Tens of billions of additional dollars could be flowing to change society if people acted on their desire to use their money to help bring about change. Thousands of people could be feeling more empowered in relation to their money. Hundreds of billions of dollars could be divested from irresponsible corporations that pollute the land and exploit workers. There *is* a price to pay for our inaction.

The most important motivation for dealing with roadblocks and shoving them aside is the inspiration in the existing and emerging social movements of our time. We have a part to play in these movements whether as givers or as people putting stamps on envelopes or both. When we know what kind of impact our dollars can have, action becomes effortless.

"Sure, this is idyllic, but there are fundamental problems here that are not being addressed."

The Police Barrio Relations Project

When Moises DeJesus, a Latino truck driver, was killed in police custody in 1995, the Latino community in Philadelphia was prepared. The Police Barrio Relations Project (PBRP) had been doing its homework, working to make institutional changes in the Philadelphia Police Department. Largely because of its efforts, the Civilian Review Board of the police department flew into action. Despite attempts to cover up the case, the officers involved were forced to testify publicly and were disciplined as a result.

The historical relationship between the Philadelphia Police Department and residents of the city's barrio, the Latino community, has been bad. Community members have routinely been harassed and abused, and people have been afraid to voice their concerns for fear of lack of appropriate police protection. While people protested individual incidents, there was no sustained community voice trying to influence the structure of the police system. PBRP changed that.

Since its founding PBRP has fought police misconduct by educating community members and police officers, seeking institutional changes, and helping victims hold police officers accountable for their behavior. Its approach to police-community relationships has four elements. The first is community education and empowerment. Through workshops that simulate interactions with the police, PBRP trainers educate community residents about their rights and responsibilities when confronted by police officers. The workshop discusses legal issues and gives practical advice on how to defuse potential tension when interacting with an officer. It has trained more than five thousand people and is making a video of the workshop for widespread distribution.

The PBRP also helps police understand the Latino culture and community. Its program provides opportunities for officers to interact with the community outside the law enforcement setting to help break down barriers of prejudice. In a new workshop police participate with young people to dissolve the stereotypes that each has of the other. Officers learn from the students about the cultures, languages, and living experiences of North Philadelphia. Director Will Gonzalez says: "It's good for young people and officers to see each other in a situation where they have three days together, rather than three minutes in a tense situation, to talk to each other. They are really building a bridge."

The third aspect of the PBRP's program is support of victims of police abuse. The organization helps victims and their families file complaints, connects them with civil rights attorneys, and follows up on disciplinary action taken against officers.

The last element is to make the law enforcement system more fair and accountable. Successful campaigns include the creation of the Civilian Review Board, improvements in the translation of department forms into Spanish, and directives about the safe use of pepper spray. This work touches all community members by changing the basic protocols of police work, but it is also the work that is most difficult to find funding for.

PBRP received its first grant from the Bread and Roses Community Fund at a time when other foundations questioned if police abuse was really an issue in Philadelphia. With the support of that first grant, and the work it was able to do as a result, the project was able to secure larger foundation and individual support. Gonzalez underscores the importance of this kind of giving. "Providing people in need with hot meals is important," he says, "but without institutional changes you don't get as much bang for the buck."

For more information on the Police Barrio Relations Project, please contact the Bread and Roses Community Fund (see Appendix A).

Part III

Getting from Here to There— Nuts and Bolts

| | Chapter 6 | |

Taking Charge of Your Money

Before you can give your money fully and freely, you need to know your total financial picture and your options for divvying up the pie. If your money is a mystery, or if you just turn responsibility for "all that" over to a lawyer, an accountant, or some other financial professional, you may never realize your full giving potential. You will be uncertain about what you want and need to reserve for yourself and your loved ones and irresolute about what you can "afford" to give, now and in the future. The balance you strike among saving, spending, and giving may not reflect your true wishes at all.

So take charge of your money! Understanding it is a critical step in sharing it, and it's not as inscrutable as you might think. Some givers even find it fun!

Caveat: Some of the material we cover here and in the next couple of chapters may seem irrelevant to your situation. This book has a wide audience, and some of the information that follows applies mainly to people who inherit or receive large windfalls. Still, much of what follows relates in some way to a variety of situations. Work with the information that seems to fit your situation.

> "**I** find that it helps to be in balance about the ownership of money; you have to be able to say, 'This money is mine.' Although it sounds like a contradiction, you have to 'own it' in order to give it away. Owning it and giving it away are like walking a tightrope. It's an art. Money is great; it is a mitzvah [blessing] to be enjoyed. A big part of the enjoyment is giving it away."—*Janet Axelrod, donor, Haymarket People's Fund*

The Starting Point: Your Documents

For many givers, the first step in understanding their money is to gather up the documents that describe it. These may include such items as bank and credit card statements; paycheck stubs; checking account registers; loan and mortgage documents; stock, bond, and mutual fund account statements; retirement accounts; partnership agreements; trust documents; recent tax returns; and insurance documents. Some of these documents may be familiar to you; some you may never have seen. Some you may find, opened or unopened, in that drawer or box of "money stuff" you've saved for years without knowing exactly why.★

Your search may extend to many sources: lawyers, accountants, investment managers, banks, trustees, family members. If you have a lawyer or financial manager, make sure you have copies of all the documents affecting you, including any powers of attorney you may have signed or powers of appointment you may hold. If family members have lawyers with documents that affect you, ask for those. If you expect to inherit from parents or grandparents, try to find out roughly what's coming and how (will it be given outright or will it be in trust?). If you currently receive money from a trust, call the bank or other institution that manages it and request a copy of the legal documents that set out its terms as well as a trust account statement. If your money comes mainly from your family, ask them for information. If you have a will or trust that you created, put that on the stack too.

The idea is to bring together in one place all the information that concerns your overall financial picture, now and in the future. Each document represents a piece of the overall picture. If you understand all your documents, great. You will be able to figure out your overall

★Use year-end financial statements if you have them. They're more convenient to work with than monthly or quarterly statements because they report annual figures, sparing you the chore of converting part-year figures to yearly. Most financial institutions send out year-end statements shortly after December 31 of each year. If you haven't saved your statements for the most recent year, call the institutions that sent them to you and ask for duplicates.

financial picture more easily. But even if you do not yet understand how it all fits together, you have taken an important first step.

Stepping on Toes

Usually gathering the information you want is no problem. Just ask, and as a rule advisers and family members will answer your questions quickly, fully, and graciously. Be prepared, though, if you encounter a different response.

Perhaps, by custom or inertia, you've never had much to do with your money. You get checks, but a parent, an uncle, or some obscure person you know only by phone sweats all the details. If you suddenly, after many years, start asking for documents, your interest may be seen as a threat rather than as a healthy declaration of independence. Parents may interpret your inquiries as an indication that you don't like what they're doing or even that you suspect them of incompetence. Longtime advisers may fear that you want to replace them, or they may resent your incursion into what they see as their turf (many advisers see your money as *their* job, not yours)

If you get a chilly response, reassure whoever is involved that you are simply attempting to gain a better understanding of your money. Don't apologize, and don't think that you must lay out a new, fully developed financial program either. At this point you may have no idea what you want your money to do. Your initial task is just to *get* the information and *understand* it. You don't have to justify that to anyone.

What Your Documents Say

Once you've rounded up your documents, sit down and spend some time with them.

> **W**hen money remains a mystery, we often avoid giving anywhere near what we could, out of fear that the well will run dry.

Your Right to Know

Obviously it would be nice to know about all sources of money that will affect your financial picture at some point. It would be nice to know too, if you have children, if someone plans to give *them* money. It would help you plan and prepare, both emotionally and financially. Don't assume, however, that legally you *must* be told.

You have the right to know only about income and assets that are legally yours to control. Information about anything that is coming later may be withheld from you unless and until it "vests" (becomes yours). For example, you have no legal right to know what's in your parents' wills. In addition, information about trusts or similar arrangements set up to benefit your children need never be disclosed to you. If little Susie's grandparents decide to leave her their entire stock portfolio outright at age eighteen, legally they may do so, with or without consulting you.

Ordinarily, if a family member intends to give you or your children money, he or she will inform you as a matter of course. Surprisingly often, though, families hide information about their money. If nothing is disclosed to you, you can always ask. But if you don't get an answer, you may just have to accept it.

"I listed our income and the value of our assets, estimated the total investment returns . . . compared the results to a specific budget that included our needs, some luxuries, a reserve for our children's futures, and enough to cover our philanthropic outlays.

"The conclusions were startling. It was as if I had literally found money. To my surprise, I discovered that we had dramatically understated our potential. We could afford to spend, or give, much more. Since we were basically happy with our standard of living, and since our income and our asset ownership left a sizable cushion for us, we concluded that we could have been sharing more of what we had. A lot more! So we weren't as generous as we had imagined.

"[T]he facts were quite clear: we could have been doing more, we should have been doing more and in consort with others, we could indeed be making substantially greater improvements to our local community and to society in general.

"So we took our own advice. We expanded our philanthropy regularly and soon learned that it was ever more pleasant to *reduce* our wealth moderately than it was to accumulate it."—*Claude Rosenberg, founder, RCM Capital Management; founder & chairman of Newtithing Group, San Francisco; author,* Wealthy and Wise: How You and America Can Get the Most Out of Your Giving

Study them, even if you'd rather have a root canal. They'll tell you plenty.

At a minimum, your documents will tell you what you've got, where, and in what form (cash, stocks, bonds, etc.). They'll tell you what you own (your assets), what you owe (your liabilities), and the difference between these two figures (your net worth). They'll tell you what's coming in (income), what's going out (expenses), and the difference between these two figures (your net income). If you're lucky, they may also tell you what's coming later on. It's worth developing a working knowledge of these concepts and how they apply to your finances because once you do, you'll have taken a giant step forward in understanding your options for spending, saving, and giving. You'll have a much better idea of what you can "afford," not only for yourself and your loved ones but also for sharing.

Understanding and taking control of your money are a process of learning by doing.

Start your research by sorting your documents into two piles, legal and financial. Now split the financial documents into two categories, personal and investment, so that altogether you have three piles of information.

Go to the personal financial documents first (bank statements, checkbooks, credit card reports). These are usually the most familiar. Entries in the debit column of your checkbook, together with bank statements and credit card reports, provide a vast amount of useful information about your expenses. Look closely, and you'll be able to nail down precisely how you spend your money. How much do you spend on necessities, like housing, electricity, and so on? How much on optional items like restaurant meals and vacations? They're all in there, and taking a close look will help you see which of your expenses can be reprioritized and which cannot.

Now pull out any mortgage and loan statements. These have a lot to say about your liabilities, money you owe to others. To estimate accurately your overall financial condition, you must consider your liabilities and deduct them from your assets. Make a list showing when each personal liability is due. Those due in less than twelve months (including your credit card balance, for example) are current liabilities; those due over a longer period are long-term liabilities.

Finally, take a look at your paycheck stubs or inside your brain to add up any income you received from full- or part-time work. In the financial world, work income is referred to as earned income, while investment income is referred to as unearned. You may have other sources of personal income as well, such as gifts or royalties from that best seller you wrote last year.

Now you're done with your personal financial documents. Before you move on, stop and make a list of everything you personally own, excluding investments: car(s), residence, jewelry, appliances, furniture, boat(s), bikes, instruments, personal computers, CD collection, etc. Estimate what you realistically could expect to be paid for each item on the open market, even if you would never consider actually selling it. Add up the total. Now you have an estimate of personal assets, which figure into your overall financial picture.

Move on to your pile of investment documents (reports on stocks, bonds, mutual funds, certificates of deposit, and other invested assets). For some, at first glance, the contents of these documents may appear unintelligible. They may contain words like "basis" and "gain" that you know are important but don't really understand. They may show negative numbers or numbers enclosed in parentheses ("( )") for reasons that are not immediately obvious. Nowhere will you find a magic number saying, "This is your total financial worth."

To understand these documents, you must learn some basic financial and accounting terminology. You can work with others, take a financial accounting class, or hire a professional to help you, but you must understand the fundamental concepts to acquire the confidence needed to make the big decisions about what you want your money to do. If you are an absolute beginner, go out and buy *Personal Finance*

A capital gain is the difference between the price you paid for a stock or other property and what it is worth now.

"I think that as people with earned or inherited money, the voices we hear are the traditional voices about 'prudential use of resources.' What's missing from that is the whole concept of social return. If you take the point of view that resources are ours to be stewards of, not owners of, then you are freed up from thinking you have to maximize return, and you can think about social benefits."—*Art Lloyd, donor, Wisconsin Community Fund*

for Dummies and/or *Accounting for Dummies.*[1] If you already have some financial acumen, try *Financial Statement Analysis* by Charles T. Woelfel.[2] In only a few hours, with book in one hand and financial reports in the other, you will begin to see the wealth of information contained in these formerly cryptic investment documents (no pun intended).

Next, take a look at your legal documents, trust documents in particular. What do they say? Beneath the seemingly impenetrable facade of "wherefore" 's and "hereinafter" 's, they set out pretty much everything you need to know about your money that the financial documents themselves didn't cover. They identify who created the trust and for what purpose(s). They specify what property went into the trust to create its "principal" and name its beneficiaries and trustee(s). They state how long the trust will last, specify what happens when it terminates, and define the rules for distributing both principal and income. They tell what's under your control, what's coming down the pike, and what's out of your reach forever.

How about your income tax return? Be careful about relying on this one. Although tax returns may serve as a starting point if you lack other documents, they are of limited use in understanding your total financial picture. First, they report only income, not overall wealth. You may own assets that do not produce income, and you may receive income from assets you do not own. Second, they report only *current* income. Your current income may or may not accurately predict the income you can expect in the future. Third, some sources of income are not reported on individual income tax returns. You may, for example, participate in a limited liability partnership or other venture that files a separate tax return and does not show up on yours.

Putting It All Together

At this point you will have assembled many individual pieces of your financial pie. To get the big picture, though, you need to put together all the various pieces and see how they work as a coherent whole.

To aid you in doing this, we have provided Net Worth, Expense, and Income Worksheets (at the end of the chapter). Use them as a guide, or make copies and fill them out as completely as possible, using your investment and legal documents for the information they reveal and your own personal knowledge for matters you handle yourself. Add or cross out categories as needed, and circle those you're unsure about. You may need to hunt for missing information or collect additional documents. You may also find it helpful to supplement the worksheets with time lines highlighting important financial events over your life or multigenerational flow charts that show when and where money comes in and goes out and what questions or intervening contingencies you may face.

When you're done putting these pieces of your pie together, you'll have a working version of the same documents a professional financial planner would start with to assess your overall financial picture. In fact, consulting with a financial planner right about now could be a great way to double-check your understanding and get remaining questions answered. Having the big picture clearly in mind also gives you a big leg up on moving forward with your wish to give.

Next Step: Defining Your Financial Goals

Before proceeding further, step away from the influence of professionals and other outsiders for a time and consider what you want your money to do. Reflect upon, define, and prioritize your personal financial goals. This is probably the most important thing you can do in taking charge of your money and in implementing a plan to move it from where it is to where you want it to be.

"Giving" clearly is one of your goals, or you wouldn't have bought this book. So start with that. But is it your only goal? Probably not. Most people have several other, sometimes conflicting financial goals. Do you want to maintain a certain lifestyle, own a house, take vacations now and then? These cost money; put them on your list. Do you want yourself or your loved ones to be protected against the financial

If you are on top of your financial situation and have a solid plan to cover all your personal wants and needs, giving away assets (principal) is not an irresponsible act. It is a choice. It depends on your values and goals.

risk of a fire, a catastrophic medical event, or an accident that leaves you or someone in your family permanently and totally disabled? Then adequate property, health, and disability insurance is a goal. Retirement? Add that. College for the kids? Another one. What about passing money on to them or to your grandchildren? If this is something you want to do, put it on your list.

What about the goal of pure wealth accumulation, accumulation not for identified wants and needs but rather for its own sake? Chances are this is *not* an objective you value. In fact, if you are committed to social change, dissipating your assets may be a goal, and a perfectly legitimate one at that. Note it.

Now that you've got a basic list of goals, refine and prioritize them. What specific lifestyle do you want? Low-maintenance or high- ? How much do you need to have set aside for retirement? How much do you want to pass on to your kids or grandkids? Enough to get them started in their first houses or enough to ensure that they'll never

"We've set aside this particular room for those who still worship the almighty dollar."

need to work? Is giving more important to you than some kinds of material security? Which kinds? Be as specific as you can.

The importance of this exercise cannot be overstated. When it comes right down to it, the path your money takes during your life depends largely on trade-offs you are willing to make among competing financial objectives. Contrary to what some people think, financial experts can't tell you your priorities. You've got to tell *them*. You control the big picture; the pros just coordinate the details. It is only after you have this point squarely in mind that you can work productively to put your financial house in order.

Share your goals with financial professionals you consult. Talk them over with a trusted friend or loved one, refining them as you go, or attend a conference or seminar that addresses these issues. Your goals don't need to be crystal clear in order to start the ball rolling, nor is it your job to anticipate all the technical implications, but at least some reflection on the big questions is a must.

> "Learning about money is like learning another language. You have to learn the vocabulary and the skills to deal with it, the same way you would to learn a language."
> —*Shad Reinstein, donor, Funding Exchange*

SYLVIA   by Nicole Hollander

Synthesizing Your Objectives with Your Financial Reality

If you are clear on how you want to live, your desires can be quantified. A competent professional can put a price tag on everything you want and need and then, having analyzed your overall financial picture, go about formulating a comprehensive and effective strategy to get you where you want to be.

For people whose money supply does not far exceed their needs, systematizing giving may simply mean making "Giving" a line item in their monthly or yearly budgets. For those whose incomes and assets are much larger, however, a host of additional factors may come into play. Income, estate, and gift taxes become relevant. So may the use of trusts, charitable and otherwise. Wills, capital gains, and estate planning considerations loom large.

In the next chapter we take an overview of some of these considerations. It is beyond the scope of this book, however, to discuss in detail every factor that may affect a particular individual's personal financial plan or range of potential giving strategies. Too many variables are involved, and besides, the options are always changing. That's why we hire experts. But remember: You decide what's best for you. No professional can tell you one definite path to follow or choice to make.

Notes to Help You with Net Worth and Expense Worksheets

⇒→ There may appear to be a lot of lines to fill in, but you need only to use the categories appropriate for you.

⇒→ Make educated estimates, if needed, and round numbers off. Don't put in the cents, just the dollars.

⇒→ After you have done this once, it is easier to do again. In future years you will know where to find the numbers. It is very useful to track this information over time.

Net Worth Worksheet

⇒→ You may want to make up your own worksheet using this as a guide for the categories to include. For example, you may have more than one checking account or different kinds of mutual funds. On your own sheet you can make a line for each and then omit the categories that don't fit your circumstances.

⇒→ Usually it is best to figure out your net worth as of December 31 unless you have some particular reason to do it otherwise.

⇒→ This is for the adults in your household. If your children have separate accounts for education, they should have their own net worth worksheets.

⇒→ Some of the categories overlap. For example, for some people it may be easier to list the total current value of an investment account rather than the current value of the stocks and bonds. Just make sure you don't list things twice.

Expense Worksheet

⇒→ Sometimes it is easier to look at your monthly rather than annual expenses. Use those lines, and multiply by 12. If you use weekly expenses, multiply by 4.3 for monthly or 52 for annual. Other expenses are annual or quarterly, so just use the annual column.

⇒→ If you are a couple, it is sometimes easier to break down your expenses for each person (e.g., life insurance). Other times it is easier or makes more sense to figure out the numbers for the household (e.g., groceries).

Net Worth Worksheet

ASSETS *(what you own)*	*Current Value*
Cash and Cash Equivalents	
Cash under your mattress	_____
Checking accounts	_____
Savings accounts	
Money market funds	_____
Treasury bills	
Short-term CDs	_____
Savings bonds	_____
Life insurance (cash value, not value at death)	_____
Other (specify)	_____
Subtotal	_____
Other Financial Assets	
General	
Stocks	_____
Bonds and loans	_____
U.S. government	_____
Municipal	_____
Corporate	_____
Community loan funds	_____
Long-term CDs	_____
Loans owed to you	_____
Mutual funds	_____
Investment real estate	_____
Limited partnerships	_____
Venture capital funds	_____
Equity in business	_____
Patents, copyrights, royalties	_____
Trusts	_____
Revocable	_____
Irrevocable	_____
Investment Accounts (not included above)	_____
Other (specify)	_____
Subtotal	_____
Retirement Related	
IRA(s)	_____
Keogh plan or SEPs	_____
Annuities	_____
Pension plan (vested)	_____
403b's	_____
Other (specify)	_____
Subtotal	_____

ASSETS *(what you own)*   *Current Value*

Personal Assets
    Residence _____
    Seasonal residence _____
    Automobiles _____
    Household furnishings _____
    Computers _____
    Jewelry, furs, silver _____
    Collections _____
    Major hobby/recreational equipment _____
    Other (specify) _____

    Subtotal _____

Total Assets _____

LIABILITIES *(what you owe)*   *Value Due*

Long-Term Debt
    Mortgage: residence _____
    Mortgage: seasonal residence _____
    School loans _____
    Car loans _____
    Business loans _____
    Other (specify) _____

    Subtotal _____

Immediate Debt
    Home equity loans _____
    Bank loans _____
    Credit cards _____
    Personal loans _____
    Margin account _____
    Investment liabilities _____
    Child support and alimony _____
    Back taxes _____
    Other (specify) _____

    Subtotal _____

Total Liabilities _____

Net Worth (assets minus liabilities) _____

Expense Worksheet

	Monthly		Annual	Notes
Housing	House 1	House 2		
Rent or mortgage	_____	_____	_____	_____
Utilities	_____	_____	_____	_____
Oil	_____	_____	_____	_____
Gas	_____	_____	_____	_____
Water and sewer	_____	_____	_____	_____
Electricity	_____	_____	_____	_____
Phone	_____	_____	_____	_____
Cable TV	_____	_____	_____	_____
Internet access	_____	_____	_____	_____
Property taxes	_____	_____	_____	_____
Home insurance	_____	_____	_____	_____
Fees: condo, parking, etc.	_____	_____	_____	_____
Repairs, improvements	_____	_____	_____	_____
Furniture	_____	_____	_____	_____
Cleaning (regular and major)	_____	_____	_____	_____
Services (lawn, trash)	_____	_____	_____	_____
Transportation	Car 1	Car 2		
Mass transit	_____	_____	_____	_____
Gasoline	_____	_____	_____	_____
Tolls, parking fees, tickets	_____	_____	_____	_____
Car repair	_____	_____	_____	_____
Excise tax, registration, license	_____	_____	_____	_____
Car repayment	_____	_____	_____	_____
Auto insurance, AAA	_____	_____	_____	_____
Insurance	Both or Person 1	Person 2		
Life insurance	_____	_____	_____	_____
Umbrella or liability policy	_____	_____	_____	_____
Disability	_____	_____	_____	_____
Food				
Groceries	_____	_____	_____	_____
At work, school	_____	_____	_____	_____
Restaurants (eat in and take out)	_____	_____	_____	_____
Spring water, vitamins	_____	_____	_____	_____

	Monthly	Annual	Notes
Health			
Health and dental insurance	_____	_____	_____	_____
Doctor, clinic	_____	_____	_____	_____
Dental	_____	_____	_____	_____
Eye care, glasses	_____	_____	_____	_____
Prescriptions, lab costs	_____	_____	_____	_____
Psychotherapy	_____	_____	_____	_____
PT, chiropractic, acupuncture	_____	_____	_____	_____
Massage, bodywork	_____	_____	_____	_____
Health club, exercise	_____	_____	_____	_____
Children			
Child care	_____	_____	_____	_____
Tuition	_____	_____	_____	_____
Lessons, camp, sitting	_____	_____	_____	_____
Supplies, travel	_____	_____	_____	_____
Allowance, miscellaneous	_____	_____	_____	_____
Education and Lessons—Adults			
Tuition, fees	_____	_____	_____	_____
Supplies, books	_____	_____	_____	_____
Conferences, workshops	_____	_____	_____	_____

Personal Care	Both or Person 1	Person 2		
Clothing	_____	_____	_____	_____
Dry cleaning, tailor, laundry	_____	_____	_____	_____
Hair care, makeup	_____	_____	_____	_____
Drugstore, toiletries, etc.	_____	_____	_____	_____

Entertainment/Leisure Time				
Travel, vacations	_____	_____	_____	_____
Parties (adults and kids)	_____	_____	_____	_____
Gifts	_____	_____	_____	_____
Movies, theater, concerts, sports	_____	_____	_____	_____
CDs, cassettes	_____	_____	_____	_____
Magazines, newspapers	_____	_____	_____	_____
Books	_____	_____	_____	_____
Alcohol, tobacco	_____	_____	_____	_____

Expense Worksheet *(continued)*

	Monthly	*Annual*	*Notes*
Office Needs			
Supplies, postage, stationery	_____ _____	_____	_____
Computer	_____ _____	_____	_____
Financial			
Lawyers, accountants	_____ _____	_____	_____
Investment fees	_____ _____	_____	_____
Financial and investment planning	_____ _____	_____	_____
Bank and credit card fees	_____ _____	_____	_____
Business			
Expenses (itemize separately)	_____ _____	_____	_____
Income Taxes			
Federal	_____ _____	_____	_____
State and local	_____ _____	_____	_____
Social Security, FICA	_____ _____	_____	_____
Other			
Pet care	_____ _____	_____	_____
Photo: film, processing	_____ _____	_____	_____
Dues, membership fees	_____ _____	_____	_____
Hobbies, collections	_____ _____	_____	_____
One-time expenses	_____ _____	_____	_____
Cash spent (not categorized)	_____ _____	_____	_____
Other	_____ _____	_____	_____
Contributions			
Tax-deductible	_____ _____	_____	_____
Not deductible	_____ _____	_____	_____
Total Expenses	_____ _____		
Savings			
Retirement	_____ _____	_____	_____
College	_____ _____	_____	_____
Prepayment of mortgage	_____ _____	_____	_____
Other accounts	_____ _____	_____	_____
Old Debts			
Education loan payments	_____ _____	_____	_____
Other debt repayment	_____ _____	_____	_____

Income Worksheet

Annual

	Both or Person 1	Person 2
Salary	_____	_____
Bonuses, tips	_____	_____
Commissions	_____	_____
Consulting and self-employment	_____	_____
Benefits	_____	_____
Employer contribution to retirement	_____	_____
Dividends	_____	_____
Taxable interest	_____	_____
Checking accounts	_____	_____
Savings accounts	_____	_____
Money market	_____	_____
CDs	_____	_____
U.S. treasuries	_____	_____
Bonds	_____	_____
Loans	_____	_____
Other _____	_____	_____
Nontaxable Interest	_____	_____
Capital gains expected	_____	_____
Rental income	_____	_____
Installment sale	_____	_____
Partnerships, business income	_____	_____
Child Support	_____	_____
Alimony	_____	_____
Social Security	_____	_____
Pensions	_____	_____
Trust fund	_____	_____
Unemployment benefits	_____	_____

	Both or Person 1	Person 2
Disability benefits: taxable	_____	_____
Disability benefits: nontaxable	_____	_____
Royalties	_____	_____
Gifts	_____	_____
Other taxable	_____	_____
Other nontaxable	_____	_____
TOTAL INCOME (Combined)	_____	
TOTAL INCOME	_____	
Less TOTAL EXPENSE	_____	
NET CASH FLOW	_____	

Personal Money Survey

This survey was developed over the years by participants at Haymarket People's Fund conferences. Many found it a good way to note their progress.

1. What is your net worth, including your home?
   (Subtract your liabilities—loans, mortgages, etc.—from your assets—stocks, real estate, jewelry, etc.)

2. What percentage of your assets do you control?

3. What was your gross earned income last year?

4. What was your gross unearned income last year (including gifts)?

5. What was your total gross income last year (sum of Nos. 3 and 4)?

6. How much did you pay in federal taxes last year?

7. How much did you pay in state taxes last year?

8. How much money did you live on last year, not including taxes and donations?

9. How much money did you give away last year to charitable organizations?

10. How much money did you give away last year to individuals?

11. How much money did you give away last year in total (sum of Nos. 9 and 10)?

12. What percentage of your gross income did you give away last year (No. 11 × 100/No. 5)?

13. What percentage of your net worth did you give away last year (No. 11 × 100/No. 1)?

14. How much money do you currently have lent out or invested at no- or low-interest rates?

15. How many hours a month do you do volunteer work (not including caring for your own family)?

16. Do you do socially responsible investing? 1—yes 2—no

17. How accurate do you think your responses are?
    1—Very accurate 2—Fairly accurate 3—Accurate
    4—Kinda accurate 5—Pack o' lies

Organizing Immigrant Workers

"When I was a little child, one of the things my parents taught me was to
respect myself and to respect others. Later on in life I realized that
unfortunately not all human beings share that respect. I have seen many
people in positions of power use it to exploit and abuse poor people. On
Long Island I worked as a laborer in a factory, where I was not only abused
and exploited but also witnessed how my Latino coworkers were
mistreated. This was how I began to learn about the rights we have. I
became conscious that when people do not respect you, you must teach
them to respect you. I believe that the only way you can do this is through
coming together and getting a good education about the law that protects
the rights of people as workers and as human beings, no matter if we are
documented or not, or speak or don't speak English."
—Samuel Chavez, The Workplace Project

Immigrant workers take the most dangerous and ill-paid jobs in the
United States. Although some are understandably afraid of organizing
because it calls attention to themselves, others are actively confronting
miserable conditions. Here are examples:

The Workplace Project, Long Island, New York

Central American immigrants on New York's Long Island often find
themselves in a huge underground economy. Employers pay off the
books (under the table), routinely underpay, and at times withhold
wages completely. Factories shut down overnight to avoid health and
safety inspections, leaving people with no jobs and no access to un-
paid wages. Employers often do not provide any kind of insurance;
consequently, workers injured on the job have no resources for support.

The Workplace Project began as a legal clinic where individual workers could find support to confront unjust employers. The project soon realized that individual actions would not improve working conditions for the entire immigrant community. It began to educate workers and to organize.

Through a nine-week course in organizing, workers learn immigrant and labor history, an overview of labor law, and organizing techniques. They develop a plan for collective action, and when they graduate from the class, they are qualified to be Workplace Project leaders. As a result of this intensive training, workers can take on issues at a number of levels: campaigns against corrupt domestic worker agencies, legislative initiatives, and a rapid-response Justice Committee, which organizes pickets, protests, and other direct actions. In 1998, for instance, a group of ten workers at an industrial cleaning plant approached the Workplace Project. They had been fired for no reason and were owed ten thousand dollars in back wages. The Justice Committee and the fired workers set up a protest in front of the business, chanting, singing songs, and handing out flyers. That day the employer paid the back wages and reinstated the workers.

A legislative initiative in New York to strengthen the penalties for employers that violate labor laws was a huge victory. By building a diverse coalition, from workers' centers (including the Chinese Staff and Workers Association—see p.104) to small-business owners, they won unanimous support for the legislation from an anti-immigrant, antilabor government! The legislation raises penalties against repeat violators of wage payment laws by 800 percent, forbids the customary 50 percent settlements the Labor Department reached, and requires the Labor Department to investigate violations for six years prior instead of just two.

The project's strategies are not just reactive. It has organized several worker-owned cooperative businesses at which fair wages and good working conditions are a given. Its Landscaping Cooperative is now an independent business. A Domestic Worker Cooperative through which women can secure domestic work independent of exploitative agencies is its current project. Co-op members are trained in all aspects of small-business development and worker ownership.

The Workplace Project received support from the Funding Exchange.

Korean Immigrant Workers Association, Los Angeles

Through the Korean Immigrant Workers Association (KIWA), progressive Koreans are able to speak out in their Los Angeles community. Community members believed that the racial tension in the city was often exacerbated by the comments of Korean professionals who acted as self-appointed spokespersons. Members of KIWA wanted to counter that influence by developing a new, alternative voice.

In order to amplify the voices of workers, they founded a center where Korean workers could develop their own leadership, organize for their rights, and join with others in broader campaigns. KIWA concentrated on the restaurant industry after finding that workers typically put in ten- to twelve-hour days, six days a week, with a base salary of $2.30 per hour. They received no benefits and generally were not covered by workers' compensation.

KIWA's Koreatown Restaurant Workers Justice Campaign organizes workers to force the Korean Restaurant Association (KRA) and restaurants in Koreatown to sign a model employment agreement that establishes an industry-wide experience- and seniority-based pay scale, a just cause termination policy, and an industry-wide dispute mediation committee. It also includes an agreement to research health insurance for workers as well as a promise to abide by basic minimum labor standards. After the most profitable restaurant in Koreatown was pressured to support the agreement, KIWA was able to leverage further concessions from the restaurant association.

KIWA held a town meeting as part of the campaign. This historic event was finally an opportunity for workers to speak out about the conditions they work under every day. Attended by more than two hundred people, including progressive politicians, media and labor leaders, the meeting proved a significant step in pushing the restaurant association members to negotiate with KIWA. Piece by piece, KIWA is making progress in securing fundamental gains, while working toward larger visions of economic justice.

This group has received assistance from the Funding Exchange and the Liberty Hill Foundation.

Chinese Staff and Workers Association, New York City

Sweatshop conditions are all too common in New York City's Chinese immigrant community. Waiters in Chinatown's restaurants work more than seventy hours for between seventy-five and one hundred dollars a week, with management illegally pocketing tips. Women garment workers, who are lucky if they make three to four dollars an hour, are unable to afford union health insurance. Their work often causes severe threats to their health: advanced repetitive strain injuries; vision problems; asthma and other diseases related to air quality. In these largely unregulated factories, unethical employers can use their involvement with organized crime and their influence over the police to silence dissent by threatening workers with blacklisting, deportation, or gang violence.

The Chinese Staff and Workers Association (CSWA) addresses the needs of Chinese people in the workplace and the community. It is a place where working people can receive information about their rights, learn English, and meet others facing similar problems. It is also a place where workers can come together and organize.

CSWA has been involved in many different campaigns since its founding. In 1997 it assisted the state attorney general in prosecuting the illegal labor practices at the largest restaurant in Chinatown. The employer is now offering a $1.1 million back pay settlement and the reinstatement of those workers who were fired illegally. Currently the association is doing environmental testing in several sweatshop work sites and strengthening its newspaper, which offers an important source of information to a community struggling to survive.

The first grant CSWA received in support of its work was from the North Star Fund.

Enlace, Portland, Oregon

In 1996 Peter Cervantes-Gautschi, an organizer in Portland, Oregon, tried to counter the isolation immigrant groups experience by taking a tour of low-wage worker organizations in the United States and Mexico. In meeting with more than eighty groups, he saw a need to create a collaborative network for them.

In 1998 twenty-three of the organizations, including KIWA and the Workplace Project, gathered to found Enlace, the Low Wage Worker Organizations' Collaborative. According to Cervantes-Gautschi, "Less than five percent of low-wage workers in North America have any kind of organization. If we're about social justice, then somehow we've got to do something dramatic to enable the organizations that focus on building that base to be more successful. With Enlace, we try to create this capability."

These immigrant worker organizations show that even those in the most desperate conditions can change their situation through the power of strategic organizing and perseverance. Money helps.

Chapter 7

Tax-Wise Giving

It pays to give. In fact, the more generously you give, the more the IRS rewards you. With good planning, you and your family can save substantially, not only on the income taxes you pay each year but also on hefty estate taxes imposed when you die. (The feds really mean it when they say you can't take it with you.) However unintentionally, our government provides a substantial subsidy to those who give generously and reject excessive wealth accumulation. If you so choose, you may take full advantage.

Notice that we said *if* you so choose. You don't have to, although most financial professionals will assume that tax minimization is a goal unless expressly informed otherwise. Many progressive people strive to reduce their taxes because they abhor the federal government's use of their tax dollars to support corporate welfare and the military. Others, seeking to promote greater tax fairness, feel strongly that they should not take advantage of inequities in the tax code that primarily benefit the rich.

Obviously tax considerations alone should not drive personal philanthropy. Desire for social and economic justice, equity, and change is a far more preferable motivator. Nonetheless it is hard to conceive of developing a systematic giving program without considering the tax implications. To that end in this chapter we survey the basic tax scene and the most common charitable planning strategies, to get you thinking about which ones might be most appropriate and effective for you.

The Basic IRS Rules

Benjamin Franklin once observed that the only things we can count on in life are death and taxes. Old Ben was right. IRS rules governing taxation of individuals get us coming and going. Every year, without fail, the federal government extracts a cut of your money by way of the income tax. It's also not over when you die. Once you're gone, it taxes what you left behind through estate or death taxes. Most charitable planning strategies aim at controlling the amount of income and death taxes you will pay.

In terms of the income tax, the basic rules are as follows: If you give cash outright to a 501(c)(3) charity, you receive a 100 percent tax deduction for amounts up to 50 percent of your adjusted gross income.

What Is a 501(c)(3) Charity?

The IRS recognizes several types of charitable organization. Best known are those it designates as Section 501(c)(3). Also known as public charities, these are charitable organizations that receive funding from a variety of donors, not just one. The section reference is to the provision of the tax code applicable to such charities. Although we make a distinction between charity and social change, the IRS does not. Many social change organizations have a 501(c)(3) tax status.

If you give stock, you can deduct up to 30 percent of your adjusted gross income (AGI). If you give a combination of both cash and stock, the combined maximum is still 50 percent, not 80 percent. For either kind of gift, if you give more than you can deduct in one year, you may take the remaining deduction anytime over the next five years. Example: Cathy's adjusted gross income in 1999 is a hundred thou-

> "I can remember when Nixon's income tax returns came out and stated that he had given four hundred dollars that year. My father said, 'My God, that's probably what I forgot to deduct.' Philanthropy was part of the family system. I can remember having birthday parties where I had people bring money for the March of Dimes."
> —Emily Morgan, donor, McKenzie River Gathering Foundation

sand dollars. That year she writes checks to her favorite charities totaling forty thousand dollars. She also gives stock worth thirty thousand dollars. For 1999, she can deduct only fifty thousand dollars of her combined seventy thousand dollars in charitable gifts. However, she can spread the deduction for the remaining twenty thousand over the next five years.

Capital gains taxes are part of the income tax. Capital gains are increases in the value of the property you own—that is, the difference between the current value of the property (stocks, bonds, real estate) and what you originally paid for it. When you sell property that has gained in value (appreciated property), the IRS taxes it at rates that vary, depending on such factors as how long you owned the property and how big the gain is. Capital gains tax rates change constantly, but at present, Uncle Sam takes up to about 20 percent of the gain.

Estate taxes, as we mentioned above, are taxes imposed on everything you leave behind when you die. Well, almost everything. Your taxable estate includes all cash and investments, all real estate (includ-

"I assume you can produce receipts for all this money you claim to have given the poor."

ing your home), and most personal property (car, clothes, jewelry, art, etc.) when the value of that property exceeds the IRS's so-called exemption amount. The rules for computing estate taxes are complicated, but they boil down to this: When you exceed the exemption amount, the federal government takes up to 55 percent of everything that's left.

> **Q:** *Is there a legal limit on how much I can give away?*
>
> **A:** In a word, no! But this is not always obvious. More often than not, when givers ask their financial advisers how much they can afford to give, the response is: "Not more than fifty percent of income." This response is simply incorrect. The IRS limit on tax deductibility imposes no legal limit on giving. It is simply a ceiling on how much of your giving you can use for tax deductions. If you wanted, you could give all your income and all your assets as well.

Common Giving Strategies

Both income and estate taxes may be drastically reduced through charitable giving. Here are some of the most common strategies.

Outright Gifts of Cash

By far the simplest and most popular giving strategy is to make a gift of cash. All you need to do is pull out your checkbook, write the check, and put it in the mail. A gift of cash is considered made on the date it is postmarked. Cash donations, as noted above, are deductible up to 50 percent of adjusted gross income.

Gifts of Stock and Other Appreciated Property

Giving cash is easy, but you can reap greater tax benefits by making gifts of stock and other property. Why? Think back on our discussion of federal capital gains taxes. When you have held stocks or other property for a long time and then sell them, the IRS taxes any increase (gain) in value. The greater the increase, the greater the tax. But if you make a charitable gift of this same appreciated property, you get a charitable deduction for the full value of the gift, and *none* of that gain is taxed. This is why gifts of stock are so appealing.

Don't be dissuaded from using this strategy because of concerns about disclosing your name to an organization. You can give stock anonymously just as easily as you can give cash. All you need to do is get the recipient's name, address, and telephone number and ask your

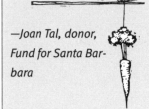
lawyer or other financial adviser to arrange for the transfer. The agent calls the recipient organization, lets it know that an anonymous donor wishes to make a gift of stock, and finds out whether the organization prefers cash from the sale of the stock or the stock itself. Then it is just a matter of completing the paper work. The recipient never sees your name.

Bear in mind that some organizations you may wish to give to may be too new, too small, or otherwise unprepared to handle stock transactions. The solution here is to go to a social change fund or community foundation and ask if it can serve as a fiscal sponsor to process the donation, then pass it on. As long as the organization you wish to give to falls within the IRS's definition of a tax-exempt 501(c)(3) charity, the fiscal sponsor may pass it on.

It is to your advantage to donate your most appreciated assets. It does not make sense to donate assets that have decreased in value. There is no capital gains benefit to you, and it's just extra work for the recipient to handle the sale. Instead you are better off selling the stock and then donating the proceeds to the organization. That way you can deduct the loss on your income tax return and take the charitable deduction too.

Insurance Gifts

Donating a life insurance policy is one of the more innovative charitable giving strategies. Often people buy life insurance policies when they are starting their families, and they name their children as beneficiaries. They hold the policies for a long time, sometimes long after the children are well established and financially secure in their own right. When this happens, it is possible to use a policy as a charitable gift.

To get a deduction, you must either name the charity as the owner of the policy or as the irrevocable beneficiary. In other words, you cannot retain any control over the policy. You cannot reserve a right to change beneficiaries. The amount of your deduction will depend on the type of policy donated.

Charitable Trusts

For individuals whose income and assets far exceed their needs and who wish to commit to a charitable giving program, a charitable trust may be the way to go. In a charitable trust the creator makes an irrevocable transfer of assets to the trust, which may be set up to last for a fixed period of years or a lifetime. During the period that the trust operates, some of the trust property gets distributed to charities of the creator's choosing, but some goes back to the creator, his or her loved ones, or other noncharitable beneficiaries. Ownership and enjoyment of the money are separated.

Because of the costs involved in setting up a charitable trust, forty thousand to fifty thousand dollars in assets are about the minimum required to consider this option, but for those who can afford charitable trusts, there can be many benefits. For example, charitable trusts funded with highly appreciated stock can save enormously on capital gains taxes that would otherwise be due if the stock were sold. They can also result in substantial savings on income and estate taxes. Even better, they can be individually structured to meet other financial goals the creator may have. For example, you can set up a charitable trust to distribute income to charitable organizations of your choosing for a period of years, then distribute the principal to your loved ones (charitable lead trust). Or, you can do the opposite, setting up the trust to pay income to you or your loved ones for life, then to distribute the principal to charity (charitable remainder trust). With either strategy, you can change charitable recipients as you go along. You can set up the trust so that activists decide who the recipients will be, or you can simply name an activist-controlled social change fund to receive charitable distributions from the trust. There are thousands of options. Amounts and types of tax deductions depend on the specific type of charitable trust created.

Setting up a charitable trust is definitely not a do-it-yourself proposition. IRS requirements are complex and constantly changing, and such trusts are not for everyone. Consult an accountant or tax lawyer if you consider this option.

Private Foundations

Private foundations are charitable organizations that, in contrast with public charities and foundations, are usually created, funded, and controlled by just one donor or family. Several types exist, but for our purposes, only conduit (or nonoperating) foundations, the most common type, are relevant. In this type of foundation a wealthy individual ir-

> "One of the things that changed when we adopted Sam was that I found I needed to save more. The moment of truth was when I did my taxes and saw that I was short on giving. Now I have money taken out of my paycheck that goes to Community Works, an alternative workplace giving program. By doing that, I was back up to giving away a couple of thousand dollars a year."—Jim McDonnell, donor, Haymarket People's Fund

revocably contributes a large chunk of assets to create the foundation, sets a rate at which the foundation assets and earnings will be paid out (the IRS requires a minimum payout of 5 percent of assets per year), and appoints a board of trustees (usually family members) to make grants to charitable causes in accordance with the donor's wishes. Many times hired employees run day-to-day operations. The foundation itself does not engage in charitable activities; all it does is make grants to organizations that do. All administrative costs are borne by the foundation.

Significant tax breaks accompany this giving structure. Cash contributions to a private foundation are deductible up to 30 percent of adjusted gross income, and contributions of appreciated property are deductible up to 20 percent. In either case the five-year carry-over provision applies. Moreover, appreciated property donated to a foundation escapes capital gains taxes. The foundation itself is tax-exempt, although the IRS imposes an annual excise tax of 1 or 2 percent on net investment income (income from interest, dividends, and capital gains).

Sound simple? It's not. First, this giving strategy makes financial sense only for individuals who can afford to commit permanently a minimum of about one million dollars to charitable purposes. Start-up and operating costs—like legal and accounting fees, site visit costs, employee wages and benefits, rent, and office supplies—add up quickly, eating into assets and earnings that could otherwise be going to charity. Foundation assets and payout must be large enough to justify the overhead, or the foundation becomes more dedicated to preserving itself than to serving any charitable purpose.

Second, IRS regulations and requirements are strict and burdensome. All applicable rules, and there are many, must be complied with or the tax-exempt status can be lost. The government enacted these constraints to curb significant abuses by foundations that, for example, operated without making any grants in a given year.

Finally, legitimate questions exist about whether private foundations are the most efficacious vehicles for addressing pressing social and economic problems. For one thing, most private foundations severely restrict their charitable payouts, many limiting it to the measly 5 percent minimum the IRS requires. The problem is that in today's stock market, foundation asset portfolios grow at many times that rate, without a proportionate increase in payout. In other words, private foundations tend to grow their wealth faster than they give it away. They are preserving themselves in perpetuity, despite the urgent need in American society for the charitable dollars they hold. In fact, in the last few years, as billions of new dollars flowed into private foundations, the percentage of foundation assets spent on grantmaking actually shrank.[1]

Some argue that the practice of accumulating wealth in private foundations is inconsistent with the charitable purposes these institutions are expected to serve. We're inclined to agree. As Rob McKay, founder of the McKay Foundation, says, "By putting money in a foundation, a funder is making a public contract with the government and the community for which they receive a generous subsidy, or tax-break. They have an obligation to give that money away."[2]

Another concern about the private foundation strategy is the extreme isolation in which grantmaking takes place. Unless a private foundation's donor is in touch with activist communities or has included activists on the board of trustees, it is easy for the foundation to fall into the habit of supporting causes that primarily benefit the donor's own class, rather than the needs of the broader community.

Still, private foundations can be an excellent giving mechanism in some circumstances. Consider the experience that one Funding Exchange donor recently shared with us:

"I was in a bind. For most of my life I owned stock in what is now a large multinational corporation, started by my grandparents at the turn of the century. My family owned a controlling interest in the company and decided to sell. At that time, in 1996, the value of my stock had appreciated from about a penny a share when I acquired it in the 1950s to over thirty-six dollars per share. My shares alone were worth over three million dollars and so were my sister's. If we did nothing, the capital gains taxes due upon the sale of our interest would have been over a million dollars each! We didn't need all that money. We wanted to use it to fund social change. I also personally hated the idea of forking over a million bucks to the government to buy more corporate welfare.

"So we didn't! Before the sale took place, we took all our stock and

put it into a private foundation, naming ourselves as trustees. It worked perfectly for everybody. Until the sale was finalized, we continued to control the disposition of the stock, which was important to ensure that our family got what it wanted from the sale of a controlling interest. Had we donated our stock to a charity or social change fund, legally we would not have retained this control. But we also avoided paying any capital gains taxes because our stock was now committed to benefiting a charitable purpose. We got a huge income tax deduction for our contribution and immense satisfaction from knowing that our money was going to support change. We don't want the responsibility of deciding where the money would go, though. So instead of making grants ourselves, we either choose recipients from lists of organizations screened and recommended by the Funding Exchange or donate the payout to social change funds around the country whose activist boards make the decisions. We structured our foundation so that its goals, payout rate, and decision-making structure can change as we change.

"This has been one of the most rewarding experiences of my life. It was just dumb luck that we ended up with this wealth. What a blessing to be able to give it back!"

With a bit of creativity, lots of work, and a well-thought-out plan, the private foundation option can work to advance social change. Payout can purposely be set high so that the foundation spends down its assets instead of hoarding them to ensure a continued existence. Organizations like the National Network of Grantmakers (NNG), a group of progressive individual givers, can keep you connected and provide inspiration and ideas. Grantmaking can be democratized by appointing activists knowledgeable about target communities and issues to the board of trustees.

But before you commit yourself to this giving strategy, be sure you are clear on why you are choosing it. Sometimes a donor-advised account within an existing social change foundation can screen potential recipients, keep you informed on issues and activities, administer grants in accordance with your wishes, and generally achieve the same results as a private foundation, but without the hassles of re-creating the wheel under the foundation aegis. The Funding Exchange and some other public foundations can also work with you if you wish to

make a large contribution but take time in deciding where the money will go.

Bequests and Other Gifts by Will

If you read this book but do nothing else, make a will. Your will is absolutely your last chance to ensure that your money goes to work for social change. Almost as important, donating your money by will can guarantee that you minimize the estate taxes imposed when you die.

There are several ways to make a charitable gift by will. Simplest is an outright or direct gift to a named charity, often called a bequest because it is made by will. You may give a specified dollar amount (a general bequest), you may bequeath a specific asset like IBM stock or a vacation home (a specific bequest), or you may simply direct that everything you own after payment of all other debts, taxes, and gifts to loved ones goes to a charitable organization (a residuary bequest). If you are not sure about precise dollar amounts, you may designate percentages to go to one or several organizations.

If you are not familiar with many charitable organizations or would rather leave the selection process to others, you may create a charitable trust or foundation in your will. This type of gift operates in much the same way as a charitable trust or foundation created during life. The trust property is transferred out of your estate to a trustee or trustees, who also receive your instructions on how to manage and distribute it for charitable purposes. A trust or foundation created by will may be set up to last either for a set period or for an indefinite period of time.

A final caveat: In this chapter we have touched on only some of the most common tax-wise methods for putting your money to work for change. There are others, and there are so many technical and legal aspects to most methods that it would be foolhardy not to seek advice from a capable accountant or attorney before taking the plunge. If you do, you will be rewarded with the highly satisfying experience that comes from sharing wealth.

Malama Makua

On the northwestern point of Oahu is Makua, a Hawai'ian name meaning "parents," a land sacred to native Hawai'ians. According to the oral history of the people of Wai'anae, it is the place where Papa (the earth mother) and Wakea (the sky father) created both the land and the people of Wai'anae. It is also the site of a military reservation notorious for its environmental abuses.

In 1992 Wai'anae residents and their supporters came together to oppose a permit application by the Makua Military Reservation (MMR) to burn and detonate hazardous wastes. The military wanted permission to burn munitions and medical wastes in a pit in the middle of the valley in Makua. The Environmental Protection Agency and the military proposed a very quiet process for approval. Public hearings were to be held in San Francisco, effectively ensuring that no members of the community could testify to its impact on their lives. Residents organized Malama Makua so they could stop the military. In collaboration with other community organizations, they were successful in getting the army to drop its application.

Since that success Malama Makua has developed its niche in a diverse coalition of community organizations committed to the reclamation of the Makua Military Reservation by the people of Hawai'i. Their goal is to remove the military from the Makua Valley and to clean up the land and return it to its appropriate cultural and environmental uses.

Community members have been petitioning the military for information about the land since the seventies. They've asked about the status of the many endangered plant species in the valley, the condition of sacred sites within the reservation, and the environmental consequences of military activity such as live firing ranges. They have threatened two lawsuits in order to receive that information. One challenges the military's failure to comply with the Endangered Species Act, and the other forces it to provide an environmental impact study. The suits are part of the preparation for the scheduled return of a piece of the military reservation to the community in 2029. "People need to be prepared for the land's return," says Roger Furrer, a member of Malama Makua's steering committee. "They need to know what's happened in the valley, what the levels of contamination are, and the location and conditions of the sacred sites. Our requests for information have been ignored for so long; we feel it's appropriate to push."

Furrer identifies the impact of colonization on the people and on the land as the biggest struggle Malama Makua faces internally and externally. The community also struggles with the racism, external and internal, that traditional colonial power relies on. Native Hawai'ians are a diverse people with a range of understandings of Hawai'i's history. Navigating the changes in culture, reclaiming tradition, and undermining colonial mentalities have created stress for the community.

Its commitment to the native community in Wai'anae means that Malama Makua's organizing strategies don't always look like those of a traditional advocacy organization, and this has made it challenging for the group to find funding. "There needs to be fiscal responsibility within any social change organization," Furrer says, "but people who support these organizations need to be very clear about where their culture—whether it's economic, political, or organizational—stops and the culture of the community begins. I give the People's Fund credit for struggling with those issues again and again."

Chapter 8

Choosing and Working with Financial Professionals

I n your quest to understand how giving can fit into your overall financial picture, you may quickly discover that there is more to it than you want to take on yourself. Without question you need a working knowledge of what you've got, where it comes from, and what you might want to do with it. But unless you are a tax lawyer or a CPA, you are not expected to know obscure provisions of the tax code or the workings of "GRITS," "GRATS," or "NIMCRUTS."★ If your finances justify it—and they almost always do—get professional help.

A good, objective financial professional can greatly ease the process of deciding what you want your money to do and where, how, and when you want it done. In fact, many givers find that hiring a financial professional is one of the most empowering steps they can take in

★Shorthand—acronyms—for tax shelters: GRIT is a form of annuity trust; GRAT is another form of trust; NIMCRUTS is a form of a charitable remainder unitrust.

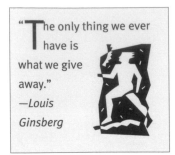

making decisions about their money. The right pro can supply solid information about everything from insurance to budgets, charitable giving, investments, trusts, and tax laws. If you are just starting out, a pro can help you understand your documents, clarify questions, get answers, and direct you toward other resources. If you are already giving, you can challenge yourself to find more and better ways of going about it by sitting down with a pro.

The trick for givers is to find the right professional. When sharing money rather than amassing it is a central goal, some financial professionals just don't "get it." After all, "preserve and grow" is the holy grail of the financial world. Many financial professionals approach giving as a tax strategy or an afterthought, not as a guiding principle. Few see the value in using money to level the playing field, and most know little about available opportunities. Moreover, it can be a challenge to find a truly independent pro. Some professionals earn their daily bread by taking a cut of your assets. Others stay employed only by selling their employers' products.

Fortunately there are financial professionals who *do* get it and who will work for your interests. In this chapter we show you how to go about finding and working with such a pro. We outline the major types of professional service and describe each. We suggest what to look for, what to bring to an initial meeting, and some questions you may wish to ask. All along we give tips on power dynamics, practical points, and your role as adviser to your adviser. Finally, we offer pointers on when and how to terminate a relationship that becomes untenable.

Who's Who

Deciding what kind of financial professional you need can be a challenge. You may need two, three, or even four if your situation is particularly complicated. Turf and boundaries are sometimes murky, made murkier when you already have someone advising you but are thinking of making a change. It can be awkward to make even preliminary inquiries when the answers depend on disclosure of private financial information. And of course, you want a reputable firm or individual.

Here are thumbnail sketches of the major players and what each does:

Financial planners are generalists who can help you review, understand, and shape your income, expenses, and cash flow needs, charitable giving potential, investments, taxes, estate planning, insurance coverage, and retirement. A good planner starts with your goals and develops a comprehensive financial plan that balances those goals with your long- and short-term needs for money. The plan anticipates possible changes from major expenditures or new sources of income and builds in flexibility to accommodate them.

Many givers seeking to define their goals, figure out where to start, or devise long-term strategies find the services of qualified financial planners invaluable. Because planners start with their clients' goals, they can screen out or bridge gaps in the often bewildering and piecemeal presentation of options offered by lawyers, accountants, and brokers and other financial specialists. Because their work crosses all aspects of financial management, they often work with specialists as coordinators on their clients' behalf.

You probably have noticed that financial planning services are being pitched to almost everyone with a bank account. Banks, insurance companies, brokerage houses, and other financial institutions promote planning services as part of a total financial services concept. It is in fact true that people from a wide variety of income levels can benefit from the services of good financial planners. But the type and quality of available services vary widely, and it is important to find a planner whose qualifications and expertise match your particular needs.

It is equally important to be wary of planners who have a conflict of interest in giving independent advice. They may be either independent practitioners or individuals employed by brokers, insurance companies, banks, or investment services who earn commissions or other benefits by selling you their employers' financial products.

To find out if there might be a conflict, ask your prospective planner how he or she gets paid. Most planners charge hourly rates or fixed fees for their services, and these are generally regarded as the preferred arrangements. Some take a combination of fees and commis-

> " For most people, money is a possession. We need to learn to see money as an instrument that can be used to help create change, to improve our lives and the lives of those around us."—*Francisco Ramos, donor, Crossroads Fund*

sions. Proceed with caution on these planners. Avoid these who work on commission only.

Tax, trust, and estate planning lawyers know the law within their specialties and can devise strategies and draft documents to ensure that your money goes where you want it. They can also be particularly helpful in deciphering documents—if they can avoid their profession's tendency toward legalese. (If your lawyer is incapable of translating the law into lay terms, you are wasting your money.)

Obviously an appropriately qualified attorney can help you write a will or set up a charitable trust that carries out your giving goals. You may also wish to consult an attorney if you have trouble getting documents or accountings from individuals who manage your affairs or if you are in a dispute with a trustee, a lawyer who works for your family, or some other guardian of your assets. The right lawyer should be able to ascertain fairly quickly what your rights are, explain them to you, and suggest a solution. A lawyer is also a good place to start

For accountant Ted Gribble, appearing on the hit show "CPA Unplugged" was a dream come true.

when confidentiality is a chief concern because the attorney you hire to represent only your interests is duty-bound to keep your confidences.

Accountants are experts in organizing and keeping track of money. They prepare tax returns, perform audits, give tax advice, and assist with gift, tax, and financial planning. Often accountants work in tandem with other financial professionals to "sweat the details" of a financial plan. Many can identify obscure provisions of the tax code or make financial projections that help clients maximize charitable giving potential. Most accountants are specialists. Some are certified personal financial planners and take on more of a generalist's role.

Beware the term "accountant." The terms is often used very loosely to describe anyone who works with financial records, from entry-level bookkeepers to CPAs. Certified public accountants (CPAs) hold the highest level of professional training and adhere to the highest standards of their profession. They charge accordingly, with fees comparable to those of an attorney. Bookkeepers and noncertified "accounting services," on the other hand, are unregulated and require no special qualifications. If you seek out accounting assistance, be sure you know what you are paying for.

Banks offer a wide variety of investment and financial management services, including

---

What Is a Trust? What Is a Trustee?

Many givers and potential givers receive income from trusts managed by one or more trustees. Very often both the nature of the trust and the duties and authority of the trustee are unclear. Sometimes trustees serve as de facto financial advisers; sometimes not. Even the terminology can be vexing. Here is a short primer.

A trust is a legal entity created by one person to hold assets for the benefit of one or several others. The creator sets the terms of the trust, saying who gets it, when, how much, and under what circumstances. Sometimes a trust has a series of beneficiaries—for example, a grandparent may name a parent as the first beneficiary, then a grandchild as the beneficiary upon the parent's death. Sometimes one beneficiary receives only trust income, while another is entitled to assets. In many instances a charity is a beneficiary (charitable trust).

A trustee is a person appointed by the creator of a trust to manage or administer the trust's assets. Often the trustee is a bank, a (usually male) relative, or a lawyer. One trust may have several trustees.

By law a trustee must administer a trust according to the terms set out by the creator. A trustee cannot spend assets of the trust in ways that were not authorized and cannot squander assets. Nor can he or she profit at the beneficiary's expense. A trust's terms, though, usually afford at least some leeway for interpretation. This can be important when a beneficiary wants to loosen restrictions on how a trust's income or assets are handled, as, for example, when the beneficiary wants the trustee to make socially responsible investments or contributions to charity. If the trust's terms permit the trustee "to make such investments and distributions as the Trustee deems advisable for the support and education of the beneficiary," there's an argument to be made that the trustee should acquiesce to your wishes.

(continued on next page)

Trustees are conservative. Many are wary of investing trust assets in anything but the largest, most well-established and profitable companies, and most will not expend assets or income on anything even remotely controversial, despite their having the legal authority to do so.

Don't despair if you are the beneficiary of a restrictive trust. If you are entitled to trust income, you can give that. Or you can check with a lawyer to see if the trust is really as restrictive as the trustee interprets it. Some givers have been able to convince or compel their trustees to change the handling of trusts so that it better comports with their values rather than the trustees'.

trust or asset management and financial planning. Sometimes a bank manages all aspects of a client's finances, whether by the client's own choice, by appointment, or by default. Some offer very personalized service. Many do not. For better and worse, bank officers often serve as trustees over assets placed in their care and hold a legal obligation to manage and preserve the assets for their beneficiaries.

By definition, banks are conservative money managers and will discourage nontraditional uses of assets. They may be especially wary when a beneficiary's desired use, such as charitable giving, cuts into principal or otherwise reduces an account's overall value. Banks want to preserve and grow your money, not share it or direct it outside the bank. In some instances their legal duties prohibit their loosening the reins. In any event many know little about alternative investments or charitable giving opportunities. There are exceptions, though, which will be highlighted in our chapter "Socially Responsible Investment"; more information can also be found through resources listed in the appendices.

Investment managers manage part or all of a client's investment portfolio (stocks and bonds). They are expected to know the stock market and make investment decisions for individuals who lack the time, interest, or expertise to make these decisions on their own. Essentially the client takes a chunk of assets, consults with the investment manager about investment objectives, then turns authority for the assets over to the manager, who makes all the day-to-day decisions about what to buy or sell. The manager provides regular updates and reports but generally has a great deal of discretion, unless the client insists on prior approval. (In the trade these are known, predictably enough, as discretionary and nondiscretionary accounts.)

An investment manager's focus is on making money for the client, not on planning, educating, or finding nonmarket alternatives. Fees usually are based on a percentage of the client's invested assets, and the manager's goal is to earn the maximum possible return. For this reason those who want to invest in community loan funds or other nonmarket alternatives usually do not ask their investment managers to handle their entire investment portfolios. They meet their alternative investment goals simply by setting aside portions of their assets to manage on their own or with the assistance of attorneys. By consulting directly with the manager of the alternative enterprise or loan fund you are interested in investing in, you can make the investment yourself.

Stockbrokers operate in the same arena as investment managers but are more involved in the actual buying and selling of securities, which they do for commissions. Decision making is up to the client. Some brokers make recommendations. Others merely execute transactions at the request of a client who knows what he or she wants. The latter (discount brokers) charge proportionally lower commissions.

As the son of a Wall Street broker, Charles Garland was born to a life of privilege. Ironically, schooling at Eton and Harvard had introduced him to Leo Tolstoy's ascetic Christianity and radical politics; when Garland's father died and left him a million dollars, the young college dropout refused the inheritance.

In 1920 American peace and justice organizations were woefully underfunded, and many of Garland's friends told him that the poor could not afford the luxury of his moral absolutism. The young man relented and placed the money into a trust to create the American Fund for Public Service.

Garland lived out most of his life on a subsistence farm in Pennsylvania, but his money was one of the few sources of funding for progressive organizing in the twenties. In addition to creating the ACLU, the fund supported American pacifism and laid the legal groundwork for the fight against segregation.

Insurance companies and others working in the area of financial risk management frequently offer financial planning or investment advice. While insurance offers some creative estate-planning opportunities, companies that sell insurance products tend to "go with what they know" in giving financial advice. Most agents know only one or two areas well and lack the skills and perspectives of more independent financial professionals. Moreover, company representatives who work on commission have a vested interest in selling their companies' products, regardless of whether or not the sales make sense in a given situation. Don't rely on an insurance company as your only source of financial advice.

Philanthropic consultants are not financial professionals as such, but rather are experts on financial aspects of giving (tax consequences, structuring gifts, etc.) and the work of various charitable organizations. A few keep well informed on social change groups and can provide guidance in identifying and selecting organizations you might want to give to. Philanthropic consultants may be independent consulting services or professionals who work for banks or foundations. Some social change foundations have contacts with such consultants and can make referrals.

Wealth counselors, relatively new on the scene, provide planning services and counseling on both emotional and technical challenges of having wealth. They work independently or for large charitable institutions and may serve either individuals or families. Sometimes you are billed for their services at a flat rate, sometimes at an hourly rate. Some large charitable institutions absorb the expense as a cost of doing business, but naturally these individuals work primarily to serve their employers' interests.

What to Look for in an Adviser

Virtually everyone who seeks advice on his or her financial affairs wants a professional who is trustworthy and whose skills, training, and expertise are appropriate to his or her particular needs. He or she wants someone who understands his or her financial goals, knows what it will take to realize them, and can communicate in terms he or she understands and can work with.

Individuals who do not subscribe to the notion of continuous wealth accumulation, or who make giving a central financial goal, face special challenges in finding good financial advice. Some advisers simply won't "get" what they are trying to do. Some will try to protect clients from themselves. A few will be downright hostile.

But you *can* find what you need. Many progressive individuals have found advisers with both top-notch professional skills and the willingness and ability to turn their clients' goals into reality. It is beyond the scope of this book to elaborate on all the factors that bear on the selection of a qualified adviser. For general advice, see one of the several good books available on the subject at most bookstores. For advice on finding pros who work well with progressive money goals, we asked the folks who've successfully gone out and found precisely what they wanted. Here are some of their tips:

»→ Don't go in to see an adviser without taking time beforehand to reflect on your broad financial goals. If you go in expecting an adviser to define your goals for you, you will be disappointed.

»→ Don't count on finding one adviser who will be able to give you all the answers to all your questions. Often it helps to see first a planner, then a lawyer or other specialist.

»→ Be wary of signs that a prospective adviser will resist your goals. On the other hand, don't mistake critical inquiries for resistance. You want someone who will point out important technical, financial, or legal implications of your goals that you may not be aware of. You *don't* want someone who derides or ridicules your goals or who regards them as an amusement.

»→ When meeting with a prospective financial adviser, be up front about your goals and priorities right off, and don't apologize for them. If you don't want the status quo, say so. If you are gay or lesbian and want an adviser attuned to protecting your own and your partner's interests, speak up. Any issue that could make or break the relationship should be put on the table. In this way you cut through the baloney, save time, minimize misunderstandings, and get a good initial take on whether you and the pro could work compatibly.

»→ If you are already working with an adviser, someone you inherited or hired a long time ago when your goals were different or undefined, determine whether the relationship still works.

Close family ties with an adviser can work for or against you. The adviser may be accustomed to taking directions from only one family member. Or he or she may welcome some fresh input. Your goals may or may not be compatible with those set out for the rest of your family. You may need independence, or you may just need to make your wishes known. Sometimes it is financially unwise to

"I tried different people over the years, and I haven't been happy. I need to switch now. When I first moved here, I gave all my money to a socially responsible investment guy everyone around here used. He was a terrible teacher, horrible. I asked, 'What's the difference between A and B?' and he said, 'It's the difference between a Cadillac and a pickup truck.' Now, I had come here from Nashville, and a pickup truck was much more valuable to me. I stopped using his services."—*Sara Cohen, donor, Bread and Roses Community Fund*

pull away from an existing family adviser, as when a whole family shares a common set of complicated financial or legal circumstances. If it would take an outsider months or years to reconstruct, it might not be cost-effective to hire someone else, especially if the only result is to have two people create the same wheel.

Unless you're really sure it will be a waste of time, sit down with your existing adviser(s) and go over your current goals and objectives. If you like, it's perfectly legitimate to consult with another adviser about your options before shaking anything up. Or if you have several advisers, you may be able to get what you need by keeping one and adding or changing another. Ultimately you will have to decide if the benefits of staying with a particular adviser outweigh the drawbacks.

➻ Always remember that a relationship with a financial professional is a business relationship, not a personal one. You hire a professional to perform a service, and your loyalty to him or her should be rooted in how well he or she does the job, nothing more. It doesn't matter if you've been working with an adviser for twenty minutes or twenty years. If you don't trust or feel comfortable with your adviser, or if you feel stymied in your efforts to get what you need or participate as you wish, you need to change the relationship.

➻ Although many social change givers want professionals who share their world view, this is not always necessary. Any prospective adviser must possesses credentials and technical skills appropriate to your needs. Beyond that, however, the single best predictor of a successful relationship is whether the adviser genuinely respects and honors what you are trying to do. We know of excellent advisers who, without either embracing or rejecting their clients' goals, have sought out the kinds of investments the clients wanted, researched social change projects, or drafted documents ensuring that the clients' money would go to social change, rather than to Uncle Harry.

➻ If it's essential to you to work with a pro who shares your outlook or works with other clients of similar mind, you can find one. How feasible it may be is another question. If you can travel occasionally and don't mind doing business by phone and fax, proximity is no longer a necessity. Make sure that costs are feasible too, though this is a somewhat subjective factor. It may be "worth" it to you to spend money on a certain planner, lawyer, or investment manager who you know to be good, even if it costs you more in time or money than you ordinarily would be willing to spend.

How to Find the Pro You Want

You could start by checking out the resources we've listed in Appendix F. For example, the Social Investment Forum's Web site has listings of financial planners, brokers, and investment managers involved in socially responsible investing. Also, Co-op America publishes an annual directory called the *Green Pages.*

You might also get good leads from professionals in related specialties. For example, an accountant who helps with your tax planning might know a good lawyer who could draft a will or charitable trust for you. A financial planner might know a mutual fund manager who targets the types of investments you want.

One of the best sources of leads on financial professionals who work with money sharers is people already working with them. Progressive foundations often know which advisers their donors use and can make referrals. Also, conferences for people with inherited or earned wealth, offered by many social change foundations, afford an excellent opportunity to meet people who have found advisers they can recommend to you.

But don't just get names and phone numbers. You can winnow out the field by asking specific questions about potential advisers. Describe what you are looking for. Ask for a quick assessment of a recommended pro's strengths and weaknesses. Find out what asset range he or she works with and what fees to expect. Finally, see if your source knows of anyone you should not use.

Beware of endorsements from professional associations to which most financial professionals belong. While these organizations can confirm if a prospective adviser meets the profession's *minimum* standards and sometimes will say if a pro has been reprimanded or suspended for conduct falling *below the minimum,* they generally offer no affirmative guidance on where to turn.

Preparing for the Initial Meeting

Once you have names, numbers, and feedback on three or four prospects, make an appointment for a personal interview. If the scheduler doesn't mention it, ask if there will be a charge for the initial consultation. Policy on this varies from professional to professional and field to field. If there is no charge, expect that the fees charged once you become a client will be structured to absorb the costs of the "free" interview.

Arrive at the meeting prepared to outline what you are looking for. Be as specific as possible on points of critical importance, and don't hesitate to say if part of what you need is education. Some of what you say will depend on the type of adviser you are interviewing. For example, a broker or investment manager will want to know your criteria for socially responsible investing. A trust lawyer will need to know your giving goals. A philanthropy consultant may need only a general idea of the types of organization you are interested in.

Take along copies of key financial and legal documents that the professional may need to review. These could help him or her zero in on your situation quickly and perhaps suggest a couple of ways to help you. Included might be estimates of your current or projected income and expenses; a recent net worth statement; trust or estate planning documents; investment account statements; and lists of your overall financial and investment goals, to the extent that you have formulated them. If there is something in one of your documents that you do not fully understand (there always is), test the adviser's communication skills by asking for a quick explanation. The response you get may speak volumes about how well you and he or she will work together. (Incidentally, if you don't want to leave copies of your private financial documents with a prospective adviser, it is appropriate to ask for their return at the end of the interview.)

In the meeting try to get a sense of how well you would work with this adviser. Is there a give-and-take quality to the discussion? Do you feel comfortable asking questions? Does the adviser respond to you with questions indicating that he or she understands your needs and concerns? Are your questions answered to your satisfaction? Do you pick up on any attitudes toward your goals or toward class, race, gender, or sexual orientation?

Some Questions to Ask

To begin with, you will want to ask some general questions about a prospective adviser's credentials, background, and technical expertise. You will also want to know precisely what services are offered, how he or she charges for them, and whether there are any costs not included in the base fee. Ask what steps or procedures the adviser ordinarily follows with clients like you, and go over such potential problem areas as confidentiality and accessibility. More specific questions, and questions applicable only to certain types of financial professionals, may be found in several of the good mass-market guides to the subject.

More important for our purposes are questions designed to draw out whether the prospective adviser would make a good fit with your goals as a progressive giver or investor. Try this: Describe your goals; then ask the prospective adviser if he or she has ever worked with clients who had similar goals. If so, how many? Ask for a recounting of one such client's situation and the specific strategies the adviser formulated to meet that person's needs. Find out whether you might be able to contact this or another client for a reference. (By the way, "No" is sometimes a legitimate response. A financial adviser should never give out the name or phone number of a client without first checking with the client.)

Also ask, after describing your goals, if the adviser has any ideas right off the bat about how to help *you*. An awkward pause or vague "I'll have to get back to you" is not a good sign. A professional in tune with your needs and competent in his or her area should be able to offer at least a couple of concrete suggestions, even at an initial meeting.

The more actively you participate in an interview, the more quickly you will sense the prospective adviser's fit with your goals and needs. Whatever you do, don't make any commitments on the spot. It is fine and expected that you are shopping around. Don't hesitate to say so. At the end of the interview just thank the adviser for his or her time and leave.

> "For years I felt completely disempowered from questioning anything my advisers were saying or doing. It all seemed so complicated and over my head, and besides, my dad had hired them at huge expense, so I thought they must be 'the best.' What a joke. Once I took the time to learn some financial and investment basics and put together my own financial goals, I could see that the emperor had no clothes! Literally . . . When I saw them, it was as if they were sitting around those mahogany conference tables in their underwear. They had no power over me anymore. They weren't bad people, but they were bad for me, so I got some new ones. My new advisers understand me, and mostly I understand them. Things are working out fine."—*Donor, Funding Exchange*

THE DANCE OF THE MALADROIT ACCOUNTANTS

When to Say Good-bye

The process of managing your money is fluid. What you need in the way of professional advice will change with time and circumstances. When you are working with an adviser, you need to monitor regularly your overall financial and estate plans, investments, and giving goals and to meet periodically with your adviser to stay current, discuss any changes or new strategies you may want to implement, and so on.

At some point you may need to bring your relationship with a financial professional to an end. Perhaps your adviser has accomplished all that you set out to do. Perhaps he or she has done nothing. Maybe it has become clear that your approaches are no longer compatible, or

   Nuts and Bolts

never were. Maybe you're at an impasse with a lawyer or an investment counselor who won't do what you want. Maybe your best friend has found a financial planner she won't stop raving about. You interviewed her, and now you want to switch.

How do you fire someone? We think that honesty is still the best policy. It might be hard, and it might not help you, but it could help the next client who passes through this adviser's door. If you can't do this, you can simply name something that you appreciated about the relationship but say that you're taking your business elsewhere. You don't have to explain why you are leaving unless you want to.

Don't hang on to a relationship that is not working just because you are concerned about hurting the professional's feelings. No matter how long you've worked together, no matter what confidences you've shared, it's business, not personal. You pay for what you are getting and deserve to get what you pay for.

One Bite at a Time

You are not alone in the wilderness. It's good to know that there is plenty of assistance available to help on your journey to take charge. You can master your documents. You can find people to help you interpret them and move closer to your goals. If you feel overwhelmed, take a moment and recall how you eat an elephant: one bite at a time.

The Community Coalition for Substance Abuse and Treatment

In the late eighties injustice was the daily diet in South Central Los Angeles. There were few groups committed to organizing for fundamental change. At the same time, crack cocaine was devastating low-income neighborhoods. In 1989 the Los Angeles Police Department responded to area drug and alcohol problems in South Central with Operation Hammer, the mass arrests of African American and Latino youth. Many longtime activists believed it was critical to change the idea that law enforcement is an appropriate solution to the substance abuse problem. Instead they wanted to address the underlying issues that drug and alcohol problems represent. But how?

Organizers understood the problem's complexity. There was the proliferation of crack, unjust law enforcement, and public manifestations of alcohol and substance abuse problems, such as the increase of liquor stores, crack houses, and motels used for drug dealing. They formed the Community Coalition for Substance Abuse Prevention and Treatment to attack issues of substance abuse from a social change perspective.

For starters, the fledgling organization decided to address the excessive number of liquor stores operating in the South Central community. There were 253 liquor stores in a district with a population of 200,000. (Contrast that with the state of Rhode Island, with 280 liquor stores for a population of 1.3 million.) In the wake of 1992's civil unrest, they were determined to prevent the reopening of liquor stores that had been destroyed. Community activists worked with city council members and others to convert these stores to other uses; this resulted in 44 new, non-alcohol-related businesses, including credit unions and Laundromats. They prevented the rebuilding of more than 100 stores. Community members closed motels and "recycling" centers known for drug-related crimes and developed a new ordinance that created stricter requirements for alcohol outlet permits in South Central L.A.

Community Coalition members see the issue of an overabundance of liquor stores as evidence of problems of sustainable economic development in low-income communities. They began to search for economic alternatives that would contribute to the neighborhood's economic and social well-being. The result was Greater Resources through Organizing and Working (GROW), an initiative that organizes neighborhoods in the two square miles around the coalition's community center to promote positive economic development. The community has conducted its own planning and needs assessments and has designed organizing strategies and such solutions as protesting the quality of food in a grocery chain in the community, researching land use issues, and seeding new economic opportunities. Its focus on positive economic development is a viable (and visible) alternative to a drug and alcohol economy.

The Community Coalition also trains young organizers and leaders. High school students in the South Central Youth Empowered for Action (SC-YEA) program have organized committees at eight high schools. The teenagers led a successful fight to reduce tobacco and alcohol advertising near South Central Los Angeles schools and replaced offensive billboards with 120 of their own antitobacco designs. They also took on the citizen committee responsible for overseeing $2.4 billion in funds earmarked for school improvements, after their research had demonstrated that the money was distributed unfairly, with older schools receiving less than schools in more affluent areas. They convinced the board to redirect $199 million into their community for additional school repairs.

The success of the Community Coalition shows that law enforcement does not have to be seen as the only solution to problems of substance abuse in low-income neighborhoods. Community Coalition's approach of organizing to confront underlying problems proves, once again, that organized people can remake neighborhoods according to their own vision.

For more information on the Community Coalition for Substance Abuse and Treatment, please contact the Liberty Hill Foundation (see Appendix A).

Chapter 9

Socially Responsible Investing: Do You Know What Your Money Is Doing?

Since the eighties, there has been an explosive growth in the number of investors, the volume of dollars, and the menu of socially responsible investment options. This growth is accompanied by a track record of good financial performance and social impact.

Some of you may be skeptical that selling off stocks in offensive corporations could make a difference. After all, if you sell it, won't someone else buy it? It is true that once it issues stock, the company has already raised the money it sought. But a company is still concerned about its public reputation, and this is a source of leverage.

To have the maximum impact, socially responsible investing must be done in consort with social movements and other actions outside the financial marketplace. There is, however, value to personal witness and your own choice not to profit from the exploitation of other people and the earth.

Though some critics still argue that it is imprudent to limit the universe of investment options with nonfinancial criteria, the financial accomplishments of socially responsible investments are measurable and often favorable. As with any investment, performance changes year to year, and not all are stellar performers. Consult the resource organizations we list in Appendix F for timely information on performance.

The earliest social investors were motivated by religious beliefs and the desire not to invest in corporations that produced liquor and tobacco. Several investment funds, like Pax World, excluded such "sin" investments. Another generation of activists used their shares in companies like Dow and Honeywell to protest the manufacturing of weapons during the Vietnam War. Activist groups introduced social-issue shareholder resolutions for stockholders to vote on.

During the sixties and seventies shareholder activism expanded to include concerns about labor and environmental issues. In Kentucky a Catholic religious order, the Sisters of Loreto, used their shares in the Blue Diamond Coal Company to draw attention to that company's policies of strip mining. Though activists rarely rallied sufficient shareholder votes to defeat management positions, they succeeded in drawing public attention to irresponsible corporate practices, and this *can* change corporate policies.

Amid this wide spectrum of activity, there are three principal areas of socially responsible investment: shareholder activism, socially screened investments, and community investments.

Shareholder Activism

Shareholder activism means using one's ownership of stock to introduce or vote on social issues that affect the governance of companies. Periodically public corporations issue proxy statements, which are essentially ballots for owner shareholders. Proxies can include a variety of financial or social issues. Shareholders either vote "with" or "against" management, with a nonvote counted as a vote in favor of management. As a result, management rarely loses, but shareholder meetings continue to be forums to raise issues.

Today shareholders organize to push social-issue resolutions concerning pollution, excessive executive compensation, and human rights practices, among others. International activists rise at the annual

"I grew up in a Quaker household during the Vietnam War, and I was appalled to find out that I had stock in Gulf Oil, and Gulf made napalm. I asked my father to sell it. He said, 'If you don't own it, someone else will.' But he did sell it."—*Donor, Bread and Roses Community Fund*

A worldwide boycott of Nestlé products resulted in the company's agreement to stop the aggressive marketing of infant formula in areas of Africa with unsafe water. So outraged was the American public over the deaths of infants for profit that boycott information was disseminated even in conservative rural areas of the United States.

meetings of Union Carbide to press for justice for the victims of the 1984 disaster in Bhopal, India. Teachers, through their major pension fund investments in large corporations, push for stronger corporate commitments to environmental and human rights concerns. The Interfaith Center on Corporate Responsibility coordinates the shareholder actions of dozens of national religious denominations and provides information for individual shareholder activists.

Shareholder activism is one avenue for using one's capital as leverage for social change. Other shareholders use the threat or actual withdrawal of investments as leverage against certain corporate behavior.

Socially Screened Investments

Many people would like to disassociate themselves entirely from corporations with repugnant records as polluters, union busters, and discriminators. These investors choose not to profit personally from investments in firms with abhorrent practices.

A growing number of individual investors are therefore divesting their holdings from such companies. A number of investment advisers now specialize in socially screened investments, avoiding the most "socially injurious" corporations.

The most stunning example of the success of removing financial support to demand systemic change was the South Africa divestment movement. At its peak more than four hundred billion dollars were withdrawn from investments in that country. Tens of thousands of individual investors and hundreds of major pension funds, universities, states, and municipal governments divested their holdings from corporations operating under apartheid. Former South African President Nelson Mandela credits the international divestment movement as one of the major forces that contributed to the international isolation of apartheid.

A new wave of reinvestment has swept into democratic South Africa. There is even an investment program that allows U.S. investors to lend funds to support community economic development projects in Black townships.

*"We still haven't worked out all the kinks
in the capitalist system, have we, J.B.?"*

Today a growing number of social investors are demanding "green portfolios," the exclusion of companies that have consistently bad environmental practices. Many environmental activists were startled to realize that they were sharing in the profits of such big corporate pol luters as Exxon, Monsanto, and Alcoa. There are now green mutual funds and an organized movement to get corporations to adopt resolutions committing themselves to sustainable environmental practices.

A variety of firms, investment advisers, mutual funds, money market funds, and other vehicles now specialize in socially screened stocks and bonds. Some have the capacity to tailor portfolios to the investor's social concerns. Investors with larger net worth (more than $150,000 in assets) work with individually managed accounts, while smaller investors may put large parts of their savings or portfolios in socially responsible mutual funds or money market funds.

Community Investments

Some investors see a limit to effecting social change through investments in publicly traded corporations and other stocks and bonds. Un-

The stock market will not be the cutting edge of social change.

less their actions are part of larger social movements that press for improved corporate behavior, the social impact of investment actions is minimal.

These investors aspire to see their investments go directly to the root of urgent problems, like the scarcity of affordable housing, the dearth of community economic development funds, and the lack of credit available for people in for low-income communities. For these investors, there are a number of options among community investments.

At a time when the gap between haves and have-nots is widening, community investments are a vehicle to bridge this gap—and to build basic security for more people. These investments include deposits in community development credit unions and banks, loans to community loan funds, and some forms of direct equity investment in community-supported ventures. Your investment professionals may be unfamiliar with (or reluctant to steer you toward) community investments. You may find yourself having to educate and push them to learn more about these opportunities. Some of this reluctance may come from the constraints that keep many investment advisers focused on traditional investment vehicles and fearful about lawsuits for engaging in fiscally imprudent activities. If this is a barrier, you may have to remove a chunk of money from an adviser's oversight to participate in the community investment field.

Community Development Credit Unions and Banks

Not all banks and credit unions have the same commitment to social goals. Banks, for instance, are obligated by their charters to address the credit needs of the communities from which they draw deposits. But many fail miserably in reinvesting in their communities, particularly low-income or minority neighborhoods, transferring funds instead to speculative ventures with the possibility of a quick or astounding profit.

There is now a generation of community development credit unions (CDCUs) and community-oriented banks that were started explicitly to reinvest in credit-starved neighborhoods. CDCUs are formed to meet the consumer credit needs of low-income communities and operate in more than four hundred communities nationwide. Banks like the Community Capital Bank in Brooklyn, New York, hold a steadfast commitment to revitalizing credit-starved neighborhoods.

The South Shore Bank in Chicago began in 1974 as one of the first community development banks in the nation. Because other banks had withdrawn credit from the South Shore neighborhood, community activists formed a new bank to meet the credit needs of that neighborhood. Now, more than twenty years later, the bank has financed the construction and renovation of twenty thousand units of housing and has lent millions to local businesses. The neighborhood has experienced an economic revival, and the bank has expanded its service area to assist borrowers in surrounding neighborhoods.

Investments in these institutions may take the form of checking accounts, savings accounts, certificates of deposit (CDs), or individual retirement accounts (IRAs). One advantage of investments in CDCUs and community-oriented banks is that they are insured by the federal government and thus very secure.

Conventional wisdom might be that loans to projects in poor communities are highly risky. The reality is that tremendous amounts of money flow through such neighborhoods, like leaks in a rusty bucket, but the residents don't control the housing, jobs, or credit institutions in their own communities. Community or intermediary lenders work to plug the economic holes by lending to community development corporations, nonprofit housing groups, land trusts, and other institutions that build local economic self-sufficiency.

Community Loan Funds

In the last dozen years more than one hundred new lending programs have been created to link socially concerned institutional and individual investors with worthy community development projects. Community loan funds are private, nonprofit institutions usually founded by religious and community activists as a mechanism to provide bridge capital, credit to get projects started before traditional bank financing arrives, to low-income housing and small-business efforts.

One of the oldest funds is the Revolving Loan Fund of the Institute for Community Economics (ICE), in Springfield, Massachusetts. Founded in 1981 with a $10,000 loan from an individual, the fund, as of March 1999, had placed over almost $32 million in 356 loans. In that period it wrote off less than $450,000 in losses, which is less than 1 percent of all funds lent. Losses were covered by ICE's loan-loss reserves without any impact on lenders to the fund. The fund pays a fixed interest rate, set by the lender, usually up to the equivalent of what one could earn in a bank CD.

The social impact has been tremendous. Loans from the fund have been critical in the construction or rehabilitation of 3,675 units of affordable housing and an estimated four thousand new jobs through small businesses. The ICE Revolving Loan Fund prides itself on enabling organizations that have been denied credit to get their first projects up and running in order to build a capacity to access traditional forms of investment.

There are now more than forty community loan funds operating across the United States. (For information on where they are, see "Resources for the Socially Responsible Investor" in Appendix F.)

Other Alternative Investment Options

Several other investment options funnel capital to worthwhile projects. These include venture capital, which is usually an equity (ownership) investment in a business or a housing development for low-income people. Such investments need to be carefully analyzed. You can receive help in evaluating projects from venture capital firms or special investment advisers. These investments may be higher risk with the potential of a higher return than loans secured by assets with a fixed term and rate of return.

There are also a small but growing number of international investment opportunities for U.S. investors who want to direct money to projects in Africa, Asia, and Latin America. For instance, the Nicaraguan Loan Fund, based in Madison, Wisconsin, enables concerned North American lenders to place loans with community development projects that help rebuild that country.

How to Do It

There are no blueprints for the perfect high social impact, high financial return investment strategy. (Bummer!) The extent to which your investments are a reflection of your own values depends on the amount of time you devote to them or your ability to find a like-minded investment professional.

There are some practical issues involved in trying to clean up an investment portfolio, particularly if you have stocks that were purchased a long time ago. It may not be advisable from a tax perspective to sell a lot of appreciated stock in one big chunk. Work with an adviser to develop a plan to make your portfolio more socially responsible over time, balancing social, tax, and financial considerations. Put the most offensive corporations on the top of your list for stock gifts or sale, and wait to unload others. In the meantime vote on social issue proxies that come in the mail, or let activists use them to attend shareholder meetings to demand change.

Questions to Consider

In evaluating the menu of socially responsible investments, consider some basic questions about your own goals and needs.

»→ What are your social change goals?

»→ What kind of impact would you like your money to have?

»→ Where do you draw your personal "value line" in terms of ethical investing? What corporate practices will you refuse to profit from? (Examples: pollution, unfair labor practices, alcohol and cigarette production, weapons and other military production, operations in countries that violate human rights.) You may have to weigh and balance different social criteria; for instance, maybe you'll be offered investments in green companies, but they may not have fair labor practices.)

»→ What corporate behavior do you want to reward? (Environmental responsibility, promotion of women and people of color, etc.)

»→ What are your investment goals? What kind of return do you want or need? Are you interested in income return (receiving timely income) or long-term equity growth (having the overall value of the assets increase)? How much liquidity, or access to cash, do you need?

»→ Are you willing or able to sacrifice some return in order to have a high social impact?

»→ Do you want to maximize overall return on investments to increase giving?

> "A lot of our money is tied up in investing in community economic development or alternative investing. Instead of 'social change funding,' I thought of the words 'economic change funding' for funding that creates new ways of doing things, reinvesting in communities and people to whom resources, funds, wealth, and capital have been denied."
> —Sue Lloyd, donor, Wisconsin Community Fund

>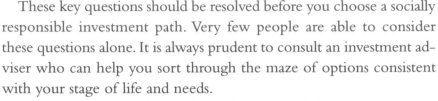
>
> "I've always encouraged any nonprofit I've been involved with to have a good investment policy with social screens. The Fund for Southern Communities has one. I'm on another board where they have no policy at all. Every meeting they know I'm going to ask, 'What are the social criteria for our investments?' And they have to say, 'We don't have any.' "
>
> —Robert Brown, donor, Fund for Southern Communities

These key questions should be resolved before you choose a socially responsible investment path. Very few people are able to consider these questions alone. It is always prudent to consult an investment adviser who can help you sort through the maze of options consistent with your stage of life and needs.

Because of the popularity of socially responsible investing, many investment advisers claim expertise in this field. Beware! Here are questions to ask when interviewing a potential adviser.

➻ What has been your overall financial performance?
➻ How long have you used social screens? What criteria do you use?
➻ How many securities do you regularly screen for corporate social responsibility (or irresponsibility)?
➻ How many social issues do you (or your firm) monitor?
➻ What are your data sources for your analysis of investments?
➻ What percentage of your clients are socially responsible investors? What volume of assets do you manage in socially screened portfolios?
➻ What is your own perspective on social investment?

Questions about Investment Options
As you become clearer about your own goals and needs, questions you might have about different investment options will become sharper. Through annual reports, promotional materials, and conversations with program staff, you can address such questions as these:

➻ How do these investments contribute to social change?
➻ Can your investment or shareholder actions contribute to broader organizing efforts for social change?
➻ Do the individuals who work for the investment firm have a commitment to social change and a history of working with social movements?
➻ Is there a minimum investment required?
➻ What is the risk? Is it an insured deposit? What are the forms of security for my investment?
➻ What is the liquidity? How easily can I convert my investment to cash?

➻ What is the organization's track record in both financial return and social impact?

Socially responsible investing is not a one-time decision but an ongoing process of reflection, education, and action. It requires you to stay informed and involved to ensure that your financial and social impact goals are met.

Social investment is a rewarding engagement that keeps you connected to the currents of social change in our society. It is one way citizens can be involved in holding corporations accountable for their conduct in our communities and around the world. Social investing can serve as a bridge in building a more fair economy by supporting the creation of small businesses, affordable housing, and community ventures in communities suffering from disinvestment in the United States and throughout the world.

The Virginia Black Lung Association

At nineteen Homer Anderson won a Bronze Star for heroism in World War II.
He returned home to work in the mines. For twenty-two years he was a loyal
worker for Clinchfield Coal, putting in as much overtime as regular time.
Then he came down with black lung disease, which is degenerative and
irreversible. Most people die from its complications: pneumonia, chronic
bronchitis, or emphysema. Damaged lungs frequently lead to heart disease
and kidney failure. According to the Federal Black Lung Act and Regulations
of 1970, if a person has lung disease and has worked for ten or more years
in the coal mines, it is assumed that he or she has black lung disease.

Mr. Anderson was awarded black lung benefits in 1978. He received benefits for ten years. In the meantime the company worked
to compile "evidence" to show that most people receiving benefits do
not in fact have black lung disease. One day Anderson received a form
letter that not only denied him further benefits but read: "You owe
$63,000. Please send this amount in 30 days." He is one of thousands
of miners in this predicament.

What's going on here?

In the early and mid-seventies, the United Mine Workers cam-
paigned to reform their union and obtain black lung benefits. The
1965 Mannington mine disaster, in which seventy-five men burned to
death in a methane gas explosion, catalyzed this effort. Until 1975 one
miner died on the job every day. There were few regulations, and the
work was done with a pick and shovel. In the mid-seventies new
technology saved many lives, but ironically, the mechanization kicked
up a finer dust that led to increased black lung cases.

Between 1970 and 1975, 75 percent of the people who applied for
black lung benefits received them. Affected miners actually helped
write the regulations in 1976.

Restrictive regulations instituted by the Reagan administration in
1981 reversed this trend by effectively denying *96 percent* of the applicants. After intense lobbying by the coal companies, the eligibility

regulations allowed the company for which the miners worked to contest claims and to demand back payments of benefits. That is what happened to Homer Anderson. The companies of course can spend infinitely more money than the miners for attorneys' fees, doctors' reports, and outside "experts" to defeat claims.

In January 1988 thirty-two miners and their wives pledged themselves to build an organization, the Virginia Black Lung Association, to right these wrongs. They have revitalized the national black lung movement, which covers all the coal-mining states in the Appalachian region as well as several midwestern and western states. Today they have twenty-one hundred members, over 95 percent of whom are disabled coal miners, widows, and immediate family members; almost all are over fifty years of age, and 80 percent are poor. About two members die every month.

"The tough thing is to watch these guys go downhill. I have one fellow, his one pet project is his truck, but he is so disabled he can no longer climb in. None of them can walk for more than two hundred feet without stopping for breath. That's the hardest thing for me and the organization: to watch the disease and then the deaths of the people I've known for ten or eleven years, people who worked hard," says Marilyn Carroll, the association's director.

The association assessed the current political climate in the late nineties and decided to target its attention on the U.S. Department of Labor. In conjunction with the National Black Lung Association, it demanded that a decision made by the Fourth Circuit Court of Appeals be the standard regulation for receiving black lung benefits. The decision says that if it can be shown that black lung disease hastened a miner's death, benefits should be paid.

The Virginia Black Lung Association changed how the courts dealt with these cases, educated local doctors about the disease, and mobilized its members and the public through quarterly newsletters and coverage in local, regional, and national media. It nurtures local leadership at monthly chapter meetings in six locations in southwestern Virginia. Members with little formal education have developed reading and leadership skills through participating on the legislative advocacy, membership, and newsletter committees. Members assist other miners so they know what to look and ask for when given medical exams by company doctors. They also help them fill out the mountain of paper work necessary to file claims. Imagine the ingenuity and tenacity it takes to organize twenty-one hundred people, most of whom are sick and poor.

The Virginia Black Lung Association has received financial assistance from the Appalachian Community Fund.

Chapter 10

Organizing . . . and Beyond!

I t's finally time to think about investing in the future by giving to social change organizing. Groups that work for change use a variety of strategies and tactics to achieve their goals. Given the range of these methods, understanding what organizing is and what it isn't can be tough. There are some vexing gray areas and no absolute hard-and-fast rules.

This chapter is about how to recognize social change. Imagine it for a moment as a three-legged stool. One leg is basic organizing and the preorganizing work that leads to it, one leg is organizing strategies that go beyond the basics, and the third is infrastructure. In this chapter we describe the three legs of the change, not charity stool. We begin with a brief review of basic organizing, which the stories between each chapter typify. Then we examine other methods to mobilize people and make change, strategies that may not at first look like organizing: community economic development, media, electoral politics, and art and cultural work. Finally, we look at the infrastructure of progressive organizing, the individuals and organizations that provide training, research and analysis, and communications assistance. These organizations do not generally stand on their own but are part of the larger movement for social change.

We also provide you with a gem of a list, the Core Criteria. Social change foundations use these kinds of criteria when evaluating groups applying for financial support. For those making substantial contributions, we make suggestions in Appendix F for how to review an organization's budget.

Basic Organizing

Organizing is collective activity that builds a group. The participants use the power of collective action to create change. Through organizing, people learn who their allies are, where the pressure points are, how issues are linked, and the necessity of a long-term commitment.

Through organizing, people can learn how society works and the ways that groups are rendered invisible, marginal, or undeserving because of their race, class, gender, age, abilities, sexual orientation, religion, and country of origin or because they are tiny Davids up against big Goliaths. Through the act of organizing, people who have neither wealth nor the privileges of class can lay claim to their rights, their needs, and their dreams. There are few things as powerful as moving from individual victimhood to collective strength, vision, and action. Through the power of organizing, David's chances against Goliath increase dramatically.

Here's one of Robin Hood's favorites, a multi-issue organization: Seniors with Power United for Rights (SPUR) is a grass roots organization founded by members of three senior centers in New Orleans. One of its priorities is to ensure that older people remain independent as long as possible, regardless of their income. To that end SPUR organized seniors from around the state to rally at the state capitol for expanded home- and community-based services for Medicaid-eligible seniors. This work resulted in the passage of two bills that mandate evaluation of the health care system, with consumer input, and development of Medicaid-funded assisted living units.

After building an organization through constituency organizing, SPUR now organizes around issues that affect a wider range of people. It successfully advocated for an eight-hundred-thousand-dollar energy assistance fund and was influential in the development and writing of a public transportation handbook that informs riders in simple language of their rights as consumers. Recently SPUR has turned its attention to organizing around policies that affect Social Security, recognizing the need for its long-term continuity as a basic safety net.

SPUR exemplifies basic organizing: People affected by a similar problem come together to find a solution. The value of coalition building and the importance of articulating ambitious goals are clear in its work. It follows up; for example, the consumer representatives on the health care evaluation team will certainly be accountable to organized groups of seniors. Finally, it understands that social change issues are connected.

The Preorganizing Stage

Some conditions create the necessity for a *pre*organizing or community-building stage. If there is no shared sense of community, there is little, if any, foundation for organizing. With a sense of community, people are more likely to feel valued, safe, and capable of collectively tackling even the toughest problems.

In the preorganizing stage it is necessary to build connections, trust, and hope among people. This can happen in a variety of ways. The classic example is a crisis. Say a neigh-

The Core Criteria

The Core Criteria can be the basis for determining whether a project is doing social change work. These are guidelines, not rules. Make the questions yours. Rearrange; add; subtract.

Goals and Plans

➤ What problem is the group working on? Given current social and political conditions, is it a significant problem?
➤ Is the group addressing the root causes of the issue?
➤ If the group is successful, what *specific* social change will take place? Does it foresee long-lasting change?
➤ How is the group going to achieve this change? What are its strategies and plans?

Constituency

➤ Who is the constituency or community the organization represents? How is the organization accountable to it?
➤ Does the group reflect the diversity, in membership, board, and staff, of the community it represents?
➤ Does it work with other organizations?
➤ How are new leaders identified, supported, and trained?

Nuts and Bolts

➤ How long has the group been in existence? What is its track record?
➤ How does it evaluate its work?
➤ Does it have a fundraising plan? How, and from what sources, does it raise its budget?
➤ How is the group's financial health? Does it produce and monitor a budget each year?

borhood comes together to demand a stop sign for a busy intersection where a child was injured and gets results from the city council. This visible victory can launch a group. Or the religious right descends on the local high school, demanding the teaching of creationism and an end to age-appropriate sex education. Parents mobilize. Sometimes staff from the local social service agency or neighborhood clinic will attempt to organize its clients over persistent issues of health and safety such as lead paint removal, unsanitary and unsafe apartments, and lack of city services.

However it happens, this preorganizing stage can be a big gray area for givers because there is just the possibility—we hope probability—that organizing will occur, but you can't bet the store on it. Making these kinds of assessments and giving seed money are things progressive foundations do particularly well.

If you are going to make an individual decision about whether to support a group at this stage, you may agree with Helen Wolcott, a Chinook Fund donor: "This is the difference between the way my father gave and the way I give. The bottom line for him was: 'Is it cost-efficient?' rather than my question, 'Do these people deserve a chance?' "

Beyond the Basics: Other Strategies for Social Change

Art and Cultural Action

Art and progressive cultural action can be the basis for creative and powerful organizing strategies. These activities can energize people to become involved and to *act*. Bringing people together is the first step in organizing. Cultural work—singing, storytelling, mural making, theater, improvisational skits, oral histories, etc.—can sustain and inspire organizers and organizations. Cultural workers can deepen people's understanding of their cultural identity and encourage people to recognize their collective rights and power. For that reason it is particularly useful in the preorganizing stage.

Here's an example: The Center for Cultural and Community Development and director Jane Sapp helps communities discover their own cultural resources. Recently the center worked with a group of ninety young African American and Vietnamese people who live in adjacent housing projects in Biloxi, Mississippi. Through seven days of intensive workshops with artists and organizers, participants came to appreciate the value of their own lives, communities, and

Arts and Cultural Work: Key Considerations

»→ Why and how was this strategy chosen?
»→ How will the use of an art and cultural work strategy build community?
»→ Will it amplify and deepen organizing?

histories. They also understood the problems they had in common. They had walked through one another's neighborhoods, attended one another's churches. A Vietnamese and an African American elder spoke to the group, detailing the obstacles of poverty and discrimination in their communities. The young people were then ready to work together to improve their communities across what had been, until this moment, insurmountable boundaries.

Progressive cultural action can help people think differently about themselves and the world they live in. Attitudes shift; behavior changes.

Cultural action can be about creating meeting places—actual physical spaces or temporary, conceptual ones—where people can come together, often across social or political dividing lines. For instance, the Mendocino People's Portrait project brought community artists to rural northern California to open an ad hoc multimedia center next door to a local supermarket, to provide a place where people could walk in and use video, audio, computers, music, and visual arts to express their views on issues facing the community.

Arts and cultural work can be fun. Organizing can be fun. That's important. Why would anyone use his or her precious free time to work in an organization where there was no time for laughter or friendship or creativity?

Media

Communication is the foundation of organizing. Organizations can use a variety of media strategies to communicate beyond the converted. A well-thought-out campaign can put a group's issue on the map—or at least in the news. Think about the AIDS quilt. It certainly touched those who sewed the squares and those who saw the immense

By linking art and community organizing, the Theater Offensive in Boston boldly addresses the needs of at-risk individuals and communities through their its theater troupe A Street Theater Named Desire. It takes on a life and death issue at its source by bringing the realities of HIV/AIDS to gay male communities by performing outside gay bars at closing time to reach men who have avoided educating themselves about the epidemic.

quilt in person. Beyond them its vivid image of the inconceivable loss that AIDS has wrought was seen and heard by millions through television, magazine, and newspaper coverage.

Social Change Organizations: Getting Mainstream Media Attention

"Grassroots groups must face the fact that mainstream media coverage is indispensable for social change and organizational growth. The mayor will treat a community group as a political player after watching them on television. The implicit sanction in a New York Times *story can persuade a major foundation to take notice for the first time. A feature article in a magazine like* Family Circle—*bought by locals at the supermarket checkout counter—will bury a label like 'crazy radicals' for good."*—The Peace Development Fund

The Peace Development Fund (PDF) funds a Media Training Project to encourage social change groups to use the media as an organizing tool. The Colonias Development Council (CDC) in Las Cruces, New Mexico, received media training through PDF. Colonias are unincorporated communities within 150 miles of the Mexican border that lack safe drinking water, adequate sewage systems, and decent, safe housing. An estimated 1.5 million people live in such settlements in the four border states.

During the media training workshops, the CDC staff and colonia residents learned how to present themselves to the media. They defined what was significant about their work, then practiced shaping information into story ideas they "pitched" to make-believe reporters in role play exercises. Finally, they chose which of their issues had the best potential to carry a media campaign.

They dug into their campaign with limitless energy. A news conference wasn't enough; they sponsored a week's worth of activities, including tours into the colonias. They organized a major benefit that a thousand people attended. Within that week their story could be read in eleven newspaper articles, seen on nine television programs, and heard on seventeen radio shows.

Good media work is like good organizing: A good strategy and personal contact make it happen. There are plenty of progressive

media consultants who can help an organization frame its message, plot a media campaign, come up with an updated brochure, or design an attractive Web site.

Organizations Make Media

Some organizations make their own media. A national organization, INFACT, produced a film called *Deadly Deception* to focus attention on General Electric's nuclear weapons business. The film was simultaneously released at events all over the country. The story was covered from coast *(New York Times)* to coast *(San Francisco Chronicle)*. The tape was a phenomenal organizing tool. Within the first year five thousand copies were distributed.

Then, in what Thomas O'Boyle, a former *Wall Street Journal* reporter, called "a historic milestone for grassroots activism against corporations," *Deadly Deception* won an Academy Award for Best Documentary. In her acceptance speech the director, Debra Chasnoff, urged one *billion* viewers to join the boycott against General Electric.

Within a year GE sold off all its nuclear weapons business. This removed a major political player from peddling its influence for more and more nuclear weapons. INFACT called off the boycott and declared victory.

It doesn't get much better than that.

Independent Productions

Independent productions are used by social change groups and individuals for education about issues and to bring the story home in a way that cannot be done as well through another medium. Independent film and video makers, radio hosts, and journalists who produce this work are sustained by social change movements, although they may not be directly accountable to them.

Here's what independent activist media can look like: *"¡Aumento Ya!* documents the largest organizing campaign in the history of agribusiness in the Northwest. In 1995 Oregon's farm workers' union, Pineros y Campesinos Unidos del Noroeste (PCUN), mobilized thousands of strawberry workers and supporters to win a 20 percent wage increase, the first one in a decade, generating one million dollars in higher wages. The grant from the Paul Robeson Fund for Independent

The motivation to give is a human response to the suffering, injustice, and needs we see around us. Our first instinct is to give immediately to alleviate the symptoms of a problem. To be an effective giver for change, however, requires us to ask difficult questions about the causes of these problems and then to assess the most effective strategy for change.

Media: Key Considerations

»→ What is the goal of using this particular kind of medium?

»→ Will it be well produced? Will people want to watch it, listen to it, participate in it, or read it?

»→ Will this project reach beyond the converted? How?

»→ What is the distribution plan?

»→ How will this media strategy, or project, amplify and extend organizing?

»→ Is the organization realistic about the costs, in both time and money?

Media of the Funding Exchange ensured wide distribution of the film to labor unions, student groups, and economic justice organizations, as well as cable television's Free Speech TV. Although the film was made by an independent producer, there were strong connections to the union.

Unless media are your field, you may wish to turn to someone who can help you evaluate projects. Sometimes you can see a rough cut or read a script of the work; other times you have to rely on the quality of past work. A producer seeking funding for a radio program will most likely have a tape you can hear.

If you are considering funding a documentary, you want to know the qualifications of the producer, director, and editor. A media activist we know says, "Good politics in a proposal for a documentary aren't enough. What makes a piece interesting is how conflict is portrayed. Are the filmmakers willing to understand what causes people to hold ideas or act in ways we don't agree with? Without this a piece will almost always preach only to the converted and will bore even them. It won't succeed in changing anyone's mind."

The Technological Explosion

Opportunities for communication through the Internet, multimedia productions, computer networking, and other interactive media are being used by a growing cohort of progressive activists. "Young people are democratizing media. If you want to support youth organizing, it's likely that you will be asked to support media strategies from 'zines [cheaply produced desktop computer magazines] to a Web site on the Internet, from microbroadcasting [pirate radio] to video cam documentation," says Jan Strout of the Paul Robeson Fund.

This project supported by the Robeson Fund shows the possibilities of technology for widespread education: *The Revolution Will Be Digitized* is an interactive multimedia CD-ROM that uses the Internet as a communications tool for peace. It is an artistic exploration of the Zapatistas' struggle in Chiapas, Mexico, which combines hyperlinked video clips, images, text, and sound to create a resonant narrative of many perspectives. It begins with the arrival of the conquistadors and stretches into the expanding future of cyberspace. Encompassing multiple aspects of history and culture, while providing a wealth of information in both English and Spanish, the project is an ideal tool for students, educators, and activists in the Americas and worldwide.

As the Internet becomes more organized, there are many good starting points for searching the Web for information on progressive social change. Check out www.igc.org; it builds connections for the progressive movement on the Web. Visit www.webactive.com. (Also see Appendix G.)

Electoral Work

Electoral politics is about access, power, and the distribution of collective resources. When used as a social change strategy, electoral work can force the political structure to live up to its democratic ideals by responding to those who have traditionally been left out. Organizing for voter registration and participation, efforts for campaign finance reform, drives to open up the electoral arena to third parties, and campaigns to promote proportional voting are strategies social change groups have used to open up the political system, to increase democracy. It can be a vehicle for leadership from the grassroots: community people can be trained and supported to serve as accountable elected officials. Issue-based coalitions and organizations, such as those that organize for a cleaner environment or universal health care, often use electoral strategies to put their issues out in the mainstream for education, debate, and action. (For information on what types of contribution to electoral activity are tax-deductible, consult the Alliance for Justice, listed in the Appendix E under "Infrastructure.")

Dissatisfied with a statewide political structure that was completely unresponsive to the needs and interests of the Black community, the organizers of Southern Echo, an African American organization based in the Mississippi Delta, began an effort that would identify, elect, and hold accountable candidates chosen by the community.

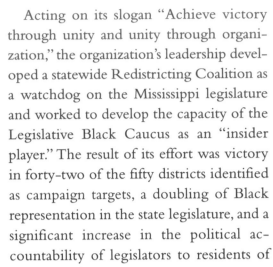

Acting on its slogan "Achieve victory through unity and unity through organization," the organization's leadership developed a statewide Redistricting Coalition as a watchdog on the Mississippi legislature and worked to develop the capacity of the Legislative Black Caucus as an "insider player." The result of its effort was victory in forty-two of the fifty districts identified as campaign targets, a doubling of Black representation in the state legislature, and a significant increase in the political accountability of legislators to residents of the African American community.[1]

Organizations resort to referendums (ballot questions that call for specific changes in laws) when they believe the public will demand a change that the legislators will not make. When progressives develop referendums, it is crucial that the campaigns build on a base of local organizing. For example, campaign finance reform often goes against the interests of current legislators, yet the public overwhelmingly supports an increase in fairness in the electoral system. "Clean election" referendums have been passed in Arizona, Maine, and Massachusetts. These wins came as a result of local organizing and coalition building prior to intensive campaigning for the referendum.

Community Economic Development

In the United States people don't usually think about "development" issues the way people do in the rest of the world. At a grassroots level, development in an international context means access to income, housing, safety, health, and the ability to participate in mutual support networks to provide those essentials. In the United States "development" generally brings to mind real estate or something vague called economic development.

Community economic development has emerged in the United States as a partial response to the narrow American definitions of development. It recognizes the need for "ordinary" people to hold a vision of what community is and how community needs will be met. Conceptualized in this way, community economic development (CED) is an important strategy for change, since when it's done right, it's about community organizing.

In this day of promoting entrepreneurship, much CED doesn't pass Robin Hood's test for social change. Truly progressive CED defines development in the broadest possible way by asking the question "What does this community need for its members to realize their full potentials as human beings?" When you consider CED as a strategy for change, looking at the how, the why, and the who is as important as the what.

Here is an example of a group supported in part by the Vanguard Public Foundation:

The Women's Economic Agenda Project (WEAP) is an economic development organization in Oakland, California, whose focus is to move women out of poverty. It organizes, works for legislative change, and, more recently, has developed job skills and technological expertise in low-income communities. With the help of a loan from the city of Oakland, WEAP purchased an office building that has become a community center for economic empowerment. Its Women and Family Center offers a Computer/Telecommunications Skills Center, housing high-tech job-training programs; a Small Business Village, which provides office space, Internet access, and management training for up to thirty start-up businesses; a Special Needs Empowerment Project for people with disabilities; and meeting and video-conferencing facilities. The building provides rental income from other nonprofits for WEAP's programs. *This may well be the first time that a nonprofit group run by a multiracial group of low-income women has used real estate ownership as a funding source for its social programs.*

WEAP is committed to ensuring that access to technology doesn't become one more way that lower-income people are marginalized. Its vision is for its center to become "a national demonstration model combining universal technology access with a focus on job development, economic security, justice, women's advancement and urban revitalization." That's a tall order, but one that is

**Community Economic Development:
Key Considerations**

⇒ Why was community economic development chosen as an organizing strategy?

⇒ On whose terms is the development envisioned?

⇒ Who benefits from the development? Who controls it?

necessary to build true economic opportunity.

"It's not just about jobs," says Ethyl Long-Scott, the director. "We see the possibilities of a city where people too poor to own a car can reach out all over the nation through computers to learn what ways others have found to resist peer pressure, to make schools safer, to hold their elected officials and law enforcement agencies more accountable, to find out what the history texts don't discuss, to increase justice."

Infrastructure

Infrastructure encompasses a broad spectrum of work that supports grassroots organizations. It can range from training to research and think tanks to progressive media. It includes national organizations that provide vital links between state and local grassroots groups.

Trainers and training organizations provide consistency and continuity for the movements for justice. They are our universities; they gather, disseminate, and add to our collective knowledge of what works. Training reduces the need for organizations to reinvent the same darn wheel. Organizations and individuals provide training in all aspects of running a successful organization, from leadership development to financial management, from long-range planning to fundraising skills. Many progressive foundations pay for or themselves provide training to social change organizations. Without this assistance, many small groups would stay small.

Information that hasn't been sanitized, distorted, or censored by the media is the lifeblood of organizing. Progressive publications (magazines, newsletters, and journals), national think tanks, and academics, as well as certain Internet sites, provide a wealth of information organizations can use to educate their constituencies. Research centers and think tanks provide reliable information and progressive analysis that organizations use to develop strategic campaigns. Progressive media provide forums for debate and discussion within the movement while the issues, strategies, and policies they investigate sometimes move into mainstream public debate.

A key consideration in assessing this kind of work is to make sure that it has connections to grassroots movements. Are the research and data accessible to activists? Can groups use the information to educate their members and build campaigns? Are policies being developed in conjunction with organizations that will follow through on organizing?

Within the progressive movement, many infrastructure organizations function in a variety of roles. (See Appendix E: Infrastructure: Organizations that Support Organizing.) They may do research and training, they may have policy institutes to back up their organizing among state and local groups, or they may provide consulting to organizations on strategic media work while playing an advocacy role in pushing progressive policies into the mainstream media.

What follows are examples of infrastructure organizations, to give you a feel for the range of work.

The National Gay and Lesbian Task Force (NGLTF) works to strengthen the gay and lesbian movement at state and local levels while connecting its activities to a national vision of change. Along with coalition-building work, NGLTF has an internal think tank, the Policy Institute, that does research and analysis. Its study *From Wrongs to Rights: Public Opinion of Gay and Lesbian Americans Moves Toward Equality* shows, contrary to the message of the dominant culture, that a growing majority of Americans support gay civil rights. This kind of information is a powerful tool for organizations developing strategies and pushing for changes in policy.

Organizations like Just Economics (JE), a training institute made up of women from all walks of life, create bridges between organizations that produce data and policy analysis and communities working for change. Their training programs make the analysis accessible and can help inform the campaigns of social change organizations.

When the Center for Third World Organizing (CTWO) began a campaign to change the California state budget, it asked JE to design training in how the budget contributed to racial injustice and sexism and how it could be used as a tool for equality. By focusing on the difference in spending between prisons and education, JE

> "I meet with donors all the time who say, 'Oh, I don't fund the arts,' or, 'I only fund locally based organizing.' In other words, we don't fit into their rigid box. People on the political right understand the importance of funding a movement infrastructure of organizations and tactics—electoral politics, grassroots organizing, political education, media, research, and ideology."
> —*Milagro Ortiz, a housing organizer from Philadelphia*

uncovered a link between the development of prisons and changes in state revenue. Because California politicians were reluctant to raise taxes for the wealthiest citizens, they were forced to borrow money from them by issuing bonds, in order to generate sufficient revenue. But bonds can be issued only for capital projects like building prisons, not for teachers' salaries, educational programs, and so on. This realization led CTWO to look deeper at the issue of state borrowing. It was able to generate new strategies to hold the state accountable for how it uses borrowed money.

The Western States Center is a multipurpose training and education center with a mission to build and invigorate democracy. It builds broad-based statewide progressive coalitions and encourages a new generation of citizen leaders to run for public office. One of its programs is: The Western Progressive Leadership Network, which helps constituency and issue groups identify goals that transcend traditional single issue approaches, helping them form permanent progressive statewide coalitions to address issues in which everyone has a stake. Five new statewide coalitions, representing women's issues, working people, environmentalists, gays and lesbians, low-income people, people of color, and educators, have been formed.

Many infrastructure organizations provide specialized research that would be next to impossible for community groups to accomplish. Political Research Associates (PRA) is a national clearinghouse on the activities, strategy, and agenda of the radical right. PRA prepares resource materials, responds to the needs of organizations and communities under attack by the right, and monitors the strategies of right-wing leaders and organizations, passing information along to communities and to the media.

The infrastructure organizations that we've just profiled serve another important function. They can break the isolation experienced by many small groups, particularly those in conservative settings. These infrastructure organizations can function like bees: They cross-pollinate, organization to organization, issue to issue. Our final group understands that isolation and has created an infrastructure to address it.

"Especially at small colleges or conservative campuses," notes the Center for Campus Organizing (CCO)'s development director, Nikki Morse, "our organization provides a vital link to wider movements, assuring isolated activists that they are not alone. We are committed to enabling students to become the next generation of public intellectuals and community activists."

CCO is creating an infrastructure to help students become more strategic in their work and develop a broad-based progressive agenda.

Its organizing guide has helped hundreds of fledgling campus groups build effective campaigns; its newsletter, *Infusion,* is distributed to more than ten thousand campus activists, providing a forum for students to explore issues and share organizing strategies; and CCO has pioneered the use of the Internet in political campaigning with its Campus Activists Network list. It has also analyzed how the right has organized on campuses and gives activists the tools to discover and oppose their impact on young people.

You can see from the examples in this chapter that organizing is a complex fabric: It can look different, it can feel different, and it can serve different functions. Having a working knowledge of the ways groups organize will help you understand social movements and help you make better funding decisions. Read on!

"The way that our ceremonies work is that when we give gifts, we create a rebalancing."— *Jeanette Armstrong, quoted in* The Honor of Giving: Philanthropy in Native America

Not in Our Town

After the white supremacist Aryan Congress declared the Northwest to be its "homeland" in 1986, hate groups in the region became bolder and more violent. In 1993 Billings, Montana, found itself the target of a series of hate crimes: Ku Klux Klan flyers were distributed, tombstones in the Jewish cemetery were overturned, the home of a Native American family was spray-painted with swastikas, members of an African American church were harassed and intimidated, and bricks were thrown through windows that displayed menorahs (candelabra) for the Jewish festival of Hanukkah.

Rather than accept the growing climate of fear and intimidation, the community took a stand. Those who were not targeted stood firm beside those who were. City officials and law enforcement officers made strong statements against the hate crimes. The painters' union formed a work force to paint over racist graffiti. Religious and community leaders sponsored human rights activities. The local newspaper printed full-page menorahs for display in homes and businesses throughout the town. Most of the ten thousand people who placed the menorahs in their windows were not Jewish; they displayed the symbols as an act of solidarity.

The people of Billings, Montana, tell their powerful story in the video *Not in Our Town*. The video includes a dramatic interview with an ex-supremacist who has renounced his past affiliations and hate crimes.

The story doesn't end there. The Working Group, producers of the video, launched an outreach campaign in coordination with the television broadcast of *Not in Our Town*. In collaboration with the Independent Media Institute, it asked communities across America to join in declaring Not in Our Town Week. Over two hundred communities across the nation sponsored activities in the weeks preceding and following the broadcast.

The video and the campaign launched a movement. Hundreds of communities from across the country have decided to take their own stand against hate by signing proclamations, organizing public screenings, holding town hall meetings, and rebuilding churches burned down in racially motivated attacks. Rather than allow themselves to be a negative example, the citizens of Billings and their story, *Not in Our Town,* have become a rallying cry for communities committed to compassion and acceptance rather than hatred and intolerance.

The Working Group received funding from the Benton Foundation for the film.

Update: The Not in Our Town (NIOT) Campaign has stretched into five years and shows no sign of ending. The example of the people in Billings continues to ignite action around the country, as more and more communities shape their own NIOT campaigns. In response the Working Group made *NIOT II: Citizens Respond to Hate.*

In its new film the Working Group highlights community responses to the Billings story. It tells the story of St. John's, a historic Black church in Columbia, South Carolina, that was a repeated target of vandals until it was burned to the ground during a wave of church burnings in 1996. As a result of seeing this story in *NIOT II,* a Texas contractor and his friends traveled to South Carolina to rebuild the church.

Here's an example of what is going on in one state, Illinois. Bloomington-Normal posted signs at each city limit stating, RACISM/NOT IN OUR TOWN. Rockford kicked off the new year with a mayoral proclamation urging all in the town to join the NIOT movement. Within four months more than fifty organizations had signed on to the NIOT principles; they are organizing a city-wide march and rally. Springfield, the capital, was the site of a "Not in Our Town, Not in Our State, Not in Our Nation" rally. In Decatur the board of education is hosting a race relations seminar featuring a NIOT member and city councilman. Peoria is beginning a campaign appropriately called "Racism—It Doesn't Play in Peoria." Knoxville, Illinois, kicked off NIOT with a mayoral proclamation and a Not in Our Town contingent in the Labor Day parade.

Both films continue to be powerful tools to bring up intolerance as a *community* issue.

Part IV

Decisions, Decisions

Chapter 11

One Way of Doing It: Social Change Foundations

You've looked at the world of giving. You've heard the case for change. You've mustered your money. Now it's time to make decisions!

Among other things, you need to decide how to give, to whom, when, in what amounts, and for what purposes. You need to decide what issues to focus on, which constituencies to target, and at what geopolitical level (local, national, or international). You need a process to follow and criteria to guide you. You need a *plan*.

Perhaps you'd prefer not to make all these decisions yourself. Maybe you lack time, energy, or expertise. Perhaps you think that the power to decide where your money goes should be shared. You *do* have choices, and here in Part IV we help you consider them. One option is to give money through a social change foundation, as discussed in this chapter. Another option is do-it-yourself giving, but with help and input from others (we'll talk about this in the next chapter). Consider these options; then, in Chapter 13, decide what works best for you and set out a plan of action.

Networks of the Progressive Social Change Foundations

Funding Exchange Network Members

Appalachian Community Fund (ACF)
Funds in West Virginia and the Appalachian counties of Tennessee, Kentucky, and Virginia

A CF is in a region of the United States known for its persistent poverty and Bible

---

Belt conservatism. The challenge in Appalachia is to overcome historical barriers of absentee and corporate landownership, removal of resources and stereotypes about the people, all of which mask a great activist tradition.

ACF's priority is to bring money and resources back to the area. In 1986, it awarded twenty thousand dollars in grants; by 1998 that total had reached over two million dollars.

Bread and Roses Community Fund

Makes grants in the five-county region of greater Philadelphia and Camden, New Jersey

After efforts to reform traditional philanthropic institutions failed, a group of Philadelphians started the People's Fund. Its descendant Bread and Roses followed in 1977.

Bread and Roses is supported by a broad base of donors, thousands of individuals who give anywhere between five and fifty thousand dollars a year. Many

Many givers turn to progressive social change foundations to carry out their giving plans. Located throughout the country, these foundations exist to help donors support social change, in the United States and throughout the world. They identify and screen potential grant recipients, particularly those in underfunded communities; they determine which projects they will support; and in general they ensure that donor dollars are well spent. Givers can support a wide range of progressive issues through foundations, or they can donate to specific issue funds. Social change foundations can make giving easy and *effective*.

This chapter shows you the range of these foundations. After a short history of alternative foundations, we delve into the characteristics of a progressive foundation. We toot the horns of those we know the best and profile a few that fund internationally. (Effective international giving almost always requires working with a foundation or other intermediary.)

To keep you inspired, we include examples of great projects all the way through.

A History of "Alternative" Foundations

Social change philanthropy has roots that predate the 1920s. We'll start, however, with the second wave, those alternative foundations organized in the 1960s to support the antiwar effort and community organizing. The very first public effort to institutionalize social change giving was the formation of the Brotherhood Crusade in Los Angeles, the African American communities' alternative to the local United Way. In 1967 RESIST was founded; it was—and still is—a foundation that gives small grants throughout the country for progressive organizing (and publishes a wonderful newsletter).

The original foundations of the Funding Exchange (FEX), today a national network of fifteen progressive foundations, followed: first Bread and Roses, then Vanguard Public Foundation, quickly followed by Haymarket People's Fund and the Liberty Hill Foundation. Except for Bread and Roses, these funds were organized by young people with inherited wealth. They adopted the slogan "Change, Not Charity!" because of their belief that systemic change rather than charity was needed.

The founders—some with "brand names"—took philanthropy out of the wealthy class, where it had comfortably resided, and deliberately gave up control over where the money went. They believed that making giving decisions was power that was best shared with activists. They saw these new foundations as community institutions, accountable to activists and donors. They knew that movements for social change were always short on cash and that it was vital for there to be places where a wide range of givers could pool their money for greater impact and where organizations without traditional access to money could go for funds.

The early members of the Funding Exchange challenged the nature of traditional philanthropy. They showed up at the venerable Council on Foundations meeting as fellow funders and asked questions of the large, established foundations: Who is on your board? How do you feel about the enormous power you have to sink or float organizations? In that indomitable manner that only the young and righteous can pull off, they let the foundation world know that the alternative foundations made the best grants because of the role of community activists.

The community funding board structure—that local activists make decisions on grants—was the most radical and far-reaching contribution to philanthropy that the Funding Exchange has made. Gradually foundations began to have discussions of accountability and accessibility. Some began disseminating information about their guidelines for funding *for the first time.* Most—from the Ford Foundation on down the line—now have community people on their boards.

No longer alternative, the funds called into question the traditional way that philanthropy operated: the secrecy, the elitism, and the "we know best" attitude. The relationship between traditional foundations and progressive social change foundations is now one of reciprocity. The progressive funds "have the unique opportunity to leverage additional resources by bringing the needs of the community, defined by the community, to the attention of larger funding agencies."[1]

The strongest evidence of the success of the Funding Exchange is that others have made this model theirs. There is an expanding move-

of its donor programs, including a new socially responsible investing group, reflect this inclusion. The fund also sponsors a popular support group for women with wealth.

Chinook Fund

Supports progressive social change in Colorado

Just as the chinook winds bring warmth, so the Chinook Fund thaws the frozen political climate. This influence is sorely needed in a state that is home to a phenomenal number of local and national right-wing and extremist religious organizations.

Before the Chinook Fund, there was no connected progressive community in Colorado. The fund recently convened a cross-issue multicultural gathering of progressive organizations to discuss strategies for countering the far right. This culminated in the birth of the Colorado Progressive Coalition, which later received a fifteen-thousand-dollar grant from Chinook.

ment of progressive funds that are supported by donations from individuals and that have activist boards. We list many of them in Appendix A and refer to some in the next few pages.

What Makes a Progressive Foundation?

What Gets Funded

Progressive social change foundations support groups working directly for social change, as well as the infrastructure organizations. Progressive foundations are willing to take risks. Many of these groups are on the cutting edge of change, bringing people together who have not worked together before, finding solutions that have not previously been tried. Donor Joe Crocker summed it up well: "The CEO of the United Way of Minneapolis told me that the Headwaters Fund is to the foundation world what venture capital is the the corporate world."

New Power Relations

When the early progressive funds adopted the slogan "Change, Not Charity," they did more than declare an end to Band-Aid solutions. They redefined the relationship between those who donate money and those who receive it as a mutual exchange, rather than as charity. Organizations do work that donors believe in; donations help keep the recipient organizations thriving.

Who Decides

In a progressive model, people active in their communities decide where the money goes and serve on the board of directors. Social change foundations strive to reflect the communities they support in the makeup of their board, staff, and funding board committees. Diversity is not "managed" but worked on and celebrated.

Esther Nieves, former board member and current donor to the Crossroads Fund, says, "Money coming into a community is about power. The beautiful thing about activists is their insights and the access they provide into communities."

Rigorous Decision Making

Each foundation has its own process for making grant decisions. Generally, after an initial screening by staff, community funding board members read proposals and interview potential grantees. This can include a site visit or a meeting that *all* grant applicants attend. Each applicant summarizes its work and funding request; funding board members and other potential recipients ask questions. This can become a forum for spontaneous connections among groups that in traditional situations would feel competitive. After all proposals have been discussed and the applicants leave, the committee gets down to the difficult job of making decisions.

It's a tough crowd to please! You can't just impress them with a well-crafted proposal. These activists know the turf, and they have to live with the achievements or failures of these projects in their communities.

Conflict of interest policies keep the process clean and fair. Who gets funded is *not* determined by who knows whom. Although local people make the decisions, it is not an insider process.

Not by Bread Alone

Most progressive foundations offer more than money to social change organizations. Many support technical assistance (TA) for their grantees; some provide it themselves. Technical assistance organizations are to grassroots groups as consultants are to business.

TA providers work with social change groups to sharpen their skills. They can offer specific information on such topics as fundraising and working with the media. On a more sophisticated level, TA providers can assist groups to develop skills in critical political analysis and movement building and to address issues of race, sex, class, or sexuality that can make it hard for diverse social change groups to work together well.

Donor Programs

Progressive foundations also offer donors more than just places to give their money. Most involve donors in all aspects of their work. Some foundations offer workshops and conferences on a variety of issues, like those featured in this book. Most publish newsletters and annual reports. Others present briefings on current issues. Most offer a community of people from different backgrounds who work together across what are at times barriers of race and class.

For over twenty-five years, Haymarket People's Fund (New England) has been organizing for people with wealth annual conferences where

that challenged the root causes of societal ills had little or no access to foundation support. In response a handful of local progressives with wealth and vision founded the Fund for Santa Barbara.

Much has changed since that time, but the struggles continue. Today the fund supports more than a hundred projects each year with cash grants as well as technical assistance.

Fund for Southern Communities (FSC)
Funds in Georgia and in North and South Carolina

FSC was started by activists tired of making trips to foundations in the Northeast to plead for funds. They envisioned an activist-led southern foundation. Begun in 1981, the fund has served as a vital link between individuals who want to support progressive endeavors in this conservative region and a broad range of community organizations that need their support. One of the bedrocks of the fund's philosophy is: If everyone gives what he or she can, it will always be enough.

Deeply committed to local organizers making the grant decisions, six community funding boards ensure that Haymarket can respond to the needs of a diverse region. One of the oldest and largest funds in the Funding Exchange network, Haymarket has more than seventy volunteers actively involved in keeping it responsive to new issues. Now it not only funds youth issues but also includes young people as decision makers within the organization. Founded in 1974 by young people with inherited wealth, Haymarket pioneered working with people who have resources, inspiring them to become involved in social change.

Headwaters Fund

Funds in the Twin Cities (Minneapolis and St. Paul)

In addition to making grants, the fund sponsors a Grassroots Capacity Building Program. Executive Director Steve Newcom says, "While many grassroots organizations are led by

participants can discuss the challenges of having both more money than most *and* a commitment to social change. "Wealth conferences changed my life," says John Lapham. "Finally, a place where I can talk about personal, technical, and funding issues that come up for me. I found a community." Haymarket People's Fund also organizes events for all givers, like a recent one-day workshop on how to fund cultural work.

The Liberty Hill Foundation in Los Angeles organizes van tours—Urban Reality Tours—of neighborhoods that many donors have never visited. "Unless you go on the Liberty Hill van tour," says Randi Johnson, a donor, "it's easy to live an incredibly insulated and provincial life since L.A. is chopped up by freeways and is very segregated." By the end of the day supporters have a more concrete idea of what their money is helping make happen. According to the staff organizer, "The grantees are ecstatic to take donors on a tour of their neighborhood. They are glad that people care!"

There are also conferences for specific constituencies. The Third Wave Foundation, in partnership with other organizations, offers an annual conference on wealth and philanthropy for young people up to the age of thirty-five. Resourceful Women in San Francisco offers classes and support groups as well as conferences for women with inherited wealth or earned assets. The Outgiving Project offers conferences for funders of GBLT projects.

Donor-advised grantmaking, described in Chapter 12, is a donor program offered by most social change and traditional foundations.

Building Community

Just as the foundation of good organizing is to build community, the same is true for progressive social change foundations. Robert Brown enjoys being on the funding board of the Fund for Southern Communities because "it is a watering hole for progressive people in the South. It's a revival for activists and people involved in progressive philanthropy." This fund has enlarged the watering hole to a veritable sea with its annual concert by Sweet Honey in the Rock (a cultural performing group of African American women) that is done in collaboration with Spelman College. More than a thousand people attend.

The Headwaters Fund (Minneapolis) sponsors an annual Walk for Justice. It's a fun-filled easy way for grassroots groups to raise money.

In 1998 about eight hundred people representing ninety-three groups walked "for justice" and raised more than eighty-five thousand dollars.

The Funding Exchange

The Funding Exchange (FEX) is the national network of the fifteen funds briefly profiled in sidebars throughout this chapter. The member funds are unified in their commitment to support community-based progressive social change and to maintain a democratic grantmaking process. Nationally FEX coordinates network-wide training and spearheads special grantmaking initiatives and technical assistance projects. In the late 1990s the network's annual cumulative grantmaking had risen to more than twelve million dollars, funding approximately twenty-five hundred community-based projects. As public foundations, the FEX and its member funds raise most of their budgets from individual donations.

FEX provides a unique array of giving options for donors. At the national level, it supports both national and international social change work, as well as local organizing in areas where there are no local funds and little progressive money. There is an extensive donor-advised grantmaking program. FEX also coordinates three national funds, each with its specific interest and its activist board:

*→ *The Saguaro Fund,* named for the saguaro cactus, which provides water in the desert, funds projects where resources are scarce and survival is difficult. Its primary focus is to support organizing in communities of color in the United States and Puerto Rico. Here's an example: *Jesus People against Pollution:* This environmental justice organization in Mississippi assists medically underserved communities to achieve hands-on medical testing, relocation, and compensation from companies that have created toxic dump sites in low-income and working-class neighborhoods.

*→ *The Paul Robeson Fund for Independent Media* is one of the few ongoing sources of money for progressive media—film, video, radio preproduction and distribution. The fund supports media artists whose work emphasizes how people come together to solve problems in society. A few of its grantees:

people from disenfranchised communities, these people should be viewed not as victims but rather as leaders of great proficiency, tenacity, and influence. By reinforcing their skills and by making opportunities for groups to learn from each other, the fund believes it can help build the capacity of the community as a whole."

Within a two-year period, two thousand Twin Cities activists participated in the program.

Liberty Hill Foundation (LHF)
Funds in Los Angeles County

The crusading writer Upton Sinclair *(The Jungle)* was arrested while standing on Liberty Hill for reading the U.S. Constitution to strikers during the great longshoreman's strike of 1923. To celebrate Sinclair's ideals, LHF organizes an annual Upton Sinclair Dinner.

In addition to its Hallmark Seed Fund for new groups, Liberty Hill's Fund for a New Los Angeles offers larger capacity-building grants, while the Environmental Justice Fund is helping build a regional voice against environmental racism. LHF also

regularly convenes activists
and donors to strengthen
progressive organizing.

**McKenzie River Gathering
Foundation (MRG)**

Funds in Oregon

MRG began when two
donors brought together a
group of progressive organizers to develop a activist-
controlled foundation.

Oregon has been the
"canary" for the far right's
attempts to limit the rights
of undocumented people,
of lesbians and gays, and
people of color. MRG's
funding of the response to
this assault provides
direction for many national
efforts to turn the tide of
intolerance and hate.

North Star Fund

*Funds within the five
boroughs of New York City*

North Star's mission was
shaped by the community
response to the New York
City fiscal crisis in the mid-
1970s, when bankers and
city officials cut essential
services, such as hospital
and housing programs.
Early grant recipients came

Taken for a Ride: A feature documentary about General Motors'
secret campaign to destroy American public transit and foster au-
tomobile dependence. GM bought up public trolley systems and
then dismantled them, leaving automobiles as the only transportation option. Screenings will be cosponsored by community groups
in cities across the country.

Democracy Now!: A daily one-hour news talk radio program on
Pacifica Radio that profiles the efforts of activists to challenge cor-
porate domination of politics and the media. It's aim is to move lis-
teners to become involved in politics and public affairs. "How
Global Economics and Politics Affect Women," "Living Wage/Min-
imum Wage Campaigns," and "MAI: The Trade Agreement No
One Is Talking About" are examples of recent shows. *Democracy
Now!* is heard in five major cities and on fifty radio stations.

➻→ *The OUT Fund for Lesbian and Gay Liberation* supports organizing
for the basic human rights for gay men, lesbians, bisexuals, and
transgendered people. Examples of OUT funding:

Esperanza: Developed a Leadership Project that builds and
strengthens progressive coalitions in San Antonio and other parts of
Texas. It used its grant from OUT to set up discussions about race,
class, gender, and homophobia within the coalitions where it works.

Living in Lesbian and Gay Families: A photo and text exhibit that
traveled to schools and community centers across the country. By
incorporating a resource guide and panel discussions in schools,
the project helps dismantle stereotypes.

In addition to these three grantmaking programs, the Funding Exchange has incorporated funds within its donor-advised grantmaking
program that are established by individuals or groups of donors to
meet specific needs. Here are a few: The Florian Loan Fund makes
loans to social change groups for fundraising projects, enabling them
to move to a higher level of financial viability. The Third Wave Foundation is a national independent activist fund by, for, and about young
women from the age of fifteen to thirty. It supports these women in
the areas of reproductive rights, microenterprise, scholarships, and
general organizing. The Ignacio Martin–Baro Fund for Mental Health

and Human Rights supports human rights and mental health projects in communities affected by violence and repression around the world.

Sister Foundations

In the past two decades the number of progressive foundations has soared. Here's what some of them look like: Businesses like Ben and Jerry's ice cream have set up progressive foundations to give a percentage of their profits to organizing. Religious groups may give from annual offerings through their own foundations, such as Church Women United. The Jewish Fund for Justice and the Shefa Fund work with Jewish givers to link Jewish social action with community action. Other religious institutions, like the Unitarian Universalist Veatch Program at Shelter Rock, give from the interest of a bequest. Foundations like the Environmental Support Center, the Ms. Foundation for Women, and Girl's Best Friend focus on one issue or constituency.

The National Network of Grantmakers

Founded in 1980, the National Network of Grantmakers (NNG) is an organization of individuals involved in funding social and economic justice. Its membership includes activist donors, foundation staff, board members, and philanthropic advisers. Today it works primarily within organized philanthropy to increase financial resources to social and economic justice work, to provide a network of mutual support for progressive givers, to share information across grantmaking issues and constituencies, and to promote the exchange of information and strategies among social change givers and community activists. It also reshapes philanthropic policies and promotes diversity and open, democratic processes.

A unique aspect of NNG is the community it offers through the caucuses and working groups that its members can join. There are caucuses for women, youth, people of color, and gay, lesbian, transgendered, and bisexual people. Some of the working groups include the Electoral Working Group, Funders Who Fund in the South, Fun-

together to defend their communities against this policy of planned shrinkage.

North Star continues to fund similar efforts and sponsors forums to support organizing, such as its conference on Organizing for Social Change: Fighting Racism and the Politics of Division, which brought together fifteen hundred organizers.

The People's Fund
Funds in Hawai'i

There is a carefully crafted myth that Hawai'i is a tropical paradise. However, behind the rows of hotels and swaying palm trees, activists are working to counter the consequences of one hundred years of colonization: poverty, attacks on Kanaka Maoli (Native Hawai'ian) sovereignty, unbridled development, serious pollution, and pervasive government corruption. The U.S. military occupies 25 percent of the land.

There is, however, a widespread resurgence among the Kanaka Maoli of their culture, language, and history and a growing movement for self-determination.

ders Who Fund Native Americans, Working Group on Media, and the International Working Group.

International Work

Let's broaden our horizons and look at foundations and intermediaries whose primary purpose is to fund social change beyond the United States.

Find a Partner

Some U.S.-based social change organizations work in partnership with community development, human rights, advocacy, and aid organizations in their target countries. Giving through a U.S. partner organization committed to social change is the best way to know that your donation will support projects developed and carried out by local people rather than pad a bureaucrat's salary or support a large-scale development project that could undermine the local economy.

On a purely practical level, these foundations can be invaluable as a source of information about the nuts and bolts of supporting social change outside the United States. (For example, how do you get funds into the hands of local groups that don't have access to banks?)

Why Give Internationally?

People give to international work (projects outside this country) and international solidarity (projects in this country that support progressive organizing in other countries) for a number of reasons.

⇥ *Global problems demand global solutions.*

Social problems cross borders. Poverty in Mexico drives desperate people to emigrate to this country, where most continue to live in poverty. Global warming has global implications. Pesticides banned in the United States endanger the lives of tens of thousands of farm workers throughout the world and arrive in this country anyway, coating our fruits and vegetables.

⇥ *U.S. corporate and foreign policy has contributed to and in some cases created conditions of poverty and lack of political freedom.*

A number of campaigns seek to mobilize consumer pressure to force corporations that have overseas plants to pay decent wages, provide humane working conditions, and eliminate child labor. Another example is Haiti, the poorest country in the Western Hemisphere. It was ruled for many years by the dictators "Papa Doc," Duvalier and his son, "Baby Doc," both of whom bled the country of its wealth and were actively supported by the U.S. government.

⇥ *We have a personal connection.*

Some of us have been touched by movements for justice that forever bind us to the people of a certain country or area. Many North American activists visited Nicaragua, El Salvador, and Guatemala during the 1980s; their experiences strengthened their commitments to work for peace in Central America. For others, the personal connection is a moral imperative: Because a vast majority of people in the world are desperately poor, we, as fellow humans, must act.

Below are just a few of the U.S.-based partner organizations; many others are listed under "International Giving Resources" in Appendix C. You can give to them and rely on their expertise to choose projects, or,

---

The People's Fund has been a key supporter of these movements.

Three Rivers Community Fund

Funds in southwestern Pennsylvania

One of the newest funds in the FEX network, the Three Rivers Community Fund reflects the local convergence of three rivers. Donors are active in all fund activities, from serving on the board to participating on the grant-making committee.

Recently supported initiatives include a Living Wage Campaign, tenant organizing to address major housing policy changes, and antiracism work. The fund also sponsors Spectrum Jams, meetings at bookstores and coffeeshops where community members can discuss a variety of diverse issues.

Vanguard Public Foundation

Funds in San Francisco and Northern California

As one of the first alternative foundations created during the Vietnam

War, the Vanguard Public Foundation has lived up to its name by funding domestic violence projects, divestment from South Africa, HIV/AIDS education, and organizing against toxic chemicals in the Silicon Valley long before these were mainstream issues.

Vanguard actively promotes socially responsible investing and helped establish the Northern California Community Loan Fund. The foundation became involved in recent affirmative action and "fight the right" struggles.

It has a well-developed donor-advised project, the Partnership Program.

Wisconsin Community Fund (WCF)
Funds in Wisconsin

WCF is proud of its statewide funding of Native American treaty rights, regulation of mining, safe water, and farm issues. The fight against the use of bovine growth hormone (BGH) in the dairy industry started here in the eighties, with support from WCF. In the nineties an unusual

in some cases, you can choose the specific project(s) you want to fund.

Grassroots International supports innovative social change projects initiated and carried out by people in Africa, the Middle East, Asia, Latin America, and the Caribbean. Contributions from Grassroots enabled villagers in rural Eritrea to build microdams to address the problem of chronic drought. Each of these community-controlled dams provides water for thousands of family farms. Grassroots International's philosophy is that "The root cause of hunger isn't bad weather. Nor is it poor technology or even overpopulation. It's lack of power to ensure the fair distribution of food and economic resources."

The Global Fund for Women is a foundation that backs the efforts of women to transform their societies and the world. Its funds work on issues as diverse as literacy, domestic violence, economic autonomy, and the international sex trafficking of women. It has an international board of women that helps it identify grantees and evaluate grant requests.

Oxfam America, one of the ten autonomous Oxfams around the world, provides grants and technical support to hundreds of partner organizations in Africa, Asia, Latin America, the Caribbean, and the United States. The assistance enables its partners to grow food, devise health and education programs, protect human rights, and encourage broad public participation in government. Oxfam-supported projects include Vietnamese peasants restoring war-damaged farmland and forests, Haitian farmers increasing food production, and Zimbabwean health workers providing health care for people with AIDS.

Take a Trip
If you are interested in funding internationally, you might want to join a partner organization on a delegation (tour). To travel to another country to understand the conditions and see the response of local people can be a life-changing experience. *The Global Exchange* organizes a variety of Peace and Democracy Reality Tours throughout the world and in the United States. Its tours have included: Ireland (Historic Turning Point?), Guatemala (Human Rights and Indigenous Culture), Cuba (Film and Music), and India (Economic Development).

Tax Tidbit
If you give to an international project through a tax-exempt organization in this country, you will receive a deduction. If you give directly to

a project outside this country and it is registered as a tax-exempt organization with the IRS, you will receive a deduction; if it isn't, you won't.

Together We Make a Difference

As always, the whole is greater than the sum of its parts. Alone, donors may give twenty-five, one hundred, or one thousand dollars here and there to many organizations. But when money is pooled through a social change foundation, grants of two, five, or ten thousand dollars—money that can make a significant impact—can be given.

Allen Hunter states it well: "Every year, when we give money, we give small amounts to a large number of organizations we know and trust and believe are doing useful work. At the same time we always give to the Funding Exchange and the Wisconsin Community Fund because there is no reason for us to believe that we know about all the useful, important organizing projects that need support. If we pool money with others and trust the collective decisions of activists who decide where the money should go, we're contributing to the broader social change we want but don't have the time to investigate."

coalition—farmers, Native Americans, sportsmen, and environmentalists—helped pass a strong mining moratorium bill, to protect the economy and the environment.

The fund has sponsored a hands-on media conference and conferences on racism, the right wing, and homophobia.

Women's Funding Network (WFN)

WFN is the membership association of more than seventy women's foundations, federations, individuals, and supporting institutions. The network promotes the development and growth of women's funds that empower women and girls. It advocates for increased funding for the needs of women and girls, encourages cooperation across barriers of race and class, and promotes participation by women of color and other women frequently excluded from philanthropic leadership.

Men Stopping Violence

What does it take to make violence against women unthinkable? According to Men Stopping Violence (MSV), an organization that embraces this goal, the first step is to understand violence against women as a community issue, requiring community sanctions and solutions. MSV seeks not only safety and justice for victims and changes in perpetrators' behavior but an end to the unjust power relations between men and women that provide the social foundation of domestic violence.

According to the U.S. surgeon general, domestic violence is the leading cause of injury to women, ahead of auto accidents, stranger rape, and muggings combined. When acknowledged at all, the problem is usually addressed by focusing on the individual problems of the perpetrator or the victim. MSV develops responses to domestic violence that firmly place it in a social context. It doesn't just ask, "What will change this particular batterer?" Rather, its question is: "What will change the community so that battering is not tolerated?"

By using this holistic approach to domestic violence, it understands that social change requires breaking down the walls of secrecy and privacy that surround the issue. This understanding directly impacts on its programs. Initial screening for participation in their program for men who batter, for example, takes place in a group setting to establish the premise that the work is not so much about individual growth as about social change. Also, men from the community, with or without histories of domestic violence, are routinely invited to attend batterers' classes so that they can understand that changing sexist norms and holding perpetrators accountable are the responsibility of the entire community.

Friends of perpetrators are invited as well to participate in building complex systems of accountability necessary to make change. MSV Director Dick Bathrick tells the story of a man in his last month of his program who wanted to start a class for batterers in his church. "His partner told him that there was so much anger in the church community as a result of his abuse that she didn't think anyone would attend. His MSV instructor challenged him to invite the men from his Sunday school class to attend his remaining classes. That way the community could understand the work he'd done to make real changes in his life, and ideally it would continue to hold him accountable to those changes."

MSV also works directly with institutions to create system-wide change. Through its participation in the State Commission on Family Violence, it has developed legislation and legal and judicial processes that emphasize accountability for perpetrators and safety and justice for victims. It also trains Domestic Violence Task Forces throughout Georgia, organizing within the system to influence individuals and procedures that contribute to the unfair treatment of domestic violence cases. "If a task force is struggling with, for example, a particular judge who is insensitive to the issue," explains Bathrick, "we will bring in a respected peer from another part of the state who understands effective and just intervention. So it's not some random person talking to a judge, but a judge working with another judge trying to change the judicial norms that have contributed to the problem."

MSV seeks to make change in social institutions where change is needed but is not necessarily welcomed. As a result, it depends on support from the broader social justice community. "Our philosophy is that the community must take on the issue of domestic violence by sending the consistent message that violence will not be tolerated," says Bathrick. "Receiving support from the Funding Exchange, with its commitment to community-based social change, fits with that philosophy quite well."

For more information on Men Stopping Violence, please contact the Fund for Southern Communities (see Appendix A).

Chapter 12

Doing It Yourself

In the last chapter we gave you the flavor of the progressive social change foundations that we know best. Obviously we are partial to foundations in which community activists participate in decision making. This method has proved to be more responsive to the unique needs of local communities than other methods of giving. It gets money to organizations with which many givers may not otherwise come into contact. We believe in the integrity of the donor and activist partnership.

Our goal, however, is to move money into social change work in all the ways it can get there. So in this chapter we explore ways of doing it yourself. Most of the options described here are for people who have substantial amounts of money to give, although there are several techniques anyone can use. This chapter covers the mechanics of giving. To do it yourself, you need to consider not only the Core Criteria (see Chapter 10) but also how to research and evaluate groups. We are specific in our suggestions. It's a lot of work to make thoughtful decisions about where to give for social change. But, as a friend says, "It's the best work there is!"

Direct Giving

Direct giving is the simplest way to give. You write a check to an organization, or if you're giving a large amount from an investment account, you can transfer stock. Some givers determine how much they will give at the beginning of the year, transfer that amount to separate bank accounts, and then write checks until they have spent it. Many others save their giving decisions until the end of the year either because they equate the holiday season with giving or because the deadline for receiving a tax break for a charitable gift is December 31. (But if you are completely stressed out during this season, this won't be a satisfying time to make giving decisions.)

Direct giving, like many choices in life, has pros and cons. On the pro side, you may keep more in touch with the groups you give to directly, and they in turn will keep you informed and, you hope, involved in their work. You will feel like part of the organization. Moreover, 100 percent of the money you give will go directly to the group.

On the con side, you may need to spend a big chunk of time to figure out where you want your money to end up. You will need to do your own evaluation prior to giving and before you give again. You will most likely find yourself on more mailing lists, you will receive more phone requests, and you may end up with a mountain of reading material. If you give large amounts of money, fund raisers will want to meet with you (which isn't necessarily a con). If your anonymity is important to you, you might have to jump through a few hoops to protect it.

Consultants

Hiring a consultant is an option if you are going to give away a large amount of money—say, *at least* $250,000. A consultant can investigate and advise you on individual gifts, provide a buffer between you and potential recipients, and take care of the paper work. If your privacy is important, he or she can protect it. How much time will a consultant have to put in to accomplish your giving program? Hiring someone *full-time* probably makes no sense unless you have a million a year to give away. As a general rule, you shouldn't spend more than 10 to 15 percent of your "pie" on overhead.

Giving Pearls of Wisdom

→ Our goal in writing this book is to provide you with the tools to make giving one of the most *satisfying* ways you can spend money. You should feel connected through your giving and proud of the work you have supported. Do not give out of guilt or obligation.

→ Forget the notion that you'll ever find the perfect group—100 percent effective, 100 percent risk-free. People who are overly concerned that their money might be wasted often give to extremely stable organizations, which tend to be well funded anyway and rarely engage in social change organizing.

→ You probably *don't* want to give to a couple of people who have an idea and only the ability to write a knock-your-socks-off request for money but no real community support. Make sure the group has roots. Ask how many people are involved, what roles they play in the organization, how the group finds new members,

and where the financial
support has come from.

→ Be cautious about giving to a group that is less than a year old, since it takes awhile to see if people can work well together and bring in others. If there are seasoned organizers in the group, we may bypass this guideline. We also may disregard this guideline in a crisis.

→ Organizations often have a hard time raising money for general operating expenses (i.e., rent, salaries, office supplies) because many people and foundations like to give to specific projects. If you believe in a group enough to give money to it, consider allowing it to determine how best to use your contribution.

→ Not every crisis *is* a crisis. If there is a tremendous hurry and you are the only one to save a group, chances are that disorganization or bad planning created the emergency in the first place. How do you know the same thing won't happen again?

→ On the other hand, sometimes emergency requests are appropriate in the case of an unexpected

There are many types of consultants, from a trusted friend to a professional who has several philanthropic clients. There are also unfortunately some unprofessional, overpriced ones, so insist on references.

When you interview a potential consultant, you will want to figure out whether you share a similar commitment to progressive change. How knowledgeable is he or she about the social change area(s) that interest you? Can this person relate in a respectful and open manner to people from a variety of backgrounds?

Ask yourself what kind of relationship you want to have with a philanthropic consultant. Do you want to interview potential applicants or would you rather the consultant do that? How much investigation and decision making do you want to handle yourself?

Direct Giving: An Assessment

The appeal of direct giving is its simplicity; the downside is the isolation of the giver. Unless you are in touch with activist communities, it is easy for individual givers to support organizations that primarily affect people like them, or are larger and well known, or where they know people. You *can* use the resources of progressive foundations to find a wide range of wonderful work to support.

Donor-Advised Accounts

Donor-advised (DA) accounts are offered by most progressive social change foundations and community foundations. People often set up DA accounts when they have had some kind of financial windfall or when they may face much higher taxes resulting from the sale of assets like a business or stock that has risen significantly in value. A DA account is similar to having your own foundation with none of the paper work or IRS reporting hassles. You set up an account, make a gift, and recommend the intended recipients. If you work with a foundation that shares your goals, staff will be able to help you find and evaluate organizations that fit your giving criteria. Legally foundations must approve a donor's recommendations, which need to reflect that particular foundation's mission. The IRS is watching.

Most of the grantmaking at the national Funding Exchange office is donor-advised. Donors make minimum commitments of twenty thousand dollars and receive detailed descriptions (called dockets) of organizations that have been screened by the Funding Exchange. Many give from this list, as well as to other organizations they may want to support. Many of the member funds also offer donor-advised accounts, as do most public foundations. The minimum contribution and the charge for administration vary.

Another major donor-advised grantmaking institution is the Tides Foundation, based in San Francisco. It has a long history of funding progressive causes, and it fosters donor-advised grantmaking through customized program services, convening and collaborative funding opportunities.

Donor-Advised Accounts: Pros and Cons

There are many benefits to a donor-advised account. You can make a contribution to your account anytime, take a charitable deduction for that year, and make grants whenever you wish. It is also easy to make anonymous contributions from a DA account.

Many individuals have established DA accounts rather than set up their own foundations, saving time and money that might otherwise go to legal and administrative costs. Fees for donor-advised accounts vary widely but are much, much less than you could expect to pay to set up and operate your own foundation.

The biggest con is that a DA account institutionalizes individual giving, rather than the models we prefer, which spread decision making among a wide range of people active in their communities. Another caution is that you can take your tax deduction, park your money, and not actually make any decisions. With so much exciting organizing going on, why do that?

Giving with Others

There's no reason you can't enlist others to help you make giving decisions. Sitting at home writing checks may not generate the excitement and the sense of being part of something bigger that can come when you work with others. It's not easy to have substantive debates

event or an extraordinary opportunity.

→ Set limits on being solicited. You can refuse to take fundraising calls during dinnertime—or refuse to take fundraising calls at all. If this is what you choose, say something like "I don't respond to phone solicitations, but if you send me something, I'll look at it." If you aren't interested in the organization, be honest: "I appreciate the work your organization does, but I give to other types of organizing. Please take my name off your mailing and phone solicitation lists."

→ Organizations love to receive multiyear grants (grants of specified amounts for two or more years) because they can *plan*. There's time to develop and train leaders, devise long-range strategies, and make a greater impact on an issue when funding is secure for a while. When you know a group well and believe in its work, consider this option.

→ If an organization receives significant support from the United Way, the government, mainstream foundations, or large corpo-

with yourself over which organizations to support! Giving with others can be fun, extremely educational, and instantly inspirational. It's an antidote to the isolation many givers feel.

Giving with others can be as simple as meeting for dinner to talk about your giving decisions. You can debate what kinds of social change work appears most critical and ask questions about group(s) you are considering. Then, over dessert, you all can write individual checks to the organizations you have decided on. (This decision-making process is particularly popular with procrastinators; you know who you are.)

If you feel up to the challenge, pool the money and collectively determine where it will go. The group will decide on funding priorities and a decision-making process. Each person can figure out how much he or she wants to contribute. You may decide to divide up potential recipients, assigning one or two groups to each participant to research. Or you may want to make a few site visits as a group to meet social change organizers on their own turf. You can also use the dockets from the foundations as described above.

There are infinite variations on ways to give with others. Here are two more:

A Weekend Celebration

"Four of us spent the weekend together, making both individual and collective giving decisions. It was a celebration! We stayed in a great cabin, cooked together, walked in the woods, and had a toasty fire going. There was something very special about the process, about all of us sitting around with our checkbooks out. It felt good to put giving out as a topic of conversation with others rather than me sitting alone doing it. It was like letting air into a closed room."

—Lynne Gerber, Haymarket donor

Funding Circles

Funding Circles are typically organized by foundations for donors who are willing to pool a substantial amount of money (e.g., five to twenty-five thousand) with other donors. The circle of givers studies an issue with the assistance of the foundation and then determines how to allocate the pool. The Ms. Foundation, the Global Fund for Women, and the Tides Foundation often organize funding circles.

Topics range from fighting the international sex trafficking of women to building statewide coalitions that press for clean elections.

The National Network of Grantmakers (NNG) and the Funding Exchange organized a combination site visit and Funding Circle on community economic development in South Africa. Each person was asked to contribute five thousand dollars to the collective pot. Participants studied the housing and job development projects in both rural and urban areas of the country and then visited those projects through a donor tour of South Africa. They met with community activists and heard about the challenges and triumphs of building a new country. They saw tenacity and vision. When they returned home, together they determined which projects to fund from their pooled resources.

Giving with Others: An Assessment

The best thing about giving with others is the lack of isolation. You can use one another's experiences, reactions, and knowledge to make better informed decisions. The time commitment and coordination of schedules is often the biggest challenge.

Your Own Foundation

In this section we look at how personal foundations, particularly family foundations, can be a base for social change giving.

Setting up your own foundation is an option for those with at least a million dollars to give away, although some start with much less. People set up their own foundations for a variety of reasons, with tax avoidance being primary. (See Chapter 7 on tax implications of private foundations.) Some want their own institution to carry out their giving priorities long after their deaths. Some people "inherit" foundations; being active in the family foundation was part of being a member of the family, like showing up for dinner.

The Personal: Family Foundations

Here's a real surprise: Family foundations tend to work *if* the participants can agree on the missions of the foundations and the decision-making process. Influencing the mission statement—goal(s) for giving—is an important part of institutionalizing social change giving.

> " Giving to social change work and being active in it has been a personal transformation. It is so great to see what a difference a contribution can make. It is a good way to spend a life." —*Nancy Myers, donor, Crossroads Fund*

If democratic decision making is the goal, the challenge is to come to joint decisions that satisfy everyone. Some families divvy up the money so each member can make decisions about his or her "share." Other families combine methods: A certain amount is decided on together, and the rest of the decisions are individual ones.

Depending on the dynamic of the foundation board and its mission, you might be able to influence decisions about where the money goes. Share information with family members about social change groups you're excited about. Explain the range of organizing going on in your community (or whatever geographical area you choose). Ask your family to accompany you on site visits. Consider the twinning strategy: If your mother supports traditional environmental organizations, she might be interested in the local community project to shut down an incinerator in an inner-city neighborhood. If your brother is fascinated by electoral politics, he might be interested in supporting the statewide organization working to get money out of politics.

Family foundations are not for everyone. If your family dynamics are difficult, then working in a foundation will probably exacerbate problems. Moreover, some family foundations, like some families, are extremely undemocratic. Family members from different generations, with different amounts of wealth and different objectives, may not be able to work well together.

There *are* several potential solutions to these situations. Some family foundations have invited nonfamily members to join the board both to add expertise and to smooth out dynamics (families tend to behave better when outsiders are present). With the proliferation of consultants who specialize in group dynamics, conflict resolution, and collective decision making, there is help. If your family is willing to call in a consultant to help work out a process of decision making or goal setting, for example, either as the foundation launches itself or in midstream, it could make a big difference. The consultant does not become a member of the board but helps set up a structure and process that permit the foundation to function smoothly.

Your Own Foundation

If you set up your own foundation, you have total control, within IRS guidelines, of what you give to, who serves on your board of directors, and who makes decisions. You can be creative. You can recruit an awesome board. In any case, we suggest you figure out how to stay connected to activist grantmakers so your contributions will have the greatest impact.

Practical Pointers

Be clear on why you are setting up a foundation. Make sure you have considered all your other options, such as establishing a donor-advised account with an existing foundation. Then, if you are sure, jump in!

You will need to work with an attorney to see which type of foundation makes the most sense in terms of your (or your family's) philanthropic goals, tax consequences, and cost. Attorney fees will be a sizable chunk of your start-up costs. *(Quelle surprise!)* Call the Council on Foundations or contact your local alternative or community fund for a referral to an attorney with expertise in these areas.

You will need to put together a board of directors. As mentioned above, many family foundations have benefited from the expertise of nonfamily members, particularly if they either represent or are connected to constituencies or issues the foundation wants to support. This suggestion can keep you from gliding into a giving rut.

After the lawyers go home, then what? Unless the foundation is going to operate out of your home, you need to furnish an office. You will want to design a letterhead and a brochure or prospectus to tell the world what kinds of projects your foundation will support.

If you want potential recipients to find you, there are lots of ways to spread the word. Tell your local social change foundation what you're up to. It may have grant proposals in your area of interest(s) that it would be pleased to share with you.

Connect with others for inspiration and ideas. We suggest you join the National Network of Grantmakers. The Council on Foundations, a more traditional organization, has a Program on Family Philanthropy (PFP), which has many resources. The Association of Small Foundations (ASF) was organized as an affinity group of the council to provide special services to small foundations, particularly around administrative and financial concerns. (See Appendix D: Organizations that Support Giving.)

> "Sometimes a grant can be pivotal to an organization's life or to a program they are trying to develop. At that moment, money for that purpose will really move them ahead. Being able to give at those moments is an art and a skill you can develop over time."
> —Anne H. Hess, donor, Funding Exchange

Foundations: An Assessment

The downside to establishing a foundation is that it uses resources for overhead that could be supporting change, and it can be a huge time commitment. While a foundation can ensure substantial tax savings, it requires tight adherence to IRS rules.

Having a foundation means you control the grantmaking, and that raises questions of access. Do you give to what you know, or do you open the doors and let organizations apply for support?

There are family foundations that have been in the forefront of social change giving. The Stern Fund's early and consistent support of the civil rights movement made a tremendous difference, as did the Field and Norman foundations.

Community Trusts and Community Foundations

Community trusts and community foundations make grants for a broad range of purposes within a community or geographic area. The differences between them are defined by the tax code. Other than tax code, there is no hard-and-fast difference between the two. Community foundations and trusts have evolved in unique ways because of why and where they were founded.

Community trusts *generally* serve as a kind of public foundation for a region. The United Way is the most ubiquitous in the United States, but there are many others, often connected to religious denominations, such as the United Jewish Appeal. People contribute, and a volunteer board allocates their contributions among a group of local social service agencies.

Community foundations provide a broad range of services to donors and their advisers, such as gift-planning information and consultation and asset management. Community foundations nearly always have an extensive donor-advised program. There is also a general fund that supports mostly social service programs. There are community foundations that fund some social change work.

Community Trusts and Foundations: An Assessment

Community foundations differ from the progressive social change foundations profiled in the last chapter primarily in their philosophical outlook. Community foundations usually don't fund groups that "rock the boat," and their perception of *who* the community is may differ. Progressive social change foundations are much more likely to have diverse boards and to support efforts that expand leadership within the community.

On the other hand, the community foundation or trust in your community could be unique. Find out its history, its pattern of leadership, what kinds of work it supports, and who makes the decisions about where the money goes.

The Mechanics of Decision Making

We trust you will find the way(s) of giving that fit you and your financial circumstances. Let's now look at some of the fundamentals of giving.

What Is a Proposal? Why Would I Want to Look at One?

If you are making a giving decision that involves a significant donation, we think you need to consider more than a direct mail appeal or a phone request *unless you know the work of the organization well*. Ask for a more detailed written request or a proposal.

A proposal is a structured request for financial support, which is what most foundations require. It generally includes an analysis of a problem, a plan for solving or ameliorating the problem, a budget, and, if the organization is large enough, a financial statement. A proposal should assure you of the organization's credibility and track record and therefore its ability to accomplish what it says it can. The Core Criteria outlined in Chapter 10 give you a good list of questions to keep in mind when reviewing a proposal. (Also, check out the pointers for reading a budget, in Appendix H.) Most donors ask for proposals only if they are considering a substantial gift (a thousand dollars and up). A simple request from an organization may include elements of a proposal without its specificity and length.

Very small grassroots groups may not have proposals, but they probably do have budgets and clear ideas of what their goals are and how

> "I had learned at a Haymarket conference not to descend like a fairy godmother, bestow a chunk of money on an organization, and then disappear. So when I found out that a project I loved was going to shut down because of finances and I bumped into the director at our local food co-op, I backed him up against the canned goods and said, 'Look, call me! I'll help.' After talking to him, I decided to give the previous year's budget and then to give in gradual sunsetting amounts over a period of five or six years, thus enabling the organization to develop its own fundraising capabilities. It worked! The organization is thriving."
> —*Janet Hicks, donor, Haymarket People's Fund*

they are going to reach them. Those are the key components you need to extract from any request.

How to Go on a Successful Site Visit

Site visits are often the best way to learn about an organization. They can be inspiring. They can also be time-intensive for both you and the organization. Some foundations have organized site visits for their donors. On a visit you can get a feel for the organization, you can ask questions, and you can meet the people doing the work. Most people would not go on a site visit unless they were going to make a substantial gift. Below are some suggestions to make a site visit work.

➻ When you make an appointment, be as honest as you can about the purpose of the visit. If you do not wish to reveal that you are considering a donation, you can simply say you are coming on behalf of individuals who are considering a donation. You may also want to let the group know *up front* that you will not be making a decision during the visit. Then stick to it!

➻ If possible, meet not only with the staff (if the organization is big enough to have staff) but also with other people involved in the organization. This may mean scheduling an evening meeting.

➻ Be prepared. Before you visit, read everything the group has sent you. Figure out what you *really* want to know. It's fine to write your questions down. The people you meet will see that you have thought carefully about their work and that you value their time.

➻ Your attitude should be one of respect and support—even if you find the organization moving in a direction you don't agree with. Be aware of your power as a potential funder. This can be a stressful situation for you and the group. This does not mean that you can't ask tough questions and follow them up if the answers you get don't make sense to you.

➻ Do your best to put people at ease before, during, and after the interview. Be truthful about the parts of the work that you think are great. Keep in mind how hard it is to keep an organization going. Once you have interviewed the people you have arranged to meet and completed your fact finding, thank them and graciously take your leave. In deference to you as a potential funder, the group will be expecting you to signal when the interview is over.

→ You should let the group know when you will be making the decision. Also, although this last bit of advice sounds as if it's coming right from your mother, we don't think it's a bad idea to send a brief thank-you note for the time people spent with you.

Evaluation

You will want to evaluate the work of organizations you've made significant donations to in order to inform your next decisions. Why? Perhaps an organization you've supported for years is now a shell of its former self while another organization you've supported at a low level may be bursting with plans based on a phenomenal statewide victory. This kind of knowledge would compel most of us to rethink—and revamp—our support.

Inspiration to give comes not just from knowing what a group plans to do with your money in the future. If you have already given,

> "I often give to places that are not tax-deductible; that's not one of my criteria. If they have a venue for tax-deductible giving, I do that, but if they don't, it doesn't matter—if they're working for the kind of social change I believe in. If I don't have the energy to become involved, I give the money."
> —Shirley Magidson, donor, Liberty Hill Foundation

"*My question is: Are we making an impact?*"

you will want to know what the organization has already accomplished. What progress has been made? This helps you know if your previous donation was effective. It helps you say, "Yes, I'll give again."

For an individual giver, evaluation can be difficult. If you decide all this is too much work, Janet Axelrod, a donor to the Funding Exchange, will be on your side. She believes evaluation should be simple: "You give it, they take it; they spend it; you are done with it. Let's hear the highlights of what happened. People spend too much time trying to impress their funders with their accomplishments. It's a big waste of everyone's time!"

What's the Point?

In evaluating social change organizing, be as clear as you can about what you want to know about a group's work. While this sounds obvious (yawn), it's more difficult to achieve than you might think. You can gather mountains of paper and miss the point. A good basis for evaluation is often the criteria that were most critical to you when you chose a particular group.

An Evaluation Model

This evaluation format is a combination of outcome and process models of evaluation. The point of an outcome evaluation is: What was produced? What impact did the group have? Foundations often use this model of evaluation. Process evaluation asks, "How did it happen? What was the process?" With our hybrid model, you can do as simple or as complex an evaluation as you wish, and you can be as systematic and thorough as you have the time and interest to be.

Your level of evaluation and organization may vary depending on the size of your contribution. For instance, you could make a folder for each organization you support. Note the dollar amount and date of the contribution on the inside of the folder, and keep all correspondence, newsletters, annual reports, etc. in it. Ten months or so into your giving cycle, go through each folder and ask yourself:

➡ What information have I received from each group?
➡ Did the group accomplish what it said it was going to?
➡ If not, why not? Was it able to accomplish other significant things?

- Have its mission, strategies, or tactics changed in the light of it's experience?
- What impact has the organization had on the issue? What effect did the organizing have on the underlying need or problem?
- What has the group accomplished besides its immediate goals? What was the process of the work like? For instance, how are new leaders identified and developed?
- How is the organization doing financially? How well did fundraising go? Has the group broadened its financial base of support?
- What questions do I still have about the organization?
- Do I want to continue funding this organization? If so, at what level?

In a nutshell, what is important is for you to know that your money is helping to make change. Figure out the best way to find that out, and go for it!

How Do You Find Out?

Here are several ways you can gather more information. Keep in mind time and effort on your part and on that of the organization.

- Call the organization and ask for its latest materials—newsletters, leaflets, etc.
- Call or write and say that you have a few questions about the work the organization has done in the past year. Then ask away!
- Ask people you know who are associated with the organization or who are working in the field about the organization's progress.
- Go to an event or activity the organization is sponsoring. This is a good way to get a feel for who the people are and what is going on.
- If you give through a donor-advised program, the evaluation of your grants is taken care of by the foundation. Written evaluations are received from recipients (it's the law!) and are available to you.
- Go on a site visit. This can be worthwhile, particularly if you gave a large amount of money and are considering giving more.

All Together Now

It's a commitment of time and energy to seek out groups pushing for change before the mainstream embraces those issues. It may feel risky, but that's the role social change givers play: out there, on the front lines.

Recovery Initiative

"Getting a mental health diagnosis is profoundly isolating. Connecting with others and challenging the stigma is a vital part of healing. When people work on healing on themselves, they want to give something back. Part of that transformation is believing 'I have had this experience for a reason, and part of that reason is to help someone else who has also been struggling.' Advocacy and organizing are a big way that people can do that, making sure, for example, that no one is subjected to some horrible study on his first admission to the emergency room."

—Jim Coleman, *Recovery Initiative*

Recovery Initiative was created by and for persons living with mental illness, known as consumers, in order to demand participation in changing the way mental health is addressed, both medically and culturally. It was founded in the belief that "consumers have the ability to manage their own illnesses and lives, with or without the help of a professional class."

Mental health research and abuses in experimentation are a major focus of the work of Recovery Initiative. The media have recently discovered what mental health consumers have long known: Researchers often use a methodology that significantly worsens symptoms. Consumers can be drafted into studies when they enter a hospital in an initial episode of their illness and thus not receive standard treatment. They are often asked to sign consent forms in the midst of an episode, clearly not the best time to make an informed choice. Jim Foreman of Recovery Initiative notes, "It's unthinkable that someone diagnosed with cancer would be treated initially with experimental methods, but it is not uncommon with mental health diagnoses."

"Everything in mental health research is really being driven by dollars," says Recovery Initiative's Mike Fontana. "There is a huge amount of greed and a lack of concern for people. Drug companies are pumping money into researchers who think they can do anything they want. There is too little regulation, both for research and for managed care." In addition to speaking out against these abuses to the media and the public, Recovery Initiative has been placing consumers on the boards that approve research projects.

Its organizing work also centers on eradicating the stigma of mental illness. A group of members monitor the media for negative images of mental illness and respond to offensive portrayals of people. Managed care and the insurance industry also have been a major focus of concern. The initiative pressured Aetna to restore health benefits to an eight-year-old girl who was denied because she was suicidal, and it got an Ohio-based insurance company to restore Prozac to its prescription list after an official admitted that it had been discontinued primarily for economic reasons. In the wake of the police killing of a person with mental illness, Recovery Initiative also brought the first self-admitted mental health consumer before the Cincinnati City Council, successfully arguing for a change in police language about psychiatric crises from "violent mental" to the less offensive Code 9. Since that victory it has been working with the police to provide better training to officers on mental health issues.

Recovery Initiative is committed to self-help. Its resource center provides free access to computers for word processing and Internet research to help people look for the basics: jobs, housing, and information about their illness. It also has a lending library of books, audio tapes, and videotapes related to mental illness and recovery. In addition, consumers run a weekly support group for people to heal both from their illness and from inappropriate treatment they may have received.

Critical to the success of Recovery Initiative is its core commitment to people organizing on their own behalf. This works on many levels, from helping individuals get access to needed resources to placing consumers on the boards of mental health agencies and other decision-making bodies. "You can't just change yourself and sit with that," says Jim Forman. "Part of the growing awareness of recovery is that you don't want others to suffer in the same way you have."

The Recovery Initiative is a Funding Exchange grantee.

Chapter 13

Doing It by Design: Your Giving Plan

Giving for social change is an art and a science. The art is to harness your vision for a better world; the science is how to turn your vision into the concrete steps that will lead you to organizations and movements you wish to fund.

This chapter is about getting from where you are to where you want to be and about challenging yourself to give more strategically and effectively. By working through the questions that follow, you can make a giving plan that reflects your vision, takes into account your previous gifts, and is realistic about the amount of time you can devote to giving.

Planning helps you move away from reactive giving, giving from a sense of obligation, or the feeling that you can't say no. You can become proactive, setting priorities and actively seeking out organizations you want to support. As a result of this more organized, focused approach, you become a more effective (and satisfied) giver. You also establish clear boundaries, making it easier to say no when you must and more gratifying to say yes when you can.

Get Out Your No. 2 Pencil!

Your Giving Plan

Section 1: Your Vision Statement and Goals for Giving

1. What is your vision of a better world? Stay with this question a moment. What things would have to change for this world to match your vision? Jot down your thoughts:

This method works! However, keep in mind:

➡ You don't have to go it alone. Go to a workshop on giving or involve a friend. Brainstorm and dream.

➡ It's okay if you do not have answers for all the questions that follow. On first pass you may simply want to get an idea of what you need to think about.

➡ Be flexible. Allow yourself the room to be spontaneous in your giving.

➡ Make your plan the framework for decision making, not just more paper on your already burdened desk!

2. With your vision in mind, brainstorm your goals for giving. (Brainstorming = creativity without boundaries.)

3. Look over your brainstorm list and pick one to four goals that are most important to you: These questions may help:
   Which goals do you think are most critical *now?*
   Which goals do you feel most strongly about?
   What areas do you have the most information about or expertise in?
   Write down your goals:

   Goal 1:

   Goal 2:

Goal 3:

Goal 4:

4. For each goal, write down its social change focus (or: What will social change look like if your goal is reached?).

Example:

Goal	Social Change Focus
To end poverty in the United States.	Make sure that food pantries are open seven days a week; increase the number of "family" shelters.

WHOOPS! Where's the *institutional* change here? Will this work lead to the end of poverty (or its drastic reduction)? Let's try again.

Goal	Social Change Focus
To end poverty in the United States.	Redistribute wealth; change economy so people are cared for; create jobs at living wages.

This is the most critical question of your giving plan. Not only does your social change focus ensure you are giving to change, not charity, but it will lead you to groups you want to support. Refer to the box below to sharpen your focus.

   Your turn! Ask yourself what precisely is going to need to change for your goals to be met.

Goal 1	Social Change Focus

Goal 2　　　　*Social Change Focus*

Goal 3　　　　*Social Change Focus*

5. Are there specific kinds of organizing or strategies that you think will best address the issues or change the conditions that concern you? Under each goal, write the types of organizing or strategies that make the most sense to you. Note why you think they will be effective. The "Organizing and Strategy List" below will help.

Social Change: A Working Definition

The goal of social change is systemic, institutional change, change that will live on beyond the participation of the current group. It is a change in the fabric of society.

Social change can . . .

»→ Change attitudes, behavior, laws, and public policy
»→ Expand democracy by amplifying the voices of those who have been left out
»→ Alter power relationships
»→ Address the root causes of inequality
»→ Involve conflict
»→ Create alternative institutions
»→ Level the playing field
»→ Have a greater degree of uncertainty about the outcome of the work, unlike traditional charity

Personal transformation and enhanced self-esteem of individuals are powerful outcomes of people's involvement in social justice activities, but the goal of social change is to make the world better for everyone.

Example:

Goal　　　　　　*To diminish racism*

Types of organizing: arts and cultural work; leadership development; training.

Why I think these strategies will work: Arts and cultural work are a good starting point for people to share experiences across cultures. Leadership and antiracism training were powerful for me.

Goal 1:

Types of organizing:

Why I think this will work:

Goal 2:

Types of organizing:

Why I think this will work:

Goal 3:

Types of organizing:

Why I think this will work:

Goal 4:

Types of organizing:

Why I think this will work:

Organizing and Strategy List★

_____ Arts and cultural work

_____ Coalition building

_____ Community organizing

_____ Constituency organizing

_____ Direct action

_____ Economic strategies

    _____ Boycotts

    _____ Community economic development

    _____ Divestment campaigns

_____ Electoral work

_____ Grassroots lobbying

★Definitions for each category are in the sidebars of Chapter 3.

_____ Grassroots organizing

_____ Infrastructure

_____ Internet site development

_____ Technical assistance

_____ Research

_____ Think tanks

_____ Funding networks

_____ Labor organizing

_____ Leadership development

_____ Legal action

_____ Long-range planning and strategic development

_____ Mass mobilization

_____ Media:

_____ Getting mainstream media attention

_____ Film, video, radio

_____ Popular education

_____ Public education

_____ Other _____

Shall I Give a Few Large or Many Small Gifts?

If you have given without a plan, you probably make many small gifts, rather than challenge yourself to give fewer, larger gifts, which can make a bigger impact.

Why is that? Most of us hate to say no. We buy our way out of phone solicitations with twenty-five-dollar pledges. We feel loyal to groups we've given to over the years, despite the fact we may no longer know if their work is effective or if they need our money.

On the other hand, some of us believe it is important to "join" organizations at the twenty-five- or fifty-dollar-level to be counted as members and thus help increase an organization's clout.

Loyalty and politeness can work at cross-purposes with your desire to make an impact. Use your giving plan to free yourself from any ruts you've fallen into.

6. Do you want to focus your social change dollars geographically or within a particular constituency (examples: older people, immigrants)? For each goal, write in the name(s) of a particular group(s) of people, and list geographic locations. Note why you have chosen these locations and these groups.

Example:

Goal 1   *To organize for a healthy environment*

My first priority is organizing in Alabama. A lot of toxic industrial waste have been dumped in or near communities of color because there wasn't the political clout to stop it. My second priority for Goal 1 is to support environmental justice projects in South Africa because this is a critical time in the rebuilding of that country. I don't have a special group of people in mind.

For Each Goal: Location, Constituency, Why

Goal 1:

Goal 2:

Goal 3:

Goal 4:

What Is a Large Gift? What Is a Small Gift?

If you want to make a difference with your money, you will probably want to make larger gifts and scrutinize your out-of-habit donations. The inevitable question is then: What is a large gift? A small gift? The answer lies in the reality of your finances and the size of the organization to which you are giving. Larger gifts obviously have a greater impact unless they are so large that they totally overwhelm an organization.

What is a large gift for *you?* One hundred? One thousand? Ten thousand? One hundred thousand? One million? *You* decide. As your financial circumstances change, your perception of these arbitrary categories may shift. Generally gifts that are less than 1 to 2 percent of your total giving budget are considered small. (If you give a thousand dollars a year, a ten-dollar gift—1 percent of your budget—is small.)

The significance of a donation also depends on the recipient organization and its budget. To a teenage group putting out a newspaper, fifty dollars may be a windfall. To a larger organization, it may be one of many fifty-dollar gifts it needs to make its budget. Because the donor and recipient often view the same donation in vastly different terms, it's always wise to consider both perspectives before settling on a gift's size.

---

7. How do you want to divide your giving dollars? This may change as you make decisions. If you answer now, you will have baseline information about your priorities.

a. What percentage will go to each of your goals?

Goal 1 _____% Goal 2 _____%
Goal 3 _____% Goal 4 _____%

b. What percentage will go toward previous charitable commitments that don't fit within the goals you've just developed? _____%

c. What percentage will you hold on to for emergencies and for spontaneous giving? _____%

(The total of a + b + c should be 100 percent.)

Section 2: Nuts and Bolts

Money

8. From what source(s) of money will you give? Indicate how much you'll use from all categories that apply (either dollar amounts or percentages).
   a. Salary _____
   b. Savings _____
   c. Investments _____
   d. Trust income _____
   e. A windfall (e.g., the sale of stock when the company you work for went public or you won the lottery) _____
   f. Under your mattress _____
   g. Other: _____

9. Grand total for your giving this year:
   _____

10. How will you give money? Check those that apply:
    a. Check
    b. Credit card
    c. Appreciated stock
    d. A family foundation
    e. An existing donor-advised account or one that you intend to set up
    f. Charitable trusts
    g. Other _____

> You can target your gifts in many ways:
>
> 1. Special projects, specific campaigns.
> 2. Capital expenses: bricks and mortar, equipment.
> 3. Endowments, the gifts that keep on giving.
> 4. Matching gifts.
> 5. Multiyear grants. Certain amounts of money are promised for certain periods of time.
> 6. General support. The organization should determine how the money can be best used.
>
> Unless a specific type of funding is requested, organizations appreciate general support gifts most of all.

> Contemplate *not* giving to organizations that don't fall within one of your goals. Ask yourself, "Why do I feel attached to this organization?" Maybe it helped you or someone you know. Or the issue may be a side interest for you. You may be giving to it because someone you know asks you for a donation every year. Maybe you see giving to the group as your civic responsibility. Ask yourself: "How would I feel if for this year I concentrated all my giving on the goals in my giving plan?" Sometimes by looking at the list of those groups that don't fit into your major goals, you identify other goals you have.

You as a Giver

11. How much time do you want to spend making giving decisions?
    _____ Some! I'm willing to spend time making decisions about issues I'm active in; I will let a progressive foundation make the rest of the decisions I have neither the time nor the expertise for.

_____ A lot! I want to spend serious time researching, visiting, and giving to groups that are changing the world.

_____ None! I'll give everything through progressive foundations, relying on their knowledge and willingness to do the paper work.

12. Do you want recognition for your gift? _____yes _____no
    If so, what kind? _____
    If you want anonymity, what kinds of protections are important to you? _____

13. Do you want to become actively involved in any of the groups you may give to? _____
    If yes, how does it affect your giving? _____
    Your anonymity? _____
    Your power in the group? _____

14. When and how often are you going to make your giving decisions?
    a) Monthly
    b) Quarterly
    c) Twice a year
    d) Once a year in the month of _____
    e) At the end of the year, when I'm stressing about the holidays

Decisions, Decisions . . .

15. For each goal, start by writing down the organizations you are considering. Include the major ones you've donated to in the past. If any of the latter don't fit under your giving goals, keep them in the category of "Groups That Don't Fit." Do not fill in an amount or a type of gift until you have chosen all those you want to give to.

    If you don't know of particular groups whose work will match your goals, write down something like "Needs more research, but I know I'd like _____ percent of my giving to go to this area." Then make a plan to get the information you need.

Example of partial plan:

Goal 1   *To help quality public education*

You don't have to do it all *this year*. Make a note of what you wish you could have concentrated on more so you can consider those issues or constituencies next year.

→ Level the Playing Field $2,000   General support
   (an organization promoting a statewide property tax to fund public education)

→ Parents for Justice $1,000   Multiyear
   I've given to them for three years. This year I'll let them know they can count on me for three more years.

→ I've heard about another organization that sounds interesting from the director of Parents for Justice. I want to check it out. I'll set aside $2,000 more for this goal.

Goal 2: *To support a grassroots movement for change.*

→ Vanguard Public Foundation $5,000   General support
   My local progressive foundation.

→ The Highlander Center $2,000   Project support
   For organizer training

Goal 3: *To ensure that Social Security remains viable.*
   I'm not sure what groups are working on this, but I know whom to ask. I'll figure this out by the end of October. I'd like about 15 percent of my giving to go toward this.

Groups I've given to before that don't fit my goals:

→ The South Africa Fund $1,000   General support
   (My sister-in-law is active in starting this new organization to bring reinvestment back to South Africa.)

→ Walk-a-thons, local PBS, membership in national and local organizations. Total of about $1,000

Now it is your turn!

My Giving Plan

Goal	Organizations to Support	Amount of Gift	Type of Gift (i.e., multiyear)	Notes
Goal 1				
Goal 2				
Goal 3				
Goal 4				

16. When you are done with your plan, look it over and ask yourself:

→ Do I feel good about this plan?
→ Do I think this plan will help create change?
→ Am I giving to the same old stuff?
→ Am I pushing myself to think about issues and people different from myself?
→ Can I afford to give away more money? How much?

17. How are you going to celebrate your gifts? *(Very important!)*

> What would it mean to you to double the size of your gift to an organization that is on the brink of an important victory?

"*I always mark my giving. When the last check is written, I often invite a friend to dinner in celebration. It is an opportunity for me to acknowledge the time and effort I put into being a thoughtful funder, to talk openly and proudly about the funding decisions I have made, and to honor and share the extraordinary work of the organizations I help support.*"—Tracy Hewat, director, Comfort Zone

Revisit, Revise, and Renew

As we said at the beginning of this chapter, your giving plan is not written in stone. Here's how to keep it fresh:

Revisit: Look at your giving plan every year or six months. Does it still reflect the kinds of work you want to support? Are there new issues you might want to add to your giving? When you write your checks, do you feel connected? Are you pleased at your choices? If yes, congrats. If no, reexamine!

Revise: Your giving plan stands ready for revision at any time. You may want to keep a copy of each year's plan to chart the evolution of your giving and notice the way your priorities change or stay the same. There are several computer software packages that can help you keep track of your donations. (See Appendix G.)

Renew: Keep your enthusiasm for social change giving by staying connected to the organizations you support and to your progressive social change foundation. Giving can truly be one of the most satisfying ways you can spend your money.

Thinking about How Much to Give Away

How you think about how much you will give away will vary depending upon how much you earn, how much you spend, and how much you own and owe (your net worth). Traditionally people have looked exclusively at income as the source of money from which to give. If you live on earned income (or wages) and you have a modest net worth, then looking at giving as a percentage of your income makes sense. The Giving from Income chart on the next page shows different income levels and giving percentages that may encourage you to greater giving.

If you have a high net worth, you can look to your assets and their growth as a source for giving. The Giving from Net Worth chart shows different levels of net worth with a variety of giving percentages to help you think about your overall giving.

Giving from Income

In thinking about what percentage of your income you want to give, you might start by looking at the table below. Find your income level; then look across the row until you see the amount that you'd like to give away. Look at the top of the table to see what percentage that is. Do both the

> Although the growth of your assets in a given year is not generally figured in when you calculate your income for the year, you could think of that as income and decide to give a percentage of that away.

amount and the percentage feel right to you? If not, where is the disparity? If you have given in the past, what percentage of your income does your past giving represent? How does it compare with the amount or percentage in the table?

If Your Income Is	*And You Want to Give*					
	2%	*5%*	*10%*	*15%*	*20%*	*30%*
$30,000	600	1,500	3,000	4,500	6,000	9,000
$50,000	1,000	2,500	5,000	7,500	10,000	15,000
$65,000	1,300	3,250	6,500	9,750	13,000	19,500
$80,000	1,600	4,000	8,000	12,000	16,000	24,000
$100,000	2,000	5,000	10,000	15,000	20,000	30,000
$135,000	2,700	6,750	13,500	20,250	27,000	40,500
$150,000	3,000	7,500	15,000	22,500	30,000	45,000
$200,000	4,000	10,000	20,000	30,000	40,000	60,000
$250,000	5,000	12,500	25,000	37,500	50,000	75,000

This year I/we want to give $_____, which represents _____ percent of my/our income.

Next year I/we want to give $_____, which represent _____ percent of my/our income.

Although the growth of your assets in a given year is not generally included when you calculate your income for the year, you could think of that as income and decide to give a percentage of that away.

Inspired by: *Inspired Philanthropy* by Tracy Gary and Melissa Kohner

> "It can be fun! Giving away money is fun! And it's really exciting to go out and see how much effect giving money away can have in changing other people's lives. It's a wonderful experience."—*Shad Reinstein, donor, the Funding Exchange*

Giving from Net Worth

In thinking about what percentage of your net worth you want to give, you might start by looking at the table below. Find an approximation of your net worth; then look across the row until you see the amount you would like to give away. Look at the top of the table to see what percentage that is. Do the amount and the percentage feel right to you? If not, where is the disparity? If you have given in the past, what percentage of your net worth does your past giving represent? How does it compare with the amount or percentage in the table?

If Your Net Worth Is	*And You Want to Give*					
	1%	*3%*	*5%*	*10%*	*15%*	*20%*
$250,000	2,500	7,500	12,500	25,000	37,500	50,000
$500,000	5,000	15,000	25,000	50,000	75,000	100,000
$750,000	7,500	22,500	37,500	75,000	112,500	150,000
$1,000,000	10,000	30,000	50,000	100,000	150,000	200,000
$2,000,000	20,000	60,000	100,000	200,000	300,000	400,000
$4,000,000	40,000	120,000	200,000	400,000	600,000	800,000
$5,000,000	50,000	150,000	250,000	500,000	750,000	1,000,000
$10,000,000	100,000	300,000	500,000	1,000,000	1,500,000	2,000,000
$20,000,000	200,000	600,000	1,000,000	2,000,000	3,000,000	4,000,000

This year I/we want to give $_____, which represents _____ percent of my/our net worth.

Next year I/we want to give $_____, which represents _____ percent of my/our net worth.

Inspired by *Inspired Philanthropy* by Tracy Gary and Melissa Kohner

Citizens for Safe Water around Badger

During the last half century the government of the United States has spent trillions of dollars in the name of national security to build and maintain its military forces. In the process it has generated millions of tons of hazardous and radioactive wastes. The lethal legacy of Cold War military production covers the map. No state or region has been spared.[1] Environmental cleanup efforts remain at a virtual standstill, held hostage to a politicized process, regulatory apathy, and a lack of federal funding.

Laura Olah lives in Merrimac, Wisconsin, an area known for gently rolling hills, dairy cows, and some of the best farmland in the country. Until her birthday on May 9, 1990, her life centered on her husband and three kids; her spare time was filled with giving music lessons and volunteering at her children's school. She gave little thought to the sprawling defunct military base only a short distance away. "On my birthday," Laura says, "my life changed. The army announced what it had known for fifteen years: The Badger Army Ammunition Plant had contaminated our soil and the groundwater. Because this information was withheld from the community, three families living near the plant drank poisoned water all that time." Levels of carbon tetrachloride were found in their drinking water at eighty parts per billion; five is the safe standard.

So Laura organized. She cofounded Citizens for Safe Water around Badger (CSWAB). "After the army's announcement people in the area were offered testing of their individual wells. They found chloroform in my neighbor's well. People began to get involved; we met around my kitchen table. We learned that between 1966 and 1970 as much as five hundred gallons of carcinogenic chemicals were dumped weekly in earthen pits at the ammunition plant. These chemicals moved through the soil, poisoning our drinking water." Both carbon tetrachloride and chloroform can cause cancer and other serious illnesses in humans. Liver tumors are the most likely, but tumors could also form in the lungs and kidneys, according to state health officials.

Within a month of its founding, CSWAB called for a meeting with army officials and successfully lobbied for off-site testing of seventeen private wells near the plant. Months later the group uncovered a deliberate effort by the Olin Corporation, the operating contractor at the plant, to edit test results from private wells that exceeded health standards. CSWAB took its evidence to the local television stations. The publicity put pressure on the army and regulatory agencies to change policies in managing drinking water data at Badger. As Laura says, "At Badger and other facilities across the country, the very contractors that made the pollution are the ones being paid to maintain the facility, monitor the pollution, and clean it up. They also often control the cleanup data. It's the proverbial fox guarding the henhouse." The EPA now requires Badger to report all test results directly to homeowners.

Later CSWAB successfully organized residents to block a $425 million superconducting magnetic energy storage (SMES) test model to be built at Badger. The electromagnetic effects of SMES, projected to extend over three thousand feet into the air, are thought by many to affect reproduction and cause embryonic changes, leukemia, and related cancers.

"Our group gets challenged about our lack of scientific credentials. I say, I may not be a chemist or a toxicologist, but I have a right to participate in decisions that may affect my well-being and the well-being of my family. To me, the soil and water in our community are either clean or they aren't," Laura Olah says.

"Collectively we are having a tremendous influence on the Department of Defense [DOD] nationwide. With very little money we have been able to monitor the cleanup of our community. A proposal to open-burn more than twenty-five hundred pounds per *day* of hazardous waste propellants was withdrawn by the army, following a twelve-month campaign by our group." (The facility would have released as much as 13,688 pounds of lead a year.)

"Open burning and detonation activities at military facilities across the country, however, place hundreds of communities at risk for elevated cancers and other deadly diseases. By our sharing our strategies and the technical information we have gathered, other communities across the country have a better chance of winning their own battles."

The group's long-term goal is to restore the biological diversity of the prairie now occupied by the army, ensuring that the land and waters will again be safe for all living things.

Where did they go for their funding? "The Wisconsin Community Fund heard about our work and invited us to apply. That's how we got our first grant."

Chapter 14

How to Be a Really Great Giver

Giving is one of the ways we burst out of our individual bubbles. It is a profound expression of our hope, our belief in the goodness of human beings, and our expectations for a better world. It is our humanness at its best.

Lewis Hyde, in his marvelous book *The Gift: Imagination and the Erotic Life of Property,* describes how gifts in traditional tribal cultures were given with no expectation of exchange or advantage. The recipient was to pass a gift along; if it sat still, it became merely a possession, withdrawn from the circle of giving required to strengthen the bonds of community. Anthropologists have documented how a single shell necklace circulated among hundreds of individuals and tribes within the Massim people of the South Sea islands. Implicit in these gift cultures is the belief that we are stewards, and that the strength of the whole comes through sharing.

Giving in a World Full of Needs

One of the realities of giving is that we are surrounded by human need and suffering. Here is one giver's reflection on mindfulness in the face of depravation:

> "The first time I traveled to Mexico I was struck by the number of people approaching me to sell food, trinkets, and crafts. Everywhere I went, even sitting at a restaurant table, I was constantly saying, "No thanks." It was hard not to feel harassed and besieged—and to avoid eye contact with the streams of vendors and beggars before me.
>
> "I began to think about the economic divide between these people and me and how to them I represented vast wealth. How could I expect anything else? This was my hourly reminder of the economic injustice in our world. Instead of tuning out, I looked people in the eye and allowed the experience to strengthen my resolve to work for justice."

In a less dramatic way, many of the community organizations working for change in the United States are operating in a world of need and insecurity. Government cutbacks have forced more charity dollars into meeting people's basic needs for food, shelter, and minimal health care. Some fickle foundations warehouse vast amounts of money, giving only the legally required minimum, and shy away from anything remotely controversial.

If we tune in, we realize that organizations seem to ask for our charitable money almost as often as advertisers try to sell us products. TV evangelists, office appeals, children selling candy bars, and official sports team charities all ask for your support. From social change organizations there are phone calls, solicitation letters, individual visits, and fund-raising events. There is an endless stream of activity devoted to inspiring, cajoling, and urging you to part with your money. In the face of this onslaught, it is sometimes difficult to set limits and remain civil toward those who ask.

Great Giver Rule: **Cultivate an attitude of respect and openness in the face of need. Don't confuse the asker with the societal conditions that created the need to ask.**

"I think it's a very worthy cause, but I've already responded to a phone solicitation."

"I try not to feel resentful toward people who ask me for money," said a giver from Atlanta. "It's easy to fall into the feeling of being assaulted and respond by pushing away. But I aspire to be welcoming, open, and honest. And I expect the same from others."

Walking in Their Shoes

"I respect door-to-door canvassers. It's hard work. They usually go on to do other great social change work."—Lally Stowell, donor, Haymarket People's Fund

"Fundraising *is* social change work! It is a good way to explain to people what's going on and what a group needs money for. If you really believe in what you're doing, and the money isn't for you, it shouldn't be hard to ask people. You are giving them an opportunity to support work that will make this a better world."
—Nancy Myers, donor, Crossroads Fund

Many social change organizations don't have professional development staff and polished materials. The people raising money are also directly involved in organizing work and may have families and other full-time jobs. Keeping a nonprofit organization alive is a labor of love and deep commitment. They know that to survive, they must balance raising money from multiple sources, such as foundations, members, and individual givers. "I feel like I'm a juggler," said the leader of a statewide tenants' coalition in Illinois. "Working in a small nonprofit, you toil long hours for little pay. Many of the foundations that fund us expect us to accomplish miracles on a shoestring."

People raising money for organizations are coached to build a relationship with you, the giver. They are urged to summon up their courage and overcome their shyness and fear of asking for money. For many, this is extremely hard. Yet many fund raisers love their work specifically because it is about building relationships and moving resources to an organization or issue to which they are deeply committed.

A fundraiser for a California women's center described the process as a dance. "I call it the fundraising tango," she said. "I'm always looking for potential dance partners, but I don't want to come on too strong, too needy. Sure, there's only two weeks' funding in the bank, but no one likes urgency. So it's a nimble dance."

Some people resent getting direct mail because of its sheer volume and the sacrifice of so many trees. It may be viewed as a scam, a way of ripping people off. But for many social change organizations, direct mail is a tried and true way of building a stable small-donor base. The Center for Constitutional Rights raised a quarter of a million dollars one year, from contributions of ten, twenty, and thirty dollars in response to direct-mail appeals.

The Power Relationship

"*One big difference between being a giver and being a fund seeker is that a giver gets their phone calls returned promptly.*"—Foundation director in Illinois

Great Giver Rule: **A good giver is mindful of the power relationship between asker and giver.**

There is an unavoidable inequality of power between grantmakers and grant seekers, givers and askers. While the fundamental difference cannot be erased, good communication and clarity can infuse the process of fundraising with comfort and satisfaction.

Social change gift seekers often reach to alter the traditional power relationship. "As a fundraiser," says Vashti Dubois from Haymarket People's Fund, "I couldn't do my job if I didn't approach each relationship with a sense of equality." Most fundraisers who seek support for social change work describe building honest relationships devoid of bowing and scraping. After all, donors who support social change are committed to a more egalitarian society.

For a giver, there are creative, even disarming ways to break out of the roles and rules straitjacket. For instance, why wait to be asked? Call up a group and offer your contribution along with encouraging words. Give more than what you're asked for. If you are meeting with a fundraiser, initiate talking about your gift first, then enjoy a more relaxed conversation about the organization's work. Send three friends information about the organization, and then follow up with them.

"One of the most refreshing meetings I ever had with a donor," reports the director of a national economic justice organization, "was when she came to me and said, 'I think your work is great, and I'm going to give you thirty thousand dollars in general support.' She didn't make me jump through hoops or ask me to tailor a project to her special needs. She was happy to be giving the money and supporting the cause."

> **D**onors are activists: Giving money requires a thought process, it requires educating yourself, and it requires action.

Letting Go

One of the joys of giving is learning how to let go. Like other rites of passage, determining when to let go—when not to micromanage other people and situations—takes insight and discipline. In the realm of giving, some people place many conditions upon their gifts or target them to narrowly defined projects. Most givers understandably want to know what their money is helping accomplish. But at a certain point placing too many conditions on a gift communicates distrust and lack of respect.

Great Giver Rule: **Never presume that your status as a giver should give you any more say about an organization's program and mission than anyone else involved with the group.**

One of the pitfalls of giving is believing that having extra money endows the giver with great insight. In other words, the giver risks losing his or her humility in the giving process. Once we find social change organizations that have broad accountability, vision, and good programs, do we really need to place conditions or require gifts to go to specific projects? What if we gave unconditional general support, empowering the leaders, board, and staff to make decisions about allocating resources within the organization? What if we gave a three-year commitment so the organization could spend more time on its programs and less time on raising money? There is tremendous joy for a giver in respecting and trusting other people to carry out a mission to which they are so dedicated.

Communication Counts

Because money, power, and giving are emotionally charged, communication around giving can be woefully inadequate. Transactions may take place by mail, sometimes anonymously. Yet a small bit of communication between givers and recipients makes a big difference in the ability of social change organizations to know how they are perceived and to plan for the future.

Let the organization know what kind of communication you want after your gift. Do you want to get its newsletter? Do you want an annual report? Do you want no mail, but a cup of coffee with a program staff person in a year to hear the latest news? This saves everyone time and organizational resources.

> "I certainly think that being involved in community activism has sharpened skills that would otherwise have been dull blades. I have learned to listen and to respond to people's direct individual concerns. I'm not thinking that I know what's best: I listen to other people's points of view."
> —*John Hicken-looper, donor, Chinook Fund*

Being uncommunicative, partly as a response to many requests, is a common problem. Many social change organizations don't want to pester a potential giver, but they need money and communication. The energy that goes into avoiding someone and playing cat and mouse is a big drag.

Great Giver Rule: **Return the phone call, letter, or E-mail. Keep a stack of postcards on your desk. Write it, whatever it is: "I can't meet with you, but I'll give," or "I can't give," or "I'm unable to talk now, try me again in six months."**

Giving outside Your Box

A great giver knows what he or she is looking for but is open to change. Being a good giver is about balancing your judgment with an openness to new information, spiced with a dash of humility. A good giver may have special interests but is constantly reassessing those interests. Giving to organizations outside your immediate geographical and personal issue area is challenging, but it may lead you to "hot" and underfunded issues and organizations.

Great Giver Rule: **Take risks.**

> "You should expect some grants not to work. If you don't ever make grants that go down, you are not giving close enough to the edge."
> —Bob Weissbourd, donor, Crossroads Fund

In the words of veteran activist and giver Anne H. Hess, "A good giver is someone willing to take chances and to put aside their own biases as much as possible in order to share the perspective of what others are trying to do. A good giver is as generous as they can be."

"A good funder is someone who has the strength to follow their own judgment without apology," says Kimo Campbell, of the Vanguard Public Foundation, "but who also has the ability to let go and understand that what we're doing is part of the work, but it is not *the* work. The *work* is being done in communities where people are struggling against very great odds—a very different circumstance from writing a check."

Giving Your Time and Talents

In the final hour it may not be the money that we give that makes the difference, but our acts of commitment and solidarity.

Great Giver Rule: **Become a true partner. Pitch in. Let no task be beneath you!**

Social change organizations need money and volunteer time. Most social change organizing work is people-intensive: calling people, leafleting, attending public meetings, stuffing envelopes. Giving your time, above and beyond your money, is to become a full partner in an organization's work. There may be situations in which it's not appropriate to volunteer or the work may require skills you may not have, but offering your time is another expression of support and a source of fulfillment.

Acknowledge that your gift helps change happen, feel the joy in it. It's more rewarding than paying the gas bill. Part of the joy is contemplating the boost that your gift can offer. "People who are organizing and struggling to make a better world get discouraged sometimes," observes giver Sue Blaustein of the Wisconsin Community Fund. "Getting a check in the mail says, 'I believe in your work.' This is part of what keeps people going, day in and day out."

"My sense of internal abundance comes from giving. There is so much tangible and enriching benefit that comes from a spirit of generosity and a belief about what it means to be part of a community that supports each other. There is a great deal of joy in the work. If someone told me how much I would learn, how many people I would meet, how hopeful I would feel about the world and how sustained I was going to be, I wouldn't have believed them. I didn't expect such an incredible return on my investment."
—*Tracy Gary, coauthor,* Inspired Philanthropy

Peace through Inter-American Community Action

Clean Clothing has become a cause for community celebration at the annual
Bangor Clean Clothes Fair, which features music, awards, games, and a
Clean Clothes fashion show.

In the mid-1980s Peace through Inter-American Community Action (PICA) of Bangor, Maine, opposed U.S. involvement in the wars raging in Central America and, like other peace groups, linked towns and cities in the United States with communities in Central America as a way to bring the war home. The Bangor PICA set up a sister city relationship with Carasque, a rural mountainous community in El Salvador. PICA members reported on human rights violations, held demonstrations, and worked with legislators to stop U. S. involvement.

After the war the relationship between Bangor and Carasque shifted. In determining the best way to continue to support the community, PICA members discovered that both places were threatened by the same global trend: the growing concentration of wealth and power in the hands of multinational corporations and the lack of corporate accountability to ethical standards of production. The pressures of the global economic system and the lack of economic alternatives were forcing community members to leave Carasque. Maine's economy, in particular Maine's textile and shoe industry, was also being done in by the global sweatshop economy. Since 1970 Maine had lost about 65 percent of its shoemaking industry, 65 percent of its textile industry, and 35 percent of its apparel industry.

PICA members decided that focusing on sweatshop conditions in the clothing industry would be an important way to unite the concerns of communities across geographic distance and national borders. Taking a lesson in organizing from the community in Carasque, PICA developed the Bangor Clean Clothes Campaign.

This campaign unites consumers and retailers in a community effort to change corporate sweatshop practices. Retailers in Bangor are invited to sign Clean Clothes pledges, committing them to develop Clean Clothes sections of their stores that feature clothing that meet certain criteria, including bearing the label of unions or independent monitors that report on the working conditions in manufacturing factories. Retailers work with PICA to research major clothing suppliers and obtain as much information as possible about the conditions under which their clothing is made.

PICA also organizes consumers to demand clean clothes. Members use slide shows and make presentations that connect sweatshop conditions in the developing world, the loss of industry in Maine, and the increasing lack of accountability of multinational corporations. They've developed a shopping guide that gives consumers the tools to learn about where their clothing comes from and how to pressure corporations to change practices that exploit workers through poverty wages, forced overtime, and unsafe working conditions.

In the 1997 Clean Clothes Campaign the Bangor City Council signed the first resolution in the country that strongly encourages retailers to sell clothing made in accordance with international human and labor rights standards. The resolution was passed with the help of seventy-five hundred community residents and more than seventy community organizations that signed petitions in support of the campaign. As a result, more retailers have joined the campaign, and Bangor has provided a model for communities across the country that are trying to respond to the growing ethical crisis in garment manufacturing.

Not only a model of antisweatshop organizing, PICA and the community of Carasque offer a model of long-term cross-community solidarity work. The relationship between Bangor and Carasque continues to be the foundation that the campaign is based on. In the spirit of true solidarity, PICA models its organizing work on the work pioneered by the community in Carasque. From identifying and understanding the issues to developing youth leadership to the way meetings are run, PICA is shaped by this sister relationship. This model offers the hope of developing strong international community to community bonds that have the power to challenge the dehumanizing forces of the global economy.

For more information on Peace through Inter-American Community Action, please contact Haymarket People's Fund (see Appendices).

Afterword

*"*D*on't mourn, organize."—Mother Jones*

As I write this afterword, I am very hopeful that together we can help provide activists with the tools to meet the many challenges of organizing in the twenty-first century. For the past four years I have had the privilege of working as the executive director of the Funding Exchange. A network of fifteen foundations and a national grantmaking program, the Funding Exchange has given away more than sixty-four million dollars since its inception in 1979 to support social change. I have met many of the grantees you have met in this book and many others whom you have not yet met, and I have learned immensely from them. I have also met hundreds of individual donors who support the Funding Exchange and the member funds and enable us to continue to raise funds for the movement. Many of these donors are activists as well. Some are working for a change in campaign finance laws; some are in the health field; some are filmmakers; some are international human rights activists. I think that all would agree that a

large part of their activism is defined by their choice to give money to social change and to be part of that change community.

Whether you have a lot of money to give away, a small amount, or something in the middle, your contribution makes you part of exciting and necessary social change. The contributions are your statement that you are willing to back up your beliefs and visions with material support. You are not satisfied to have your life determined by others but instead want a voice and a stake in the future.

As we step into the next century, the work that social change activists and donors do will determine how we will live our lives on this planet. We will continue to face the challenges of the consolidation of corporate power and the globalization of economic policy. Social change activists struggle with the effects of these policies on local economies and in their day-to-day lives. The results of the strategic adjustments that arise from world economic policy result in increased privatization, in the shrinking of public resources, and in the severe cutting back of social programs for the poor. These are worldwide issues. Debates about the privatization of hospitals and public education are taking place throughout the world. The consistent thread is that poor people the world over are in danger of losing their access to basic services.

One important arena for organizing is the workplace, where organizing has changed in the face of increased globalization. For example, despite gains in wages, collective bargaining, and health and safety made by low-wage workers organizing, most immigrant factory workers in the clothing industry still work without union contracts. The movement continues to support these workers, but its focus now includes a broader struggle for international human rights. The National Labor Committee and other international organizations have brought to the attention of the world the atrocities of manufacturing in Haiti, China, and other countries that refuse to adhere to decent economic business principles. They have helped us understand that the clothing we wear is made by children who are earning a few cents a day and are living in horrible conditions.

These are only some of the challenges facing social activists today. As you have read, there are groups that organize every day to combat the wage and wealth inequities in this country. Activists fight against toxic dumping and against the destruction of Native American sacred sites by huge multinational corporations. Gay, lesbian, bisexual, and transgender organizing for political equality and sexual liberation continues to unify diverse constituencies in coalitions to stave off conservative ballot initiatives and to develop standards of equity in the workplace. Although the list of challenges is long, our commitment to building a broad-based movement has never been greater.

As funders and donors we can help meet these challenges. If we are to support movement building, we need to be funding base-building, cross-issue organizing, media, and communications. We need to support local, national, and international organizations that share an analysis of the problems and a vision for a world of peace and equality. To do this, social change activists need new tools every day.

Activist groups need resources to bring together people who are organizing in different arenas to learn from one another, to develop a shared vision, and to put a unified strategy into action. Never before has this internal communication been so crucial. This point was brought home to me a few years ago when the Funding Exchange sponsored a funders' tour of the Rockies, a trip that brought donors to the Rocky Mountains to meet with groups and to understand better the challenges of organizing in Montana and Idaho. As part of the tour we convened a conference for the social change groups to meet with one another and with us. Many Native American activists who had been working together long distance over the years met face-to-face for the very first time at this gathering. They movingly told us how arduous the travel was through the mountains by car yet how crucial it was to be able to meet with other activists. We learned how important it is to support groups meeting together to strategize and to build solidarity. Travel time and travel money are scarce but necessary in the current climate. This is a crucial part of movement building.

We also must support efforts to increase the media and communications strategy of social change organizations. We need to get our message out. That was part of the reason for writing this book. I am sure that you have been fascinated by some of the stories of organizing that you read in this book. Some may be in your own neighborhood or city, and you may wonder why you never heard about them. In fact, the right wing has succeeded not only because it raised millions of dollars and supported a multitiered strategy for organizing but also because it mounted and financed a large, strategic media campaign. Media were a factor in the ability of conservatives to move the policy debates so far to the right. Media and communications take money. Lots of money.

I hope that this book will encourage giving to social change and will help us meet these challenges. I hope that the next time you receive a direct-mail solicitation from an organization or charity you will stop and ask yourself some of the questions raised in this book. Does this organization support change? Does it address the root causes of the issues? Will my contribution, large or small, support a strategy for social change over the long haul? Am I supporting a community foundation that values civic participation and shared decision making with community activists?

I hope that this book will reach many, many new donors and that we can dramatically increase the number of people who donate their money and time to social change. I hope that you will buy a copy of *Robin Hood Was Right* for a friend or a relative.

Even on the most dismal days I have hope. When I meet with activists, when I read their proposals or visit their sites, my hope is always renewed. I think about all the work that is being done in the name of justice on the comparatively small amounts of money being raised for social change. Imagine what these groups could do with more resources, with the ability to hire more staff, obtain training, harness new technology, and develop media strategies.

I want you to have hope too. And from that hope I want us to have a belief in the possibility of social justice, and from that belief, I want us to take action. I want us to raise money, to become active in a social cause, and I want us to fight like hell for our future and for future generations.

Ellen Gurzinsky
Executive Director
The Funding Exchange
April 12, 1999

Notes

Chapter 1: Understanding Charity

1. *Giving USA 1998* /American Association of Fund-Raising Counsel Trust for Philanthropy.

2. Table, *Uses of Contributions,* Giving USA, American Association of Fund-Raising Counsel, 1997.

3. Ibid.

4. Twentieth Century Fund, *Top Heavy: A Study of the Increasing Inequality of Wealth in America* (The Century Fund, 1995).

Chapter 2: Change, Not Charity

1. Andrew Szasz, *EcoPopulism, Toxic Waster, and the Movement for Environmental Justice* (University of Minnesota Press, 1994).

2. Laurent Parks Daloz, "Can Generosity Be Taught? Essays on Philanthropy," Indiana University Center on Philanthropy, 1998.

Chapter 6: Taking Charge of Your Money

1. Eric Tyson, *Personal Finance for Dummies,* 2d ed. (IDG Books Worldwide, 1996, ISBN: 0764550136). John A. Tracy, *Accounting for Dummies* (IDG Books Worldwide, 1997, ISBN: 0764550144).

2. Charles T. Woelfel. *Financial Statement Analysis: The Investor's Self-Study Guide*

to *Interpreting and Analyzing Financial Statements,* rev. ed. (Probus Publishing Company, 1993, ISBN: 1557385327).

Chapter 7: Tax-Wise Giving

1. National Network of Grantmakers, "Private Foundations and Public Charities: Is It Time to Increase Payout?" Autumn 1998, quoting Claude N. Rosenberg, Jr. *Sharing the Wealth, American Benefactor* (Spring 1998).

2. Ibid.

Chapter 10: Organizing . . . and Beyond!

1. Politics Unusual, a report from the Applied Research Center, by Madeleine Adamson, 1966.

Chapter 11: One Way of Doing It

1. Dan Delany, "Change, Not Charity: The Alternative Community Fund and Social Change Philanthropy."

Citizens for Safe Water around Badger

1. Daryl Kimball, Lenny Siegel, and Peter Tyler, "Covering the Map: A Survey of Pollution Sites in the United States," Physicians for Social Responsibility and the Military Toxics Project, 1993.

Appendix A

Progressive Social Change Foundations

The organizations listed below are local and national public foundations. You can give directly to them, and you can find out from them about social change organizations in your areas of interest. Their annual reports and newsletters describe groups they have evaluated and funded.

Astraea National Lesbian Action Foundation. Provides economic and social support to projects that actively work to eliminate all forms of oppression that affect lesbians and gay men. Contact 116 East 16th St., 7th floor, New York, NY 10003, 212-529-8021, anlaf@aol.com; www.astraea.org

Global Fund for Women. A grantmaking institution supporting women's groups internationally, especially female human rights,

women's access to media and communications, and economic autonomy of women. Provides assistance to groups overseas that wish to establish philanthropic organizations benefiting women. 425 Sherman Ave., #300, Palo Alto, CA 94306, 650-853-8305, gfw@globalfundforwomen.org; www.igc.org/gfw

Jewish Fund for Justice. A publicly supported national foundation providing grants to organizations addressing the causes and consequences of poverty. JFJ's Youth Endowment Fund Program gives young people a unique opportunity to become personally involved in thoughtful philanthropy. 260 Fifth Ave., Suite 701, New York, NY 10001, 212-213-2113.

Ms. Foundation. Funds projects for women and girls nationally. It also offers donors' circles for women. 120 Wall Street, 33d floor, New

York, NY 10005, 212-742-2300, info@ms. foundation.org; www.ms.foundation.org

National Alliance for Choice in Giving. An association of cooperative fundraising organizations. Provides national support to local and statewide federations to participate in workplace fundraising campaigns. Works with fifty-three federations covering thirty-two states. It can provide information about the alternative federation near you. Contact 2001 O Street NW, Washington, DC 20036, 202-296-8470, E-mail: 74041.2454.

National Black United Funds. Promotes expansion of African American philanthropy nationwide by obtaining access to employee charitable giving campaigns, conducting training institutes and conferences, and supporting self-help initiatives identified as community priorities. Twenty affiliates, twelve local federations, and a national Black United Federation of Charities with forty-eight affiliates. Contact: 40 Clinton St., Newark, NJ 07102, 210-643-5122, www.nbufen.org

National Community Capital Association. Represents forty-nine member community development financial institutions (CDFIs) that provide capital, training, and other services for community-based development projects in low-income urban, rural, and reservation-based communities throughout the United States. Offers a range of capacity-building, performance-based financing and public policy programs. 924 Cherry St., 2d floor, Philadelphia, PA 19107, 215-923-4754, ncca@communitycapital.org

Peace Development Fund. Provides grantmaking and technical assistance to peace and social justice projects. Through its donor-advised program, staff works with individuals to fund peace efforts in Central America, the Caribbean, and North America. 44 N. Prospect St., Amherst, MA 01004, 413-256-8306, pdf@peacefund.org; www.peacefund.org

RESIST. Funds small-budget groups across the country that struggle toward a broad vision of social justice. Publishes a wonderful newsletter. 259 Elm St., Suite 201, Somerville, MA 02144, 617-623-5110, resistinc@igc.org; www.resistinc.org

Shefa Fund. Provides donor-advised services to people who wish to make grants supporting Jewish social responsibility. Offers pooled funds that support North American work for Middle East peace, Jewish feminism, and Jewish gay and lesbian activism. 805 E. Willow Grove Ave., #2D, Wyndmoor, PA 19038, 215-247-9704, shefafnd@libertynet.org

A Territory Resource. Provides funding and technical assistance to grassroots groups in the northwestern United States. Programs include conferences, workshops, and donor-advised accounts. 603 Stewart St., Suite 1007, Seattle, WA 98101, 206-624-4081, www.atrfoundation.org

Third Wave Foundation. Combats the oppression of young women in our society. Organizes an annual conference on wealth and philanthropy for men and women under thirty-five. 116 East 16th St., New York, NY 10003, 212-388-1898, thirdwave@aol.com; www.feminist.com/3dwave.htm

Tides Foundation. Administers donor-advised giving funds for individuals and families. Offers flexibility in program design and personalized service to individuals, families, and organizations, helping them establish effective grant programs. Box 29903, San Francisco, CA 94109, 415-561-6400, www.tides.org; http://209.236.133.tides.cfm

Women's Funding Network. Brings together more than ninety public and private women's foundations and individual donors to promote the development and growth of funds that empower women and girls. Some local women's funds offer conferences for women of varying financial means to increase their financial literacy. 332 Minnesota St., Suite 3-1320, St. Paul, MN 55101, 612-227-1911, info@wfnet.org; www.wfnet.org

Funding Exchange
NATIONAL OFFICE
666 Broadway, Suite 500
New York, NY 10012
212-529-5300 • fax: 212-982-9272
Contact FEX Web site for current links to all member funds: www.fex.org

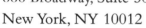

Member Funds

Appalachian Community Fund
107 West Main, Suite 202
Knoxville, TN 37902
423-523-5783 • fax: 423-523-1896
West Virginia and the Appalachian counties of Virginia, Kentucky, and Tennessee.

Bread and Roses Community Fund
1500 Walnut St., #1305
Philadelphia, PA 19102
215-731-1107 • fax: 215-731-0453
www.breadroses.org
Greater Philadelphia and Camden, NJ

Chinook Fund
2418 W. 32d Ave.
Denver, CO 80211
303-455-6905 • fax: 303-477-1617
Colorado

Crossroads Fund
3411 W. Diversey, #20
Chicago, IL 60647
773-227-7676 • fax: 773-227-7790
Chicago and metropolitan area

Fund for Santa Barbara
735 State St., Suite 211
Santa Barbara, CA 93101
805-962-9164 • fax: 805-965-0217
Santa Barbara County

Fund for Southern Communities
4285-G Memorial Dr.
Decatur, GA 30032
404-292-7600 • fax: 404-292-7835
Georgia, North Carolina, South Carolina

Haymarket People's Fund
42 Seaverns Ave.
Boston, MA 02130
617-522-7676, x303 • fax: 617-522-9580
New England

Headwaters Fund
122 W. Franklin Ave.
Minneapolis, MN 55404
612-879-0602 • fax: 612-879-0613 ★2
Minneapolis and St. Paul

Liberty Hill Foundation
2121 Cloverfield Blvd., Suite #113
Santa Monica, CA 90404
310-453-3611 • fax: 310-453-7806
www.libertyhill.org
Los Angeles County

McKenzie River Gathering Foundation
6707 NE Martin Luther King, Jr. Blvd.
Portland, OR 97211-3037
503-289-1517 • fax: 503-289-1598 and
454 Willamette Street
Eugene, OR 97401
541-485-2790 • fax: 541-485-7604
www.mrgf.org
Oregon

North Star Fund
305 Seventh Ave, 5th floor
New York, NY 10001-6008
212-620-9110 • fax: 212-620-8178
New York City

The People's Fund
1325 Nuuanu Ave.
Honolulu, HI 96817
808-526-2441
Hawai'i

Three Rivers Community Fund
100 N. Braddock Ave., #207
Pittsburgh, PA 15208
412-243-9250 • fax: 412-243-0504
www.trfn.clpgh.org/trcf
Southwestern Pennsylvania

Vanguard Public Foundation
383 Rhode Island St., #301
San Francisco, CA 94103
415-487-2111 • fax: 415-487-2124
www.vanguardsf.org
San Francisco Bay area and Northern California

Wisconsin Community Fund
122 State St., #507A
Madison, WI 53703
608-251-6834 • fax: 608-251-6846
and
1442 N. Farwell, Suite 500
Milwaukee, WI 53202
414-225-9965 • fax: 414-225-9964
www.wisconsincommunityfund.org
Wisconsin

Appendix B

Great Social Change Groups

Following is a sampling of grantees from the Funding Exchange Network. For a full list of wonderful social change groups or for more information about the ones listed here, please contact the fund(s) listed in parentheses.

Civil and Human Rights

A.C.E.-OUT, Inc., New York, NY
(Funding Exchange, Saguaro Fund)
Founded and organized by female ex-offenders, infected with or affected by HIV/AIDS, and battling issues of substance abuse and violence. A.C.E.-OUT helps incarcerated women successfully reintegrate into their communities and deters youth from the real possibilities of incarceration.

American Disabled for Accessible Public Transit (ADAPT), Chicago, IL and Denver, CO (Crossroads Fund and Chinook Fund)
A direct-action organization working to secure access for people with disabilities to public transit, public accommodations, health care, and home service programs.

Anthony Baez Foundation, Bronx, NY
(North Star Fund)
Headed by Iris Baez, the mother of a police brutality victim, the foundation works with student, parent, and community groups to educate about legal rights and demand accountability for police misconduct.

California Latino Civil Rights Network (CLCRN), Oakland, CA (Vanguard Public Foundation)

Organizes statewide civic participation projects, providing technical assistance to community agencies on conducting naturalization and voter education campaigns.

Coalition for Human Immigrants Rights of Los Angeles (CHIRLA), Los Angeles, CA (Liberty Hill Foundation)
A multiethnic coalition established in 1981 to promote and protect the human and civil rights of immigrants and to foster better relations among the many communities in Los Angeles.

Colorado Legal Initiatives Project (CLIP), Denver, CO (Chinook Fund)
A nonprofit legal agency that provides pro bono legal services to the gay, lesbian, bisexual, and transgendered communities of Colorado, focusing on cases most likely to set positive legal precedents.

Committee against Anti-Asian Violence (CAAAV), New York, NY (Funding Exchange)
CAAAV's pan-Asian and multi-issue community organizing strategy seeks radical reforms of oppressive and exploitative institutions and is committed to being an effective training ground for a new generation of Asian activists, as well as a site for strengthening the political development of experienced organizers.

Coordinadora Paz para la Mujer, Inc., Rio Piedras, Puerto Rico (Funding Exchange and Saguaro Fund)
A coalition of shelters, service providers, advocates, researchers, and feminist and human rights activists monitors the compliance of the law, affects public policy, provides support to service organizations, and organizes communities to eliminate violence against women.

Direct Action for Rights and Equality (DARE), Providence, RI (Haymarket People's Fund)
Organizes low-income families in communities of color to ensure economic, social, and political justice. Has been successful in improving workplace conditions, challenging police abuse, and increasing access to day care for the community.

Disabled in Action (DIA), Philadelphia, PA (Bread and Roses Community Fund)
A grassroots, cross-disability civil rights organization dedicated to independent living principles for all people with disabilities. Committed to freedom, integration and inclusion, DIA uses an effective combination of direct action and coalition politics to fight for the enforcement of the Americans with Disabilities Act.

Equality Begins at Home—Grassroots Organizing, Santa Barbara, CA (Fund for Santa Barbara)
Pacific Pride Foundation organized a diverse group of Santa Barbara residents to represent and advocate for equal rights for the GBLT community at a statewide level and to participate in a series of political actions as part of the national "Equality Begins at Home" initiative.

Gay and Lesbian Visibility Alliance (GALVAnize), Madison, WI (Wisconsin Community Fund)
GALVAnize has organized Madison's Gay Pride marches since 1989. The group works in coali-

tion with dozens of groups to produce the marches, which have been attended by tens of thousands of people and received national media coverage.

Ho'okolokolonui Kanaka Maoli (People's International Tribunal Hawai'i), Honolulu, HI (People's Fund)

A tribunal of nine judges convened from around the world to try the U.S. government for human rights violations against Na Kanaka Maoli (Native Hawai'ians), with the goal of bringing the injustices and violations of international law to the international human rights arena.

Justice is Blind/Mothers against Injustice (JIB/MAI) Chicago, IL (Crossroads Fund)

A grassroots group that organizes families and friends of those who have been falsely arrested, charged, and convicted of crimes resulting from police misconduct, or who have been murdered by the police, to fight injustice in the criminal justice system.

Kentucky Fairness Alliance (KFA), Frankfort, KY (Appalachian Community Fund, Funding Exchange, and OUT Fund for Lesbian and Gay Liberation)

Works with allied organizations to address issues of fairness across lines of race, class, gender, and sexual orientation; fights for anti–hate crime policies; and provides training, technical assistance, and political education on these issues.

Las Americas Immigrant Advocacy Center, El Paso, TX (Funding Exchange)

Trains immigrant women in leadership development and community organizing in the highly oppressive conditions of this city on the Texas-Mexico border. Women learn to act on behalf of their communities, challenge local and national policies and laws, and change the institutions that shape their city.

National Coalition to Abolish the Death Penalty (NCADP), Washington, DC (Funding Exchange)

NCADP's national, state, and local affiliates aim to do more than provide loyal opposition. The organization works strategically to influence citizens across demographic and political spectra, and challenge the assumptions that connect justice to executions.

Pittsburgh Coalition to Counter Hate Groups, Pittsburgh, PA (Three Rivers Community Fund)

Mobilizes the community to speak out against hate, provides assistance to communities and victims of hate groups, and sponsors educational programs on the nature and extent of hate groups.

Positive Action Committee, Sylvania, GA (Fund for Southern Communities)

Originally organized to help schools better educate kids, this group quickly moved to winning court and public battles against race tracking and successfully raising issues of public employment discrimination in rural southern Georgia.

Pride at Work, Washington, DC (Funding Exchange and OUT Fund for Lesbian and Gay Liberation)
Mobilizing the organized labor movement and the GBLT movement to advocate for full equality in the workplace and against all forms of discrimination.

Rural Organizing Project (ROP), Scappoose, OR (McKenzie River Gathering Foundation and Funding Exchange)
Connects and supports organizing by seventy-seven groups in conservative rural Oregon, addressing bigotry and economic justice locally and statewide.

St. Paul Ecumenical Alliance of Congregations (SPEAC), St. Paul, MN (Headwaters Fund)
A justice advocacy organization of nineteen low- and moderate-income congregations in St. Paul's twenty lowest-income census tracts, working for economic and racial justice and developing leaders.

Vermont Refugee Assistance, Montpelier, VT (Haymarket People's Fund)
Founded by sanctuary movement activists, monitors treatment of refugees by the U.S. immigration department, and provides legal assistance to those unjustly imprisoned.

Economic Justice

Alliance for Metropolitan Stability, Minneapolis and St. Paul, MN (Headwaters Fund)

A coalition of religious, social justice, and environmental organizations that advocate for public policies that promote community reinvestment and responsible land use in the metropolitan area.

Asian Immigrant Women Advocates, Oakland, CA (Vanguard Public Foundation)
Low-income Asian immigrant women develop language and communications skills, leadership, and organizing skills and advocate for social and economic justice by identifying common issues and building campaigns.

Black Workers for Justice, Greensboro, NC, and College Park, GA (Fund for Southern Communities and Funding Exchange)
Working across unions and industries, this mass group of predominantly Black workers in the South has been organizing the working poor for the past seventeen years on issues of economic injustice and the needs for systemic, institutional change.

Calumet Project, Chicago, IL (Crossroads Fund)
Focus includes the redevelopment of brownfields (abandoned contaminated lands); creation of quality jobs with benefits for local residents; training of workers to recognize the early signs of plant closures; and organizing of community residents around environmental justice issues.

Centro Independiente de Trabajadores Agrícolas, Florida, NY (Funding Exchange and Saguaro Fund)

CITA organizes immigrant workers to achieve change in workplace rights, community poverty, and discrimination issues.

Community Voices Heard, New York, NY (North Star Fund)

A membership organization of mostly poor Black and Latino women that works to ensure that people on welfare have access to adequate job training, education, and child care.

Fair Housing Partnership of Greater Pittsburgh, Pittsburgh, PA (Three Rivers Community Fund)

Dedicated to eliminating housing discrimination and promoting fair housing.

Fight Back Now! Burlington, VT (Funding Exchange)

Exists to fight lies and myths about poverty and low-income working people and to expose the forces that shift wealth from the poor and working class to the rich.

Housing Advocacy Coalition, Colorado Springs, CO (Chinook Fund)

This group is comprised of homeless and low- and moderate-income people who advocate for decent and affordable housing in Colorado Springs.

Inquilinos Unidos para Mejores Viviendas (United Tenants for Better Housing), Santa Barbara, CA (Fund for Santa Barbara)

Addresses substandard housing conditions and successfully challenged a notorious Santa Bar-bara slumlord through legal action. The group is now working toward the creation of a tenant-owned housing cooperative.

Island Tenants on the Rise, Honolulu, HI (People's Fund)

A growing island-wide coalition of public housing and tenants' rights activists working to unify public housing tenant organizations for dignity, affordable housing, and community strength.

Kensington Welfare Rights Union (KWRU), Philadelphia, PA (Bread and Roses Community Fund)

Based in one of Philadelphia's poorest neighborhoods, KWRU is a multiracial membership group dedicated to organizing welfare recipients, the homeless, the working poor, and all people concerned with economic justice.

The Maine Coalition for Food Security, Portland, ME (Haymarket People's Fund)

Works to eradicate hunger and ensure adequate access to food for all of Maine's citizens. The group promotes far-reaching food policies and antihunger programs.

9 to 5, southeastern Wisconsin (Wisconsin Community Fund)

A national membership group of women office workers that organizes to win raises, rights, and respect. The group was founded in Milwaukee, and WCF has funded local chapters in Racine, Milwaukee, and Milwaukee County.

Southern Appalachian Labor School (SALS), Kincaid, WV (Appalachian Community Fund)

Developed the Community/Union Project to counter the attack on the safety net for the poor and working poor. Distributed fifty thousand Welfare Rights Guide Sheets. Has a housing component to address rural housing needs; works with unions and workers around employment issues; and coordinated action and outreach with a community polluted by PCBs.

Tohono O'odham Community Action (TOCA), Sells, AZ (Funding Exchange)

Creates sustainable, culturally appropriate economic development, revitalizes the traditional food system, rejuvenates traditional cultural practices, and nurtures a new generation of community leaders for the Tohono O'odham Nation.

Workers Organizing Committee (WOC), Portland, OR (McKenzie River Gathering Foundation and Funding Exchange)

Recently opened a workers' center to serve and organize low-wage workers who are predominantly women, people of color, and recent immigrants. It builds community among those who are often isolated and vulnerable because of racism, language, and immigration status.

Environmental Justice

Citizen Alert/Native American Program, Reno, NV (Funding Exchange)

Provides support, information, and assistance in strategy development about military expansion, nuclear waste, radiation, and Native American burial grounds to the nations of the Goshute, Northern Paiute, Southern Paiute, Washo, and Western Shoshone within the Great Basin region.

Clean Water Action Council (CWAC), Green Bay, WI (Wisconsin Community Fund)

Works to prevent and clean up toxic chemical contamination of water to protect public health, wildlife, property values, and quality of life. After years of organizing, CWAC recently got the Fox River valley listed as a federal Super Fund site.

Clean Water Fund, Minneapolis and Greater Minnesota and Pittsburgh, PA (Headwaters Fund and Three Rivers Community Fund)

A research and education organization that promotes environmentally sound policies for water, waste, toxics, and natural resources. Organizes research, training, and public outreach.

Colorado People's Environmental and Economic Network (COPEEN), Denver, CO (Chinook Fund)

Organizes low-income communities of color to protect communities from health-threatening and environmentally destructive practices by businesses and governments.

Committee for Economic Recovery, Chicago, IL (Crossroads Fund)

Arranges for programs at public schools about environmental racism and injustice and is working to hold government, landowners, and corporations accountable for the cleanup of hazardous waste and environmental pollution.

Communities for a Better Environment,
Los Angeles, CA (Liberty Hill Foundation)
Combines science-based research and advocacy with legal action, community organizing, and public education. Has a long-standing commitment to work with and develop coalitions among ethnically and economically diverse community groups.

Community Labor/Refinery Tracking Committee (CLRTC), Philadelphia, PA
(Bread and Roses Community Fund)
A multiracial coalition of workers and residents in South and Southwest Philadelphia who are gaining health and safety improvements at the Sun Oil Refinery in their community. CLRTC addresses toxic emissions, the use and transportation of dangerous chemicals, and the lack of safety and warning mechanisms in the event of an accident.

Environmental Justice Action Group,
Portland, OR (McKenzie River Gathering Foundation)
Multiracial grassroots group identifying and challenging toxic exposure in Portland's predominantly African American neighborhood with a current project involving a youth leadership development initiative.

Gateway Green Alliance, St. Louis, MO
(Funding Exchange)
Addresses the intertwined issues of corporate influence on public policy, monopolization of food production, food safety, patenting of seeds and other life forms, and worldwide trade in human plant genetic material.

Ohio Valley Environmental Coalition (OVEC), Huntington, WV, eastern Kentucky, and southeastern Ohio
(Appalachian Community Fund and Funding Exchange)
A citizen group serving a three-state area that halted plans to construct the largest pulp mill in North America; forced the Marathon Ashland refinery to set aside forty-three million dollars for air pollution compliance; and organizes massive opposition to mountaintop removal and valley fill strip mining.

Safe and Responsible Farms Project,
Santa Barbara, CA (Fund for Santa Barbara)
This project was organized to reduce pesticide use—especially methyl bromide—and to improve air quality in agricultural areas. It educates consumers on the effects their buying practices have on farm workers, their families, and their communities.

The Seacoast Anti-Pollution League,
Portsmouth, NH (Haymarket People's Fund)
An environmental watchdog organization for the coastal areas of northern New England. Works to rid the seacoast of the dangers presented by the Seabrook nuclear reactor and the Portsmouth Shipyard toxic waste site.

Tri-Valley Cares, Livermore, CA (Vanguard Public Foundation)
Seeks to transform the Lawrence Livermore Lab from a nuclear weapons design and testing

facility to one that is more environmentally responsible.

Youth United for Community Action (YUCA), Los Angeles, CA (Funding Exchange)

Led by young people of color, YUCA trains youth to organize in partnership with progressive institutions. It has created a safe space for high school youths to come together to examine critically and act on issues that concern them.

International Solidarity

Action for Community and Ecology in the Rainforests of Central America (ACERCA), Burlington, VT (Haymarket People's Fund)

A nationally respected environmental watchdog group that monitors the endangered Central American rain forests and the communities dependent on them.

Centro de Educación para el Desarrollo Comunitario (CEPAC), San Luis, Distrito Nacional, Dominican Republic (Funding Exchange)

Provides assistance to communities in San Luis, enabling them to address poverty and severe environmental concerns. Communities have organized the construction of private and public latrines, developed public education programs about the contaminated drinking water, and established treatment facilities for sick children.

Colombia Media Project, New York, NY (North Star Fund)

Provides information that is not available in the mainstream media about human rights struggles that stem from the impact of U.S. policy in Colombia. Organizes public forums and delegations to and from Colombia in an effort to build U.S. solidarity.

Colombia Support Network (CSN), Madison, WI (Wisconsin Community Fund)

Works to educate Wisconsin residents about violence and human rights abuses in Colombia and the role of the United States in that country.

Comité de Reconstrucción y Desarrollo Económico, Social de las Comunidades de Suchitoto, Cuscatlán, El Salvador (Funding Exchange)

Creates an economic and social base for a new future in war-torn El Salvador by helping displaced communities return to their places of origin and develop economic activities to sustain them physically and emotionally.

Delaware County Pledge of Resistance, Delaware County, PA (Bread and Roses Community Fund)

Advocates for U.S. policies in Latin America that promote economic justice, human rights, and lasting peace. The group works in coalition with other Philadelphia-based organizations on issues related to NAFTA, GATT, and the restoration of democracy in Haiti.

Development Education and Leadership Teams in Action, Cape Town, South Africa (Funding Exchange)

Promotes a women's movement that is fully

representative and will enable women to participate in sustainable development through an integrated program of training, education, organizational development, support, and networking.

Guatemala Radio Project, Chicago, IL
(Crossroads Fund)
By organizing community members and youth, Guatemala Radio Project produces a weekly radio program that covers political situations in Guatemala and other countries, including the oppressive role of the U.S. government.

International Indian Treaty Council,
Palmer, AK (Funding Exchange)
An organization of indigenous peoples of North, Central, and South America and the Pacific working for the self-determination, recognition and protection of indigenous rights, treaties, traditional cultures, and sacred lands.

International Peace Project, Santa
Barbara, CA (Fund for Santa Barbara)
Concerned about the effects of bombing and economic sanctions on the Iraqi people, participants traveled to Iraq to record firsthand the conditions under which people are living. They delivered food and medical supplies and disseminated information when they returned.

Pittsburgh Labor Action Network for the Americas (PLANTA), Pittsburgh, PA
(Three Rivers Community Fund)
Highlights labor rights violations and fosters this region's cross-border organizing effort.

Portland Central America Solidarity Committee (PCASC), Portland, OR
(McKenzie River Gathering Foundation)
PCASC, which opposes military and economic intervention in Latin America, is a key member of the Cross Border Labor Organizing Coalition and the organizers of an immigrant rights' theater group that performs in labor camps.

Rethinking Tourism Project,
Minneapolis, MN (Funding Exchange)
Collaborates with indigenous partner organizations and communities concerned about the impact of the rapidly expanding tourism industry. It works to strengthen the capacity of indigenous people to analyze tourism development and create strategies and projects to protect biological diversity, culture, and traditional economies.

Rocky Mountain Peace and Justice Center, Boulder, CO (Chinook Fund)
Formed in 1983 as a base for research, education, and action in nonviolence. It works for the rights of prisoners, especially in maximum-security prisons, and for public safety issues at Rocky Flats.

Sentenaryo ng Sambayanan (People's Centenary), Quezon City, Philippines
(People's Fund)
A joint project of political leaders, historians, artists, activists, and academics to provide a progressive historical perspective to the commemoration of the centennial of the 1896 Philippine Revolution and the subsequent Filipino-American War.

Tennessee Industrial Renewal Network (TIRN), Knoxville, TN (Appalachian Community Fund)
Works to address issues related to plant closings and industrial flight, including public workshops on the effects of NAFTA and an exchange program with North American workers and workers in maquilladora plants. TIRN mounted a living wage campaign for city workers, and it coordinates and mobilizes community and labor organizations to change economic policies.

Twin Cities CISPES (Committee in Solidarity with the People of El Salvador), Minneapolis, St. Paul, MN (Headwaters Fund)
A solidarity organization influencing the political and economic root causes of oppression and marginalization.

Media and Cultural Activism

Appalshop, Whitesburg, KY (Appalachian Community Fund)
Community-based media that produce video documentaries about Appalachian political, social, and cultural issues, such as AIDS, domestic violence, and land exploitation. Also operates a community radio station and produces theater and films on traditional culture, social history, and current issues.

Asian Media Access, Minneapolis, St. Paul, MN (Headwaters Fund)
Connects the community through movie exhibition and media education, and production. Uses these activities to identify community issues and arrive at participatory solutions.

Atlanta African Film Society, Atlanta, GA (Fund for Southern Communities)
In addition to public film festivals, this group takes films into schools and leads discussions about their content. Recently sponsored workshops on creative political uses of the Internet for African American artists.

Barrio Warriors de Aztlan, Denver, CO (Chinook Fund)
A Chicano youth organization dedicated to self-determination works to unite youth through cultural expression, to raise social consciousness through education, and to develop peer networks to foster resiliency and community organizing.

Center for the Study of Political Graphics, Los Angeles, CA (Liberty Hill Foundation)
An educational archive that collects, preserves, documents, and exhibits domestic and international posters relating to historical and contemporary movements for peace and social justice.

East Bay Institute for Urban Arts, Oakland, CA (Vanguard Public Foundation)
A youth program that works with community organizations to develop strategies for using art as a tool for recruitment, public education, and membership development.

End of the Line, Boston, MA (Funding Exchange and Paul Robeson Fund for Independent Media)
Video focusing on the increasing demand for government assisted housing and its decrease

in support. The video is a tool for local, state, and national housing organizations to educate and motivate policy makers about the need for an affordable housing initiative.

Family Name, New York, NY (Funding Exchange and Paul Robeson Fund for Independent Media)
An award-winning documentary examining the legacy of slavery in America today by focusing on three contemporary families, two African American and one Euro-American sharing the same last name and having ancestors that lived together as slaves and slave owners.

First Friday: Unauthorized News, Honolulu, HI (People's Fund)
A monthly live one-hour public access television show by Kanaka Maoli (Native Hawai'ian) sovereignty activists that provides analysis of news, events, issues, interviews, and community updates, rebroadcast island-wide weekly.

HEArt (Human Equity through Art), Pittsburgh, PA (Three Rivers Community Fund)
Publisher of a quarterly journal of literature, reviews, and essays that promotes the role of artists as human rights activists devoted to confronting racial, sexual, gender, class, and other forms of discrimination.

The Inner City Community Coffee House/The Homeless Theater Troupe, New Haven, CT (Haymarket People's Fund)
A collective of soup kitchen guests and homeless people who produce original theater plays based on their lives. These dramatic produc-

tions educate the public on the realities and hardships of homelessness.

La Voz de la Mujer, Miami, FL (Funding Exchange and Paul Robeson Fund for Independent Media)
A Spanish-language radio show bringing low-income immigrant women's voices and concerns to Miami's airwaves. Features women who share their experiences and community leaders speaking on topics of interest to immigrant women.

Labor at the Crossroads, New York, NY (North Star Fund)
In addition to a monthly public access TV show that provides a critical perspective on labor, this group conducts a eight-week Worker Video Training Program.

Marriage Project Hawai'i, Honolulu, HI (People's Fund)
Produced an educational video for broadcast on public access television that featured heterosexual people addressing homophobia around the same-gender marriage campaign in Hawai'i.

North American Congress on Latin America (NACLA), New York, NY (Funding Exchange)
First-rate resources for news, commentary, and networking are crucial for solidarity movements. NACLA continues to be a major alternative source of information and has provided consistent in-depth journalism in the voices of writers from Peru, Mexico, Venezuela, Nicaragua, Cuba, El Salvador, and Brazil.

Out of the Past, New York, NY (Funding Exchange and Paul Robeson Fund for Independent Media)

The first film to document gay and lesbian history in America for high school students. The film interweaves historical portraits of lesbians and gay men from the past with a contemporary story of a young Utah woman's struggle to found a gay-straight alliance at her public school.

Philadelphia Community Access Coalition (PCAC), Philadelphia, PA (Bread & Roses Community Fund)

A citywide coalition of individuals and organizations that uses education, direct action, and advocacy to pressure the city of Philadelphia to provide public access cable television to grassroots community groups.

Portland Taiko, Portland, OR (McKenzie River Gathering Foundation)

This Asian-American drum performance group uses a community-based creative process to develop projects, including a piece that connects World War II Japanese internment camps with present-day anti-immigrant bashing.

Teen Thought Theater Troupe, Santa Barbara, CA (Fund for Santa Barbara)

This group of young women creates and presents live theater pieces that address race, class, gender, violence, peer pressure, and sexuality to inspire teenagers to find innovative ways of confronting these tough issues.

Video Machete, Chicago, IL (Crossroads Fund)

A collective of youth, community activists, and community-based artists that uses video as a tool to involve youths in an examination of their lives and the world around them.

Resources for Organizing

Autonomous Zone (A-Zone), Chicago, IL (Crossroads Fund)

An egalitarian resource center for education and social action that organizes educational programs and serves as an incubator for progressive collectives.

Brecht Forum, New York, NY (North Star Fund)

The forum provides community organizing training as well as classes, lectures, and roundtables led by new and established activists and scholars who supply progressive political, social, and economic analyses.

Bromfield Street Educational Foundation, Boston, MA (Haymarket People's Fund and Funding Exchange)

Established to protect the civil rights of gay, bisexual, lesbian, and transgender people, the Bromfield Street Educational Foundation publishes *Gay Community News,* organizes conferences for GBLT writers, and runs a project for gay prisoners.

Centers for Young Women's Development, San Francisco, CA (Vanguard Public Foundation)

Prepares young women living on their own to be self-advocates, while challenging public policies that keep them from participating in the development of their communities.

Chrysalis Point Mental Health Project, Santa Barbara, CA (Fund for Santa Barbara)

Organizes people with mental health challenges to advocate for their own needs, to steer public mental health policy, and ultimately to create a safe off-hours alternative to incarceration of individuals in crisis.

Colorado Progressive Coalition, Denver, CO (Chinook Fund)

A statewide coalition of progressive organizations and individuals representing more than twenty-five cities and towns whose goals are to strengthen the progressive movement in Colorado and to fight the destructive efforts of the right.

Honor Our Neighbors' Origins and Rights (HONOR), Omro, WI (Wisconsin Community Fund)

A secular and human rights coalition that focuses on Native American issues. Formed in Wisconsin, the group now has a national focus.

Ka Huliau: Linking Struggles, Honolulu, HI (People's Fund)

The People's Fund sponsored Ka Huliau: Linking Struggles, a successful networking conference. It convened over 250 activists from throughout the islands to hear speakers from the United States and the Philippines, to participate in twenty different issue workshops, and to develop strategies.

National Coalition of Education Activists, Rhinebeck, NY (Funding Exchange)

A resource and training organization for parents, union and community activists, school staff and teachers to create strategies for progressive school reform and to take on right-wing initiatives and forms of institutional bias.

Netcorps, Eugene, OR (McKenzie River Gathering Foundation)

Assists progressive Oregon groups to conserve resources, develop coalitions, improve communication, and increase time for their program work through optimum use of technology.

North Carolina Lambda Youth Network, Portland, OR (Funding Exchange and OUT Fund for Lesbian and Gay Liberation)

A youth-led statewide leadership development network for lesbian, gay, bisexual, transgender, and allied young people, ages thirteen to twenty-four, to cultivate leaders who improve communities and organize for social change.

Organizing Apprenticeship Project, Minneapolis, St. Paul, MN (Headwaters Fund)

Helps low-income communities and social change organizations identify and develop diverse and well-trained community organizers.

Philadelphia Public School Notebook (PSN), Philadelphia, PA (Bread and Roses Community Fund)

An independent quarterly newspaper (circulation forty thousand) founded to build a constituency-based movement for education reform in Philadelphia. Its focus is to support the efforts of parents, teachers, students, and communities to organize for improved conditions in schools, particularly those that serve low-income families of color.

Project South: Institute for the Elimination of Poverty and Oppression, Atlanta, GA (Fund for Southern Communities)

Works with low-income residents to do community research and analysis of issues and prepares popular education materials to promote community awareness. Also sponsors a monthly Book Club, bringing writers and researchers into dialogue with community residents working on a variety of issues.

Southern Empowerment Project, Maryville, TN (Appalachian Community Fund)

A multistate association of member-run, member-based organizations that provide training in fundraising and community organizing to people of color, young people, and small grassroots organizations. Provides on-site training and consultation.

Southerners on New Ground (SONG), Louisville, KY (Funding Exchange)

Founded in the vision of Black and white southern lesbians, SONG develops transformative models of organizing that connect race, class, gender, and sexual orientation and builds lasting relationships between people and their organizations.

Strategic Actions for a Just Economy (SAJE), Los Angeles, CA (Liberty Hill Foundation)

Established SAJE House, where working-class people gather to develop their own economic development strategies.

Still More Social Change Groups

Human Services Network, Los Angeles (Liberty Hill Foundation)

An umbrella organization that unites human service recipients, service providers, and activists to advocate for quality services in the fallout of the 1996 Welfare Reform Act.

Land Rights Council, San Luis, CO (Chinook Fund)

An organization of residents of the San Luis Valley working to reestablish traditional use rights for local people in the southern portion of the valley.

Minnesota Welfare Rights Committee, Minneapolis, St. Paul, MN (Headwaters Fund)

A high-impact multiracial organization of welfare recipients and low-income people working in response to the growing attacks on welfare recipients.

Padres Unidos, Denver, CO (Chinook Fund)

An organization of parents fighting racism in Denver public schools, with a focus on organizing Chicano and Mexican parents.

Peace and Disarmament—Stop Project ELF (SPE), Luck, WI (Wisconsin Community Fund)

SPE's mission is to shut down the Navy ELF (extremely low frequency) facility in Wisconsin and halt development of ELF nuclear missile submarine communications system any-where.

Philadelphia Student Union (PSU),
Philadelphia, PA (Bread and Roses
Community Fund)
An organization of public high school and
middle school students who advocate for a
school system that provides every student with
a safe environment and a solid education. The
group trains students in grassroots organizing
skills, holds monthly forums, and organizes actions for change.

**Stop Abusive Family Environments
(SAFE),** Welch, WV (Appalachian
Community Fund)
Created a transitional housing facility for battered women and children from an abandoned
rural school; addressed inequity and abuse in
judicial system's treatment of domestic violence
victims through a community research project;
and offers the only services and sanctuary for
abused women and children in a three-county
rural area.

Youth Force, Bronx, NY (North Star Fund)
With programs that range from a state-recognized
youth-led court to a campaign to counteract
housing discrimination for young people, this
group is committed to providing skills and opportunities for young people to participate in the
running of their own schools, neighborhoods,
and city.

Youth United for Change (YUC),
Philadelphia, PA (Bread and Roses
Community Fund)
Located in eastern North Philadelphia, YUC
trains high school students to act on their own
behalf to improve the quality of education in
their schools. Through a process of institution-
based community organizing, students organize
in their local high schools and receive extensive
leadership training, enabling them to explore
issues and devise ways to take action to address
their concerns.

Appendix C

International Giving Resources

American Friends Service Committee (AFSC), a Quaker organization, works to relieve suffering, nurture grassroots development, and promote quiet diplomacy in more than 150 sites across the world. Contact: 1501 Cherry St., Philadelphia, PA 19102, 215-241-7151, www.afsc.org

The **Development Gap** provides analysis and practical alternatives to U.S. and multilateral policy makers, the media, and the general public on the effect of foreign aid, trade, and economic policy on the poor in other countries. In the belief that good policy cannot be fashioned without an understanding of local environments and cultures, the group works to close the gap between those realities and how they are perceived by policy makers. Since 1977 Development Gap has worked with a wide range of grassroots, governmental, and public institutions in some forty countries in Latin America, the Caribbean, Africa, and Asia. Contact: 202-898-1566, dgap@igc.apc.org

The **Funding Exchange National Grants Program** is an example of a funder that primarily supports domestic social change but assists donors to make donations in other countries. The Funding Exchange (FEX) regularly incorporates groups from other countries in its biannual dockets (summaries of staff-reviewed projects). The staff can help you research grant-making opportunities. 666 Broadway, Suite 500, New York, NY 10012, 212-529-5300, FEXEXC@aol.com

The **Global Exchange** organizes a variety of Peace and Democracy Reality Tours throughout the world and in the United States. Among its recent tours: Ireland (Historic Turning Point?), Guatemala (Human Rights and Indigenous Culture), Cuba (Film and Music), and India (Economic Development). 2017 Mission St., #303, San Francisco, CA 94110, 415-255-7296, gx-info@globalexchange.org, http://www.globalexchange.org

The **Global Fund for Women** provides financial assistance to groups working on women's political participation and leadership, poverty and economic autonomy, reproductive freedom, the rights of sexual minorities, and the prevention of violence. 425 Sherman Ave., Suite 300, Palo Alto, CA 94306-1823, 650-853-8305, gfw@globalfundforwomen.org; http://www.globalfundforwomen.org

Grassroots International supports innovative social change projects initiated and carried out by people in Africa, the Middle East, Asia, Latin America, and the Caribbean. 617-524-1400, grassroots@igc.apc.org

The **Ignacio Martin-Baro Fund for Mental Health and Human Rights** supports human rights and mental health projects in communities affected by violence and repression. This fund is administered by the Funding Exchange.

The **International Development Exchange** (IDEX) provides small-scale assistance to community-led development efforts in Africa,

Asia, and Latin America. IDEX links sponsors, such as student groups, religious organizations, and individuals, in the United States with community projects overseas; sponsors select the projects they wish to fund, and 100 percent of their contributions are sent directly to those communities. 827 Valencia St., Suite 101, San Francisco, CA 94110-1736, 415-824-8384, idex@igc.apc.org; http://www.idex.org

The **Jerusalem Fund** supports the development of grass roots Palestinian initiatives in Israel and in the occupied territories of the West Bank and Gaza. The fund channels direct humanitarian aid to nongovernmental organizations that assist those in need. 202-338-1958, jfcpap@radix.net

Madre, a twenty-thousand-member national women's organization, promotes the economic, social, and political development of women. It provides medical and educational support and services to women and children in Central America, the Caribbean, central Africa, the Middle East, the former Yugoslavia, and the United States. 121 W. 27th St., #301, New York, NY 10001, 212-627-0444, www.madre.org

The **New Israel Fund,** a joint effort of Israelis, North Americans, and European Jews, provides grants and assistance to social change organizations in Israel that safeguard human rights, promote religious tolerance, nurture Jewish-Arab equality and coexistence, advance the status of women, reduce economic gaps, and pursue environmental justice. 1625 K St.

NW, Suite 500, Washington, DC 20006, 202-223-3333, info@nif.org; http://www.nif.org

Oxfam America, one of the ten autonomous Oxfams around the world, provides grants and technical support to hundreds of partner organizations in Africa, Asia, Latin America, the Caribbean, and the United States. The assistance enables these organizations to grow food, devise health and education programs, protect human rights, and encourage broad public participation. 26 West St., Boston, MA 02111, 800-77-OXFAM, www.oxfamamerica.org

Appendix D

Organizations that Support Giving

Association of Small Foundations. Provides technical support and administrative resources for foundations smaller than one million dollars in assets. 733 15th St. NW, Suite 700, Washington, DC 20005, 202-393-4433 or 888-212-9922, asf@erols.com

Comfort Zone. Encourages young adults with wealth to take charge of their money, connect with peers, and support social change. PO Box 400336, Cambridge, MA 02140, 617-441-5567.

Council on Foundations. The largest association of foundations in the United States. Provides services for different sectors of philanthropy, including family foundations, community foundations, regional associations of grantmakers, and affinity groups in philanthropy, including various annual conferences and guides on practical aspects of philanthropy. 1828 L St. NW, #300, Washington, DC 20036, 202-466-6512, www.cof.org

Donor Organizers' Network. An association of individuals and organizations that helps people with wealth become active partners in social change. Offers regional and national conferences, study groups, and other programs that encourage collaboration among its members. The network is a working group of the National Network of Grantmakers. 1717 Kettner Blvd., Suite 110, San Diego, CA 92101, 619-231-1348, nng@nng.org; www.nng.org

International Donors Dialogue. Hosts an ongoing conversation about expanding and enhancing the experience of international giving. 2261 Market St., #178, San Francisco, CA 94114, idd@internationaldonors.org; www.internationaldonors.org

Jewish Funders Network. A national network of individual and institutional Jewish funders. Holds an annual conference. 15 E. 26th St., #1038, New York, NY 10010, 212-726-0177, www.funders.org

Journey into Freedom. A nonprofit ecumenical ministry offering money and spirituality workshops, retreats, and trips of perspective to Africa, India, and Haiti. 4620 SW. Caldew St., #E, Portland, OR 97219, 503-244-4728, journey@teleport.com

Ministry of Money. Helps people deepen their faith and explore their relationship to money from biblical, psychological, and sociological perspectives. Publishes a newsletter, holds weekend workshops, and leads trips to third world countries. 11315 Neelsville Church Rd., Germantown, MD 20876, 301-670-9606, minmon@rols.com

National Committee for Responsive Philanthropy. Seeks through research and advocacy to make mainstream philanthropy more responsive to marginalized communities and progressive causes. 2001 S Street NW, #620, Washington, DC 20009, 202-387-9177, info @ncrp.org; www.ncrp.org

National Conference on Black Philanthropy. Promotes increased giving and volunteerism on the part of African Americans. Offers national biannual conference and regional conferences. 777 N. Capitol, N.E., Suite 807, Box 807, Washington, DC 20002, 202-289-3593, nationalconferenceonblackphilanthropy@juno.com

National Network of Grantmakers. An organization of progressive funders. Grantmaking affinity groups exchanging information on specific populations include Interfaith Funders, Women's Caucus, and People of Color Caucus. 1717 Kettner Blvd., Suite 100, San Diego, CA 92101, 619-231-1348, nng@nng.org; www.nng.org

Network for Social Change. A network of people in Britain who pool their money and time to evaluate and fund innovative projects in the areas of peace and preservation of the earth, human rights and solidarity, health and wholeness, and arts and media. Members meet a couple of times a year to explore financial strategies and personal development. BM 2063, London WC1N3XX, thenetwork@gn.apc.org.

Outgiving Project. Offers a biannual conference for funders of gay and lesbian projects. 1225 I St., NW, #930, Washington, DC 20005, 202-898-6340, outgiving@gillfoundation.org; www.gillfoundation.org

Resourceful Women. Offers an array of classes, support groups, and conferences for women with inherited or earned assets. Resourceful Women also coordinates the Women's Donor Network. Presidio Building, 1016, 2d Floor, PO Box 29423, San Francisco, CA 94129, 415-561-6520, distaff@rw.org

Women's Philanthropic Institute. Offers a newsletter, conferences, workshops, and other services to help educate women about philanthropy and financial decision making. 1605 Monroe St., Suite 105, Madison, WI 53711-2052, 608-286-0980, www.women-philanthropy.org; deanne/@women-philanthropy.org

Working Group on Funding Lesbian & Gay Issues. Advocates for increased support of gay, lesbian, bisexual, and transgendered issues within organized philanthropy. Provides an information center for individual and organizational grantmakers and grant seekers, a national directory of funders who support GLBT projects and programs, a guide for grantmakers, presentations, and local and regional seminars. 116 E. 16th St., 7th Floor, New York, NY 10003, 212-475-2930, www.workinggroup.org/resource.httm; info@workinggroup.org

Youth on Board. Offers training and consulting to empower young people to take leadership on nonprofit boards. 58 Day St., 3d Floor, Somerville, MA 02144, 617-623-9900, youthboard@aol.com

Appendix E

Infrastructure: Organizations that Support Organizing

The organizations below are a sample of the progressive infrastructure that provides technical information, research support, training, and policy development to social change organizations. Much of this information was provided by Political Research Associates (PRA), which maintains a comprehensive list at www.public-eye.org. Consult PRA's list for its extensive group of civil rights and legal defense organizations. All these organizations are not for profit and they welcome contributions.

Alliance for Justice
A national association of advocacy organizations. Works to strengthen the public interest community's ability to influence public policy. It has produced many guides regarding IRS regulations, nonprofits and foundations, advocacy, and lobbying. 2000 P St. NW, Suite 712, Washington, DC 20036, 202-822-6070, www.afj.org; alliance@afj.org

Alternative Radio
Supplies interviews, public affairs and documentary programs to more than 120 noncommercial radio stations across the United States and Canada. It has a catalog of tapes, including many relevant to challenging the political right wing. PO Box 551, Boulder, CO 80306, 800-444-1977, ar@orci.com

Applied Research Center
Emphasizes issues of race and social change in the development of public policy, education, and research. 3781 Broadway, Oakland, CA 94611, 510-653-3415, arc@arc.org; www.arc.org

Center for Constitutional Rights

Nonprofit legal and educational organization dedicated to advancing and protecting the rights guaranteed by the U.S. Constitution and the Universal Declaration of Human Rights. 666 Broadway, 7th Floor, New York, NY 10012, 212-614-6464.

Center for Media and Democracy

Does investigative reporting on the public relations (PR) industry to enable journalists, researchers, and others to recognize and combat manipulative and misleading PR practices. 3318 Gregory St., Madison, WI 53711, 608-233-3346, stauber@compuserve.com; www.pr watch.org; 74250.735@compuserve.com

Center for Popular Economics

A collective of political economists who work to demystify economics for people working for social change. 413-545-0743, popec@econs. umass.edu; www.ctrpopec.org; info@ctrpo pec.org

Center for Third-World Organizing

Helps communities of color organize, develop leadership, and build alliances with other communities. Includes the Minority Activist Apprenticeship Program, which provides young organizers with training and field experience. 1218 E. 21st St., Oakland, CA 94606, 510-533-7583, ctwo@ctwo.org; www.ctwo.org.

Center for Women Policy Studies

Focuses on policy issues affecting the social, legal, and economic status of women. Produces numerous publications addressing current women's issues. 1211 Connecticut Ave. NW, Suite 312, Washington, DC 20036, 202-872-1770, cwpsx@aol.com, www.centerwomen-policy.org

Center on Blacks and the Media

Independent research and information center working to correct imbalances in the media and empower the Black community. 770-322-6653, www.afrikan.net/hype

Chardon Press

Publishes books on philanthropy, fund raising, and organizing for social change. 3781 Broadway, Oakland, CA 94611, 510-596-8160 or 888-458-8588, www.chardonpress.com; chardon@chardonpress.com

Clearinghouse on Environmental Advocacy and Research

Works to expose the corporate agenda of the wise use movement. 1718 Connecticut Ave. NW, Suite 600, Washington, DC 20009, 202-667-6982, www.ewg.org; clear@ewg.org

Coalition on Human Needs

Alliance of more than a hundred organizations that promotes public policies to address the needs of low-income and other disadvantaged populations. Publications include a biweekly update, action alerts, fact sheets, and reports. 202-736-5885, chn@chn.org

DataCenter

Research by contract into a variety of topics with special expertise in corporations and current political issues. 1904 Franklin St., Suite

900, Oakland, CA. 94612-2912 510-835-4692 or 800-735-3711, datacenter@datacenter.org; www.igc.org/datacenter/

Equal Partners in Faith

Coalition of clergy and faith-based activists challenging the Promise Keepers' use of Christian teachings to create a divisive and potentially dangerous message. 2026 P St. NW, Washington, DC 20036, 202-296-4672, epf-nat/10fc@aol.com; www.us.net/epf

Gay and Lesbian Alliance against Defamation

Promotes fair, accurate, and inclusive representation of individuals and events in all media. Challenges homophobia and other discrimination based on sexual orientation and identity. 212-807-1700 or 1-800-GAY-MEDIA, glaad @glaad.org; www.glaad.org

HateWatch

Monitors the growing threat of hate group activity on the Internet. PO Box 380151, Cambridge, MA 02238, 617-876-3796, www.hate watch.org; info@hatewatch.org

Independent Media Institute

Electronic news service and information clearinghouse for editors, journalists, and activists. 77 Federal St., 2d Floor, San Francisco, CA 94107, 415-284-1420, congress@igc.org; www.mediademocracy.org

Institute for Food and Development Policy.

A people's think tank and education for action center with a commitment to establishing food as a fundamental human right. It has great publications. 398 60th St., Oakland, CA. 94618-1212, 510-654-4400, foodfirst@igc.atc.org

The Interfaith Alliance

Alliance of religious leaders concerned about the narrow vision of the religious right. 1012 14th St. NW, Suite 700, Washington, DC, 20005, 202-639-6370, mail@tialliance.org; www.tialliance.org

Media Vision

Helps organizations learn the tools of the media trade and develop the capacity not only to execute long-term media strategies but also to respond quickly to breaking news. It offers training and consulting. Based in Boston, New York, and Washington, DC. P.O. Box 1045, Boston, MA 02130, 617-522-2923, www.mediavision.org; E-mail: mediavi@aol.com

Midwest Academy

Trains groups and individuals on effective community organizing and provides written resources on social change activism. One of the nation's oldest schools for community organizing. 28 E. Jackson St., #610, Chicago, IL 60604, 312-427-2304, mmwacademy1@aol.com; www.mindspring.com/~midwestacademy/

National Abortion and Reproductive Rights Action League

Organizes to secure and protect reproductive rights while advocating for programs and policies that improve women's health, reduce unintended pregnancies, and make abortion less necessary. 202-973-3000, www.naral.org; naral@newmedium.com

National Council for La Raza
Works for economic development and social change for Latinos/Latinas. 1111 19th St. NW, Suite 1000, Washington, DC 20036, 202-785-1670, info@nclr.org; www.nclr.org

National Gay and Lesbian Task Force
Provides national, state and local advocacy around GBLT issues. 1700 Kolonama Rd. NW, Washington, DC 20009-2624, 202-332-6483, ngltf@ngltf.org; www.ngltf.org

National Network for Immigrant and Refugee Rights
Alliance of local, regional, and national organizations and individuals working to protect the rights of all immigrants. 310 Eighth St., Suite 307, Oakland, CA 94607, 510-465-1984, nnirr@nnirr.org; www.nnirr.org

Political Research Associates
Extensive publication archive on right-wing movements ranging from new right to white supremacist groups. Excellent Web page! 617-661-9313, publiceye@igc.org; www.public-eye.org

Project South: Institute for the Elimination of Poverty and Genocide
Develops popular political and economic education and action research for organizing. 9 Gammon Ave., Atlanta, GA, 30315, 404-622-0602, projectsouth@igc.apc.org; www.peacenet.org/projectsouth

United for a Fair Economy
Works to revitalize the nation through a more fair distribution of wealth. Publishes *The Activist Cookbook: Creative Actions for a Fair Economy.* 37 Temple Pl., 2d Floor, Boston, MA 02111, 617-423-2148, stw@stw.org; www.stw.org

We Interrupt This Message
Offers specialized media training and technical assistance to grassroots organizations that serve the poor, youth, and other communities currently marginalized by the media. 415-537-9437.

Western States Center
Provides training and education on grassroots organizing and leadership. Works with organizations to build broad-based statewide progressive coalitions. PO Box 40305, Portland, OR 97240, 503-228-1965, info@wscpbx.org, www.epn.org/westernstates

Appendix F

Resources for the Socially Responsible Investor

Organizations

Co-op America

Provides resource listings for products, investments, and boycott information. Distributes a planning guide for socially responsible investors called *You, Your Money and the World*. 1612 K St. NW, Suite 600, Washington, DC 20036, 202-872-5319, 800-584-7336, www.coopamerica.org

Interfaith Center on Corporate Responsibility

Coordinates social issue shareholder actions and resolutions for religious congregations and individuals. It publishes the newsletter *Corporate Examiner* and *A Directory of Alternative Investments*. 475 Riverside Dr., Room 566, New York, NY 10115, 212-870-2293, www.iccr.org

National Community Capital Association

An association of more than sixty community development loan funds around the United States. 924 Cherry St., 3d Floor, Philadelphia, PA 19107. 215-923-4754, www.community-capital.org

National Federation of Community Development Credit Unions

The national association of credit unions with an explicit commitment to meeting the credit needs of lower-income communities. It distributes a directory of members. 29 John St.,

Room 903, New York, NY 10038, 212-513-7191.

Responsible Wealth

Coordinates shareholder resolutions around a variety of economic justice concerns. A national alliance of business leaders, investors, and high-net-worth individuals concerned about growing income and wealth inequality. 37 Temple Place, 2nd Floor, Boston, MA 02111, 617-422-2148, rw@stw.org.www.stw.org.

Social Investment Forum

A national trade association for socially responsible investment practitioners. It publishes *Social Investment Services,* a directory of investment opportunities, and a periodic "social balance sheet" comparing the performance of socially screened investments with the returns of other funds. 1612 K St. NW, #600, Washington, DC 20036, 202-872-5319, www.socialinvest.org

Books

Investing with Your Values: Making Money and Making a Difference, by Hal Brill, Jack Brill, and Cliff Feigenbaum. A comprehensive book that includes sections on shareholder resolutions, community banking, special-interest mutual funds, and "The Healing of Wall Street." Princeton, NJ: Bloomberg Press, expected publication date, May 1999.

Socially Responsible Financial Planning Handbook, by Co-op America. Provides worksheets, basic financial planning tips, and a national contact list of social investment professionals. Available from Co-op America, 1612 K St. NW, #600, Washington, DC 20006, 800-584-7336.

Appendix G

Bibliography

Much of the following bibliography was taken from *Taking Charge of Our Money, Our Values and Our Lives,* a sixty-page resource guide published by the Impact Project. The Impact Project helps affluent people more effectively use their giving, investing, spending, and community involvement to make a better world. For the $18 resource guide or more information, contact IP at 21 Linwood St., Arlington, MA 02474, 781-648-0776, mtmnews@aol.com

Books

Money: The Technical

Choosing and Managing Financial Professionals, by Deanna Stone and Barbara Block. Guides the inexperienced investor in the selection of a good financial adviser. Available from Resourceful Women, Presidio Bldg. 1016, 2d Floor, PO Box 29423, San Francisco, CA 94129.

The Complete Book of Trusts: Everything You Need to Know to Protect Yourself and Your Estate, by Martin Shenkman. A clear, step-by-step explanation of handling various kinds of trusts. Includes forms and sample documents. New York: John Wiley & Sons, 1997.

Head and Heart: A Woman's Guide to Financial Independence, by Susan Weidman Schneider. A supportive guide to women's taking charge of their financial decisions, such as negotiating salary, writing cohabitation contracts and prenuptial agreements, dealing with taxes, and planning for retirement. Pasadena, CA: Trilogy Books, 1991.

The Inheritor's Handbook: A Definitive Guide for Beneficiaries, by Dan Rottenberg. Guides the layperson to handle the financial, legal, and emotional issues involved in inheriting money. Princeton, NJ: Bloomberg Press, 1998.

Invested in the Common Good, by Susan Meeker-Lowry. Offers hundreds of suggestions on how average people can invest money and time in building a new economy in harmony with life-affirming values. Philadelphia: New Society Publishers, 1995.

Personal Financial Planning, 4th ed., by G. Victor Hallman and Jerry S. Rosenbloom. New York: McGraw-Hill, 1987.

Prince Charming Isn't Coming: How Women Get Smart about Money, by Barbara Stanny. Drawn from a personal account of financial crisis, this book offers practical financial advice and anecdotes to women so they can be prepared to take control of their security. New York: Viking, 1997.

War Tax Resistance: A Guide to Withholding Your Support from the Military, by Ed Hedemann. The most comprehensive guide to war tax resis-tance. It includes why and how people resist war taxes, discusses risks and how people have dealt with them. It lists sources of counseling for those interested in resisting and alternative funds for tax money. Philadelphia: New Society Publishers, 1992. Available from NSP, Box 189, Aabriola Island, BCVORIXO, Canada, 604-247-9737.

Money: The Personal

Building Community, Creating Justice: A Guide for Organizing Tzedakah Collectives, by Betsy Tessler and Jeffrey Dekro. A guide to establishing tzedakah collectives, small groups of people within Jewish communities who pool their funds for collective giving. Philadelphia: Shefa Fund, 1994.

The Golden Ghetto: The Psychology of Affluence, by Jessie O'Neill. This book portrays an honest picture of the benefits and problems of afflu-ence. Center City, MN: Hazelden, 1997.

The Inheritors' Inner Landscape: How Heirs Feel, by Barbara Blouin. Interviews from a variety of people on their experiences of inheriting money. Halifax, NS: Trio Press, 1999. Available from the Inheritance Project, PO Box 933, Blacksburg, VA 24060, 540-953-3977.

Jews, Money and Social Responsibility: Developing a "Torah of Money" for Contemporary Life. Explores Judaism's teachings on economics, wealth, indi-vidual responsibility, and communitarian values in order to fashion a contemporary Jewish ethic of money and society. Available from the Shefa

Fund, 805 E. Willow Grove Ave., #2D, Wyndmoor, PA 19038, 215-247-9704.

Money Talks. So Can We. A resource guide for people in their twenties. Compiled by young people with wealth working with foundation and nonprofit staff, *Money Talks. So Can We* encourages young adults with wealth to take charge of their money, connect to their peers, and support social change. Divided into personal, political, technical, and giving sections, it includes articles, personal stories, and resource lists. Comfort Zone, P.O. Box 400336, Cambridge, MA 02140, 617-441-5567. Books are available for $15 (for profit) or $12 (nonprofit/individual). Checks should be made out to "TSNE/Comfort Zone" and sent to the above address.

Overcoming Overspending: A Winning Plan for Spenders and Their Partners, by Olivia Mellan. Looks at the personal devastation of a "billion-dollar addiction hiding in closets all over the country." Offers compassionate insight and ways for individuals and couples to achieve spending control and money harmony. New York: Walker and Co., 1995.

The Overspent American: Why We Want What We Don't Need, by Juliet Schor. A groundbreaking book that not only suggests ways for increasing saving and cutting spending but explains how aggressive spending was made a patriotic activity. New York: Harper Perennial, 1998.

Unplug the Christmas Machine: A Complete Guide to Putting Love & Joy Back into the Season, by Jo Robinson and Jean Coppock Staeheli. A how-to book on enjoying Christmas as a soul-satisfying celebration rather than an extravaganza of commercial consumption. New York: William Morrow, 1991.

The Way of Real Wealth, by Mark Waldman. A guide to personal and spiritual growth through exploring how we relate to money. Center City, MN: Hazelden, 1993.

Who Is My Neighbor? Economics as if Values Matter. A study guide for Christians to make sense of personal economic choices as well as global economics. Includes a resource section and concrete models for creating a new economy. Available from Sojourners, 2401 15th St. NW, Washington, DC 20009, 800-714-7474.

Giving

African American Tradition of Giving and Serving: A Midwest Perspective, by Cheryl Hall-Russell and Robert Kasberg. A brief analysis, based on 180 interviews, focuses on informal giving patterns "under the radar" of foundations. Indianapolis: Indiana University Center on Philanthropy, 1997.

Can Generosity Be Taught?, by Laurent Parks Daloz. This essay discusses three ideas important for understanding how a greater generosity of spirit might be fostered in our society. Indianapolis: Indiana University Center on Philanthropy, 1998.

Charity Begins at Home: Generosity and Self-Interest among the Philanthropic Elite, by Teresa

Odendahl. A critique of how elite philanthropy primarily benefits the rich. With many quotes from the author's 140 interviews with funders and advisers to the wealthy. New York: Basic Books, 1990.

The Coors Connection: How Coors Family Philanthropy Undermines Democratic Pluralism, by Russ Bellant. An examination of the Coors family's role in the support of the American right-wing movement. Boston: South End Press, 1991.

Family Foundation Library, by Virginia Esposito, ed. A series of four volumes on management, grantmaking, governance, and family issues for family foundations; an in-depth resource on all the details of such ventures. Washington, DC: Council on Foundations, 1997.

The Honor of Giving: Philanthropy in Native America, by Ronald Austin Wells. A portrait of contemporary Native American cultures of giving. Indianapolis: Indiana University Center on Philanthropy, 1998.

Inspired Philanthropy, by Tracy Gary and Melissa Kohner. Guides reader through the process of developing a personal giving plan. Berkeley, CA: Chardon Press, 1998. Chardon Press can be contacted at 3781 Broadway, Berkeley, CA 94611, 510-596-8160.

Money for Change, by Susan A. Ostrander. An interesting case study of social change philanthropy focused on the history of the Haymarket People's Fund in Boston. Philadelphia: Temple University Press 1995.

Moving A Public Policy Agenda: The Strategic Philanthropy of Conservative Foundations, by Sally Covington. Hard-hitting analysis of how rightwing foundations have effectively dominated public policy debate over the last two decades. Offers advice for funders who seek to further a more progressive agenda. Washington, DC: National Committee for Responsive Philanthropy, 1997.

Social Change Philanthropy in America, by Alan Rabinowitz. An analysis of progressive philanthropy in the United States, including a portrait of social change funders and grantees and an examination of ninety-one sample grants. New York: Quorum Books, 1990.

Taking Giving Seriously, by Paul Schervish. An anthology of personal and analytical writings that deals with the problem of sharing resources wisely. Indianapolis: Indiana University Center on Philanthropy, 1993.

Wealthy and Wise: How You and America Can Get the Most Out of Giving, by Claude Rosenberg. Offers a sensible, concrete, and provocative model of how to think about how much to give. Boston: Little, Brown & Co., 1994.

We Gave Away a Fortune, by Christopher Mogil and Anne Slepian. Profiles sixteen people who devoted themselves and much of their wealth to help make a better world. Highlights such common issues as what's our fair share, security, and how to have our giving make an impact. Philadelphia: New Society Publishers, 1993.

Welcome to Philanthropy: Resources for Individuals and Families Exploring Social Change Giving, by Christopher Mogil and Anne Slepian. Written for the seasoned philanthropist and for those new to giving. Information on how to use different resources, an appendix of organizations and literature, and personal stories. San Diego: National Network of Grantmakers, 1997.

Social Change

The Activist Cookbook: Creative Actions for a Fair Economy. This "cookbook" provides a hands-on manual for media stunts, street theater, and many other creative cultural and arts tools from the labor and social justice movements. Available from United for a Fair Economy, 37 Temple Pl., 3d Floor, Boston, MA 02111, 617-423-2148.

Beyond Identity Politics: Emerging Social Justice Movements in Communities of Color, ed. by John Anner. A collection of articles and essays discussing topics from building ethnic and class solidarity to fighting for immigrant rights. Boston: South End Press, 1996.

Black Wealth / White Wealth: A New Perspective on Racial Inequality, by Melvin Oliver and Thomas Shapiro. This book presents research and analysis on private wealth, combining quantitative data from more than twelve thousand households and in-depth interviews with black and white families, revealing the depth of the racial divide in the United States. New York: Routledge, 1997.

Bridging the Class Divide . . . and Other Lessons for Grassroots Organizing, by Linda Stout. Tells the inspiring story of Stout, the daughter of a tenant farmer, as a self-taught activist and as a leader in the progressive movement. Boston: Beacon Press, 1996.

Chaos or Community? Seeking Solutions, Not Scapegoats, for Bad Economics, by Holly Sklar. A compelling look at economic injustice through unemployment, low wages, and the increasingly weakened stance of labor in the United States. Boston: South End Press, 1995.

Class Warfare: Interviews with David Barsamian, by Noam Chomsky. A collection of interviews that highlight questions seldom asked, such as what are the implications of fundamentalism, "family values" agendas, and the extreme right. Monroe, ME: Common Cause Press, 1996. Order direct: 800-497-3207.

The Corporate Planet: Ecology and Politics in the Age of Globalization, by Joshua Karliner. A behind-the-scenes look at the role of transnational corporations in environmental destruction. Karliner recounts stories of communities creating their own "grassroots globalization" movements. San Francisco: Sierra Club Books, 1997.

Dangerous Intersections: Feminist Perspectives on Population, Environment, and Development, ed. by Jael Silliman and Ynestra King. A project of the Committee on Women, Population and the Environment (CWPE). Original critical essays by well-known feminist scholars and activists present a multicultural, international scope on the major global issues of the day: environment, development, and population control. Provides crucial alternative voices that make a reasoned and impassioned argument that women should be the central agents of their own fate. Boston: South End Press, 1999.

Economic Apartheid in America: A Primer on Economic Inequality and Insecurity, by Chuck Collins and Felice Yeskel. An action-oriented introduction to the problem of income and wealth inequality in America and what we can do about it. New York: The New Press, 2000.

Glass Ceilings and Bottomless Pits: Women's Work, Women's Poverty, by Randy Albelda and Chris Tilly. A discussion of women's economic problems in the United States, from barriers faced by professional women to those faced by women in poverty. Boston: South End Press, 1997.

Global Spin: The Corporate Assault on Environmentalism, by Sharon Beder. Reveals the techniques used by conservative forces to try to change the way the public and politicians feel about the environment. Offers effective means of solving environmental problems. Chelsea Green Publishing Co., 1998.

Looking Forward: Participatory Economics for the Twenty-first Century, by Michael Albert and Robin Hahnel. Describes in convincing detail how participatory economics could work as an alternative to capitalism and communism. Full of cartoons and quotes. Boston: South End Press, 1991.

One World, Ready or Not: The Manic Logic of Global Capitalism, by William Greider. An in-depth explanation of the global economy as it impacts on people's lives. New York: Simon and Schuster, 1997.

Race: An Anthology in the First Person, edited by Bart Schneider. Twenty-one essays—personal, provocative, and challenging—from many of our country's great contemporary authors and social leaders make this book a must-read. New York: Crown Trade Paperbacks, 1997.

Race, Class and Gender in the United States, ed. by Paula Rothenberg. An updated classic anthology of provocative readings on social difference, hierarchy, and oppression. New York: St. Martin's Press, 1998.

Race Matters, by Cornel West. A look at current racial politics, including strategies for effective antiracist work. Eloquent and inspiring. Boston: Beacon Press, 1993.

Shifting Fortunes: The Perils of the American Wealth Gap, by Chuck Collins, Betsy Leonard-Wright, and Holly Sklar. Chronicles the changing distribution of wealth in the United States in the last twenty years and proposed remedies to wealth inequality. Boston: United for a Fair Economy, 1999.

There's Nothing in the Middle of the Road but Yellow Stripes and Dead Armadillos, by Jim Hightower. Hightower focuses his sharp Texas wit on our country's political, economic, scientific, and media establishments. He shows what's wrong and how to fix it. And he makes you laugh. New York: Harper Perennial, 1998.

Toxic Sludge Is Good for You: Lies, Damn Lies, and the Public Relations Industry, by John Stauber and Sheldon Rampton. This book blows the lid off today's multibillion-dollar propaganda-for-hire industry. Monroe, ME: Common Courage Press, 1995.

The Truth that Never Hurts: Writings on Race, Gender, and Freedom, by Barbara Smith. A collection of two decades of political thought and literary criticism by a Black lesbian who makes connections between race, class, sexuality, and gender. New Brunswick, NJ: Rutgers University Press, 1998.

United Nations Development Report. A biennial analysis of the state of the world, and impact of the growing global disparity of rich and poor. New York: United Nations, 1996.

Who Rules America? Power and Politics in the Year 2000, by William Domhoff. An up-to-date exploration of income and wealth distribution in the United States, encouraging people to think critically about the American power structure and its implications for democracy. Mountain View, CA: Mayfield Publishing Co., 1998.

You Can't Be Neutral on a Moving Train: A Personal History of Our Times, by Howard Zinn. A personal history of working for social change that spans thirty-five years. Boston: Beacon Press, 1994.

Volunteering

A Guide to Effective Community Service and Social Action: The Giraffe Project Handbook. Inspirational encouragement, advice, and stories for people wishing to "stick their necks out" for the common good. Langley, WA: Giraffe Project, 1991.

Alternatives to the Peace Corps: A Directory of Third World and U.S. Volunteer Opportunities, by Becky Buell et al. A short resource guide for those interested in voluntary service helping community-based development work and constructive U.S. foreign policy. Includes information on how to contact organizations that can sponsor you abroad. San Francisco, CA: Institute for Food and Development Policy, 1992. Available from the IFDP, 145 Ninth St., San Francisco, CA 94103.

The Quickening of America: Rebuilding Our Nation, Remaking Our Lives, by Frances Moore Lappe and Paul Martin DuBois. Defining "quickening" as the "first stirrings of life," this book describes how people across the country are making change in their communities, schools, workplaces, and lives. San Francisco: Jossey-Bass, 1994.

Periodicals: Giving/Financial

Black Philanthropy. Profiles Black philanthropists and giving within the African American community. PO Box 3092, Oakton, VA 22124, 703-255-2447.

Co-op American Quarterly. Features articles on personal finance, local economics, fair trade, low-impact consumption, and socially responsible investing. 1612 K St. NW, #600, Washington, DC 20006, 202-872-5307.

The Giraffe Gazette. Stories of people who stick their necks out for the common good. The Giraffe Project, PO Box 759, Langley, WA 98260, 360-221-7989.

Green Money Journal. Provides an overview of mutual fund financial and social performance. W. 608 Glass Ave., Spokane, WA 99205, 509-328-1741.

More than Money. A quarterly journal of personal stories, articles, humor, and resources primarily by and for affluent people. Each twenty-page issue focuses on a theme, such as money between friends; how much is enough?; women, money, and power. For a free sample issue or a journal subscription: More than Money, 800-255-4903, impact@efn.org or www.efn.org/~ impact

Women's Philanthropy Institute News. Features articles written by and about women, why they give, and how they can expand their spheres of influence through philanthropy. 1605 Monroe St., Suite 105, Madison, WI 53711, 608-286-0980.

Progressive Magazines

ColorLines. Focuses on race, culture, and community organizing. Subscriptions are fifteen dollars for six issues. ColorLines Subscriptions, PO Box 3000, Denville, NJ 07834 or (credit card only) 888-458-8858. A free sample issue can be ordered from www.arc.org

E: The Environmental Magazine. A bimonthly independent magazine reporting on key environmental issues, campaigns, and events. For subscription information: 203-854-5559, www.emagazine.com

Earth Island Journal. Started in 1982 as a class project at Stanford University and is now a quarterly magazine providing coverage of environmental and social issues. For subscription information or a sample issue: 415-788-3666, www.earthisland.org

Extra! Fairness and Accuracy in Reporting publishes this bimonthly magazine that examines biased reporting, censored news, media mergers, and right-wing influences in the media. For subscription or free sample issue: 212-633-6700, fair@fair.org; www.fair.org

GCN (Gay Community News). The only progressive GBLT periodical with a national subscriber base that centrally addresses organizing, in both practical and theoretical ways. For twenty-five years *GCN* has provided an independent progressive voice of the gay and lesbian movement. 29 Stanhope St., Boston MA 02111, 617-262-6969.

In These Times. Founded in 1976 with a commitment to provide readers with in-depth analysis of news, politics, and culture. For a free sample issue: 888-732-3488 x239, www.inthesetimes.com

Infusion. A national newspaper for progressive campus activists. Distributed bimonthly by the Center for Campus Organizing, it provides updates, research, action ideas, and analysis on current social issues. For subscription information or a sample issue: 617-725-2886, www.cco.org; E-mail cco@igc.org

Mother Jones. A progressive journal providing both investigative reporting and commentary to inspire action toward social change. For subscription information: 800-GET-MOJO, www.motherjones.com

Ms. Magazine. An advertising-free bimonthly magazine featuring a mix of national and international women's news, personal narratives, humor, fiction, and poetry. For subscription information; 800-234-4486, E-mail Ms@echonyc.com

Multinational Monitor. Tracks corporate activity, export of hazardous substances, worker health and safety, labor union issues, and the environment. Subscription or sample issue: 202-387-8030, www.essential.org/monitor

The *Nation.* Established in 1865 to be an alternative voice in American journalism. Provides independent reporting and commentary on politics, culture, and the arts. For subscription information: 800-333-8536, E-mail info@The Nation.com.

The *Progressive.* A voice for peace and social justice in America. It includes a monthly "On the Line" section that features some of the "unsung heroes" of social change work today. Free sample copy: 608-257-3373, www.progressive.org.

Souls. An interdisciplinary quarterly journal of Black politics, culture, and society sponsored by the Institute for Research in African-American Studies at Columbia University. Subscription: Westview Press at 303-444-3541.

Southern Exposure. Award-winning investigative magazine of politics, culture, and social change published by the Institute for Southern Studies. One-year subscriptions are $24; sample copy: $5; send check to SE Circulation, PO Box 531, Durham, NC 27702. Or call 919-419-8311, x21, or E-mail SEcirculation@aol.com

Utne Reader. Selections from "the best of the alternative press." Six issues per year for $19.97 U.S; $30 CAN, Box 7460 Red Oak, IA 51591 0460. 800-736-UTNE.

YO! Youth Outlook. Monthly newsletter by and about young people, connecting young activists. They also run a radio show, a speakers' bureau, and training workshops. 415-438-4755, www.pacificnews.org/yo

Z Magazine. Monthly independent magazine of critical thinking on political, cultural, social, and economic life in the United States. For subscription information: 508-548-9063, E-mail lydia.sargent@zmag.org

Internet Resources

Institute for Global Communications (IGC). An on-line service provider geared toward activist and grassroots communities. In addition to providing access to the Internet, E-mail, and on-line conferences, it runs four networks: PeaceNet, EcoNet, WomensNet, and LaborNet. Its greatest resource is its "Progressive Directory," which lists groups by issue, including media. http://www.igc.org

Philanthropy Journal. Both an E-mail digest and on-line magazine covering philanthropy-related and nonprofit stories. 5 W. Hargett St., #805, Raleigh, NC 27601, www.pj.org

Philanthropy News Digest. A weekly compendium of philanthropy-related articles and features culled from print and electronic media outlets nationwide. 79 Fifth Ave., New York, NY 10003, 212-620-4230, asf@fdncenter.org; www.fdncenter.org

WebActive. Originally dubbed *What's New in Activism Online?, WebActive* is a project of Progressive Networks, the Seattle-based company that developed RealAudio. A well-done and professional digest of activism on-line, *WebActive* uses RealAudio to supplement interviews with activists and provide access to progressive media, such as FAIR's radio show, Counter-Spin, and Hightower Radio. It also features a directory of more than 1,250 links to progressive sites on the Web and opportunities to get involved in issues. www.webactive.com; webactive@webactive.com

Software

Living Trust Maker. Includes forms to make a revocable living trust for singles, couples, and children's subtrusts. On-screen program and legal help. This program does not create tax-savings "A-B" Trusts. Nolo Press, 950 Parker St., Berkeley, CA 97410, 510-549-1976 or 800-992-6656, www.nolo.com

Proxy Voter. Enables proxy record keeping, provides access to information about shareholder and management resolutions, and creates reports. Investor Responsibility Research Center, 1350 Connecticut Ave. NW, Suite 700, Washington, DC 20036, 202-833-0700, mkt@irrc.org; www.irrc.org

Quicken Financial Planner. Helps you get an overall picture of your personal finances and determine the implications of numerous what-if scenarios about future earning, investing, spending, and giving choices. (Available as a separate software package or as part of Quicken Suite 99.) Intuit Inc., 2535 Garcia Ave., Mountain View, CA 94043, 800-446-8848, www.intuit.com/qfp

WillMaker. Lets you make your own legal will and living will and document your final arrangements. Allows you to name a guardian for children, make property bequests, and direct your health care if you're unable. Nolo Press, 950 Parker St., Berkeley, CA 97410, 800-992-6656, www.nolo.com

Appendix H

Pointers for Reading an Organization's Budget

Things to Remember

It's appropriate to review an organization's budget when you're making a substantial gift.

→ Organizations are required to conduct financial audits if their budgets are over $250,000, and the audits are available to the public upon request. (Those with budgets between $100,000 and $249,000 must be reviewed by accountants; you could request a copy.)

→ Because there is no standard way to prepare a budget, budgets vary in format from organization to organization. If you're looking at a budget for a start-up effort or for a very small grassroots organization, it may not be as detailed or extensive as that for a large, well-established organization.

What to Look For

1. A variety of income sources or a plan to diversify funding to include individuals, foundations, and grassroots strategies such as bowl-a-thons and parties.
2. Evidence of local community support in the form of member contributions or grassroots fundraising income.
3. The budget as a reference point. Make sure it reflects what the group is and what it does. For example, has a statewide organization budgeted for statewide work by including travel expenses? If a group works in a low-income community, does its budget show that it is truly accessible to the community—through adequate child care and transportation expenses, for example?
4. The fact that some fundraising strategies not only cost money but also have a programmatic benefit. This is particularly true of direct mail and special events, which raise visibility and educate the public. Remember that you have to spend money to raise money.
5. The income side to see if there is a great deal of government or corporate funding. Does this funding place a constraint on the type of organizing the group performs?
6. If there are accountability structures in place; are there mechanisms in the organization for fiscal oversight? Who sets the direction for the organization, and what input do they have into financial decisions? Are the people who write checks the same as those who receive the checks?
7. If the salaries line item is reasonable in terms of paying staff living wages with benefits. Look for salary differentials that indicate inequality among different staff positions. If a budget is all salaries, it can be a warning that the work is entirely staff-driven and that community involvement is lacking.
8. Deficits. Look for big changes in income and expenses from one year to the next. Both these indicators can show instability.

Index

Community Coalition for Substance Abuse and Treatment, 134–35

community development credit unions (CDCUs), 141

community economic development (CED):
  community organizing and, 49, 158–60
  key considerations in, 160

community foundations, progressive social change foundations vs., 192–93

community investments, 137, 139–42
  purpose of, 139–40
  types of, 140–42

community loan funds, 141–42

community organizing:
  arts and, 46, 152–53
  economic development and, 49, 158–60
  electoral work and, 49–50, 157–58, 163
  long-range planning and strategic development for, 51
  popular and public education and, 54
  preorganizing, 149, 151–52
  progressive cultural work and, 46, 152–53
  technical assistance and, 52, 160, 161, 162

Community Reinvestment Act Statement, 140

community trusts, 192–93

Community Works, 111

computer software, for investments and personal records, 274

conduit (nonoperating) foundations, 111–16

conferences and workshops, on giving and social change, 73, 76–77, 173, 193

confidentiality, lawyer-client, 122–23

Congress of Racial Equality (CORE), 40

constituency organizing, 47

consumer culture, social movements and, 61

Co-op America, 129

Cooperative Economics for Women, 31

core criteria, for evaluating social change work of projects, 151, 184, 193

corporate welfare, 106, 113

corporations:
  boycotts of, 139
  multinational, 16, 113, 225–26, 228–29
  shareholder activism and, 137–38

Council on Foundations, 171, 191

crack cocaine, 134

Critchlow, Eliza, 60

Crocker, Joe, 172

Crossroads Fund, 27, 52, 121, 172, 189, 194, 219, 223

cultural work, progressive:
  community organizing and, 46, 152–53
  key considerations in, 153
  media organizations and, 247–49

cynicism, in American culture, 60–61

Daloz, Laurent Parks, 41

DDT, 39

Deadly Deception, 155

deductions, charitable, 106–16

Defense Department, U.S., 215

DeJesus, Moises, 79

Democracy Now!, 176

Depression, Great, 40

"development," U.S. vs. world view of, 158

Dewey, John, 50

Diallo, Amadou, 54

dioxin, 67

direct action, 48

direct giving:
  consultants on, 185–86
  pros and cons of, 185

direct-mail solicitations, 220

disability rights, 55–56

discount brokers, 125

divestment campaigns, 49, 138

documentaries, 155–56, 176

domestic violence, 34, 182–83

donor-advised (DA) accounts, 174, 175, 176, 186–87

donors:
  as activists, 221, 227–28
  anonymous vs. visible, 74–75
  conservative vs. progressive, 42
  generosity of, 30–31
  gift conditions of, 221–22
  giving decisions of, 207–8
  historical social change and, 39–40
  "How much is enough?" question of, 69–70
  moralistic attitudes of, 28, 29
  organizations evaluated by, 195–97
  power relationship between askers and, 28–29, 171, 220–21
  and preorganizing stage of organizations, 152
  progressive foundations and, 173–74
  as self-interested, 29–30
  uncertain about impact of gifts, 75–76

Douglass, Frederick, 39

drought, 180

Dubois, Vashti, 221

Dyson, Michael Eric, 40

economic justice, 103
  charity and, 28, 31, 32
  immigrants and, 101–5
  organizations supportive of, 241–43

economic strategies, for organizing social change, 49

education, popular and public, 54

education issues, 21, 50–51, 135, 161–62

Robin Hood Is *Still* Right!

☐ Yes, I'd like a free copy of the *Gift-Giving Guide,* a guide to tax-wise giving with <u>up-to-date</u> information about tax laws. (Limit one order per person, please.)

☐ Send me information about the Funding Exchange and the FEX member fund in my region.

Name: _____

Address: _____

City: _____ State: _____ Zip: _____

☐ Send information about the Funding Exchange and the closest local fund to my family member/friend/colleague.

Name: _____

Address: _____

City: _____ State: _____ Zip: _____

Please return to:

The Funding Exchange
666 Broadway, Suite 500
New York, New York 10012